THE LABOR OF DEVELOPMENT

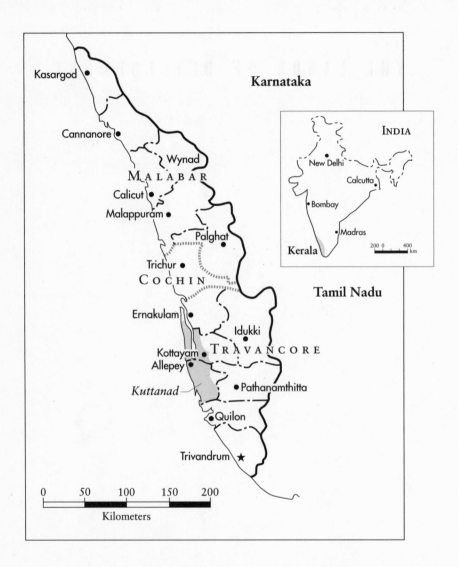

Kasargod

Karnataka

Cannanore

Wynad

M A L A B A R

Calicut

Malappuram

Palghat

Trichur

C O C H I N

Ernakulam

Idukki

Kottayam

T R A V A N C O R E

Allepey

Kuttanad

Pathanamthitta

Quilon

Trivandrum

Tamil Nadu

INDIA

New Delhi

Calcutta

Bombay

Madras

Kerala

200 0   400
km

0   50   100   150   200

Kilometers

The Labor of Development

Workers and the Transformation of Capitalism in Kerala, India

PATRICK HELLER

CORNELL UNIVERSITY PRESS

Ithaca and London

First published 1999 by Cornell University Press
First printing,Cornell Paperbacks, 1999

Printed in the United States of America

Library of Congress Cataloging-in-Publication Data

Heller, Patrick.
  The labor of development : workers and the transformation of capitalism in Kerala, India / Patrick Heller.
    p. cm.
  Includes bibliographical references and index.
  ISBN: 0-8014-3590-0 (cloth). — ISBN 0-8014-8624-6 (pbk.)
  1. Labor movement—India—Kerala—History. 2. Labor unions—India—Kerala—History. 3. Working class—India—Kerala—History.
4. Peasantry—India—Kerala—History. 5. Agriculture—Economic aspects—India—Kerala—History. 6. Kerala (India)—Economic conditions. I. Title
  HD8689.K452H45 1999
  331.88'0954'83—dc21   99-43546

Cloth printing   10 9 8 7 6 5 4 3 2 1
Paperback printing   10 9 8 7 6 5 4 3 2 1

To Max and Rosemarie Heller

Contents

Tables

Acknowledgments

A very wise and famous sociologist once told me that good scholarship was first and foremost about humility. He then went on to say that if you think you have an original idea, it only means you have a lousy memory. This book is the sum total of many ideas that I have absorbed, pilfered, and possibly mangled, from many different people, some of whom I remember, some of whom I don't. My thanks, and apologies, to all of them.

I owe my greatest intellectual debt to Michael Burawoy, Peter Evans and Michael Watts. The ways in which their ideas have shaped this book will be obvious to those familiar with their work. As much as their patience and support carried me through this project, it was their commitment and dedication to teaching that time and again restored my faith in the academic enterprise, which is, after all, about passing on knowledge. I owe special thanks to Michael Burawoy, who read more versions of this work than either he or I care to remember, and who sets a standard for working with students that few can claim.

Much of the argument I develop in this book would not have been possible without Ron Herring's pioneering work and the countless discussions we have had over the years. Not only did he help me finally understand Polanyi, but the empirical richness of his own fieldwork in Kerala was a constant inspiration. To Paul Lubeck I owe thanks for exposing me to the wonderful world that can be sociology. Arun Swamy has taught me much of what I know about Indian politics. Many people have read and commented on parts of the manuscript. I'd like to thank Charlie Kurzman, Karen Barkey, Robert Lieberman, K. P. Kannan, Richard Franke, Pranab Bardhan, Atul Kohli, and Olle Törnquist. David Stark, Phil Oldenburg,

Gay Seidman, and Amrita Basu read the entire manuscript and provided invaluable critiques and suggestions. For their friendship, advice, and ideas, thanks to Subir Sinha, Tony Marx, Shubham Chaudhuri, Alex Pfaff, Arvid Lukauskas, Marc Garcelon, Judith Tendler, and John Hartman. I, and anyone who reads this book, also have Fran Benson, my editor at Cornell University Press, to thank. She convinced me, against my perfectly wrongheaded judgment, to make the text shorter and sweeter.

In Kerala there are hundreds whose time and generosity made my research possible. If there is any measure of the degree and extent to which the practice and the institutions of democracy have taken root in Kerala, it is in the refreshingly vital and passionate manner in which Keralites from all walks of life discuss politics. Only once did someone turn down my request for an interview. Ministers, politicians, farmers, workers, unionists, students, and academics all gave freely of their time. My only regret is that in this world of uneven and unfair development, Western academics, myself included, reap largely unrequited rewards from their informants.

I thank the students at the Centre for Development Studies in Trivandrum who filled me with so many exciting ideas (and so much soothing rum). K. T. Ram Mohan deserves special thanks for his tireless efforts to educate me in the ways of local politics. K. P. Kannan and T. M. Thomas Isaac gave freely of their time, their ideas, and their extraordinary knowledge of Kerala politics and economics. Vanita and Chandan Mukherjee gave me a home away from home. I am also grateful to P. Sahadevan for being such an enterprising research assistant and such a wonderful friend; my fieldwork could never have been completed without his help. The research for this book was made possible by two grants from the American Institute of Indian Studies. Priscilla Stephan helped with the bibliography, Margaret Phillips provided invaluable library assistance, and Elizabeth Mandel spared me many embarrassments through her diligent reading of the final text.

Finally, I owe the deepest gratitude to my wife, Jo Lee, without whom the last fifteen years would have been too lonely and too serious.

P. H.

Abbreviations

AITUC	All-Indian Trade Union Congress (CPI-affiliated)
AKKV	Akila Kuttanad Karshaka Vedi
BJP	Bharatiya Janata Party
CDS	Centre for Development Studies
CITU	Congress of Indian Trade Unions (CPM-affiliated)
CMIE	Centre for Monitoring of Indian Economy
CPI	Communist Party of India
CPI(M) or CPM	Communist Party of India, Marxist
DKS	Deseeya Karshaka Samajam
EPW	*Economic and Political Weekly*
GOI	Government of India
GOK	Government of Kerala
IAS	Indian Administrative Service
INTUC	Indian National Trade Union Congress (Congress-affiliated)
IRC	Industrial Relations Committee
KAWA	Kerala Agricultural Workers Act
KSKTU	Kerala State Karshaka Thozhilali Union
KCSP	Kerala Congress Socialist Party
KKS	Kerala Karshaka Sangham
KLRAA	Kerala Land Reforms Amendment Act
KSSP	Kerala Sastra Sahitya Parishad
LDF	Left Democratic Front
MLA	Member, Legislative Assembly
PACS	Primary Agricultural Credit Societies
SNDP	Sree Narayana Dharma Paripalana
TKTU	Thiruvithamkoor Karshaka Thozhilali Union
TLA	Travancore Labour Association
UDF	United Democratic Front

THE LABOR OF DEVELOPMENT

Introduction:
Kerala in Theoretical Perspective

In the 1960s, social historians reminded us that subordinate classes, to borrow from E. P. Thompson, were present at their own making, and that indeed, they helped make the modern world.[1] Scholars of revolutions, democracy, the welfare state, and the labor process have since emphasized the role that peasants and workers played in the great transformative events of the twentieth-century, including shaping the structures and institutions of modern capitalism. Though this concern with "bringing the masses back in" has informed much of our thinking about social and economic change in advanced capitalist countries, as a coherent body of concepts and hypotheses it has had a far less pronounced impact in the study of the developing world.

In both its academic and policy incarnations, the development literature has tended to see peasants and workers as either victims or beneficiaries, but rarely as active agents of economic and political transformation. In exploring the determinants of economic development, scholars have focused either on the market and its social carrier, the bourgeoisie, or on the developmental state and its technocratic elites. In the literature on political development, including much of the recent work on democratization, the transition to more open and plural systems of representation has either been functionally tied to the ascendance of market economies or ascribed to the strategic actions of political elites. In all of these scenarios, peasants

[1] Among the most important contributions were those of Thompson (1963), Moore (1966), Wolf (1969), Tilly (1978), and more recently Burawoy (1985) and Rueschemeyer, Stephens, and Stephens (1992). I use the terms "lower," "subordinate," and "working" classes interchangeably to refer to both urban and rural wage workers.

1

and workers are reduced to passive objects of forces beyond their control and, implicitly, their understanding.

In part, the scholarly neglect of these classes reflects the fact that in most developing countries political participation has been carefully controlled. The exclusion or co-optation of workers and peasants has been so pervasive among late developing countries that it has been elevated to the status of a theoretically informed necessity: satisfying "populist" demands is incompatible with economic growth, and political modernization requires the taming of social mobilization. The former proposition flows from conventional economic wisdom (both Marxist and neoclassical) that assumes a zero-sum trade-off between growth and social consumption; the latter, most famously associated with Samuel Huntington's classic work (1968), is reflected in the current concern with problems of governance, institution building, and political leadership. A functionalist (that is asocial) bias informs these views, in which development is understood as the unfolding of institutional properties associated with modern markets or modern democratic states. These views either entirely discount the effects of social conflict and mobilization (economic theory) or prejudge them as inherently destabilizing (political modernization).

In examining the case of the state of Kerala in southwestern India, I propose to turn these assumptions on their head. I maintain that development in Kerala has been driven not by market forces or by an emerging bourgeoisie, but by the mobilization of subordinate classes. This process has been uneven, at times contradictory, and always contested, but has nonetheless resulted in the consolidation of an institutionally robust and politically stable form of social-democratic capitalism.

Three phases can be identified in the developmental trajectory of this densely populated state of thirty-one million inhabitants. In the first phase, mobilization of poor tenants and landless laborers produced an agrarian transition and precipitated the demise of the landlord-dominated social order. Periodic electoral victories by pro-labor parties and sustained lower-class mobilization led to significant redistributive reforms and the rapid expansion of the welfare state. These developments underscored, and indeed were facilitated by, the consolidation of a rich fabric of democratic institutions. In a second phase, labor militancy and continuous challenges to private property triggered a crisis of capitalist accumulation, and specifically a crisis in the labor-squeezing logic of peripheral capitalism. This crisis took its toll on the economy, but unlike many Latin American cases, it did not result in the decomposition of the popular sectors. For reasons that are explored in detail in this book, organized class interests and strong state institutions combined to produce a third phase marked by the institutionalization of class conflict and the effective, if uneven, forging of class compromises across agrarian and industrial sectors. Though in conventional economic terms Kerala remains an "underdeveloped" economy, the labor movement and the state have taken significant steps to promote capitalist growth while maintaining hard-won distributive and social gains.

I highlight the significance of Kerala through two comparative frameworks that explore two different sets of arguments. First, the degree to which both rural and urban wage-earning classes in Kerala have been politically and economically incorporated is systematically contrasted to the disorganized and largely excluded condition of lower classes in the rest of India. Such divergent outcomes within the same nation-state and its democratic institutions, and within the same national economy and its largely underdeveloped capitalist structures, point to the significance of local histories of state-society engagements. Kerala's departure from the national pattern has resulted from specific patterns of class formation and the institutional linkages that emerged from repeated cycles of class-based contestation and state intervention.

The second framework, situating Kerala in the comparative political economy literature, allows for broader claims about the relationship between subordinate-class politics and developmental outcomes. In contrast to predictions that high levels of social mobilization in developing countries necessarily overload fledgling democratic institutions, class-based mobilization in Kerala has actually institutionalized democracy and made it work better. Similarly, a redistributive trajectory of development, rather than inhibiting capitalist development, has in fact created many of the social and institutional prerequisites (for example, human capital, civic associations, robust bureaucracies) for sustainable economic growth. Simply stated, capitalism and democracy in Kerala have not only coexisted but prospered from the political and economic inclusion of peasants and workers. The case of Kerala suggests that lower-class mobilization can, in effect, be the engine of democratic development.

The elite-dominated or authoritarian political systems of the postcolonial world have provided few formal avenues for the articulation of demands from below. But recent events have brought the question of subordinate-class politics to center stage. Neoliberal proclamations of the "end of history" notwithstanding, difficult transitions in eastern Europe, Russia, and South Africa and increasing social unrest in East Asia only confirm what scholars of Latin America have long known: the relationship between capitalism and democracy is an uneasy one, and making the "double transition" poses unique problems.

The affinity of capitalism and democracy has never been a given. It has only been forged, and very unevenly at that. The challenge to Europe between the two world wars was to reconcile the rise of mass politics with the consolidation of free-market economies. The cost of failure was fascism (Polanyi 1944; Luebbert 1991). Much of the developing world today faces a similar dilemma of reconciling the demands for social citizenship with the imperative of stimulating growth in a private-property economy—summed up by a woman from a South African squatter settlement who wrote to a local newspaper in 1990: "Mandela has been released, now where is my house?" (cited in Murray 1994:4).

There have, of course, been calls for managing these dilemmas from above. The "Washington consensus" has explicitly advocated insulating economic decision making from political pressures.[2] In this technocratic vision of frictionless reform, democracy is acceptable only "within reason" (Centeno 1994). As for the Salinas presidency in Mexico, Centeno observes "the legitimacy of popular participation was accepted only as long as it would support the correct policies" (1994:4). This model has come under increasing criticism not only on normative grounds, but also because there is mounting evidence that neoliberal policies do not promote economic growth and that insulated and autocratic policy regimes are less than efficient (Przeworski 1995; Stark and Bruszt 1998). Because there are no quick fixes and no blueprints, and because various trade-offs have different distributions of social costs, we must come to terms with the simple proposition that development is and should be contested. If there is one lesson of relevance here to be drawn from European history, it is this: the terms under which subordinate classes are incorporated have a profound impact on the prospects for consolidated democracy and sustainable growth (Luebbert 1991; Przeworski 1995). There are good reasons why the question of the "entry of the masses" into politics has long preoccupied scholars of advanced capitalist states. It is now time to extend that preoccupation to the developing world and to understanding the challenges of the double transition.

The recent wave of democratization in the developing world has shed new light on this problem. Theorists of democratic transitions, once primarily concerned with the dynamics of elite-pacted transitions, have turned their attention to the problems of subordinate-class incorporation (Przeworski 1995; O'Donnell 1993). Because most new democracies are

---

[2] The most oft-cited statement of the "Washington consensus" is Williamson 1993. For a comparatively informed perspective that treats politics more charitably but nonetheless makes a case for insulation, see Haggard and Kaufman 1995.

poorly institutionalized and dominated by entrenched political oligarchies, fragmentation and exclusion of lower classes remains the rule (Weyland 1996; O'Donnell 1993). There are, however, important exceptions, in which democratic openings have been accompanied by organized demands for the extension of social citizenship. In such cases, as Spain (Maravall 1993), post-Pinochet Chile (Roberts 1997), and Czechoslovakia (Stark and Burszt 1998), the transition to the market has been negotiated through concertations with popular classes. Economic transformation in South Africa is also clearly destined to be shaped by lower-class demands. In each of these cases the rise of labor as an organized actor was the result of rapid industrialization, managed from above through various forms of bureaucratic authoritarianism and predicated on the political exclusion of labor. Subordinate-class interests were politically suppressed even as they were being formed. Democratization has changed the equation, but the dilemmas of the double transition have only just begun to manifest themselves.

In India, the sequence is reversed. On the one hand, modern industry and the industrial proletariat represent only a small part of the equation. The "agrarian question" still looms large. Capitalism remains in its formative stages, and the material base of compromise has been and will remain for the foreseeable future very narrow. On the other hand, because democracy in India predates capitalist transformation, it has formally empowered economic groups—unskilled workers, peasants, and landless laborers—that have more often than not been the victims of capitalist development. But the antinomies of citizenship and property have yet to be starkly posed. In a society where caste and ethnicity continue to serve as the primary avenues of political mobilization, demand-group politics have predominated over redistributive class politics (Rudolph and Rudolph 1987). Populism and patronage have never threatened the interests of propertied groups. Within India there are, however, important exceptions, of which Kerala is the most notable. Democratic opportunities have been seized, and subordinate classes have had a decisive role in shaping the terms of capitalist transformation. Democracy and capitalism have confronted each other directly. Thus Kerala represents an extended case study of the double transition.

Both within India and internationally, the case of Kerala is indeed unusual. But the unusual often sheds more light on dynamic processes than the usual. In his brilliant study of Lesotho, James Ferguson points out that its status as a magnet of development aid and as a labor reserve for South Africa certainly makes it peculiar. But by the same token, he remarks that "the exaggeration it produces, if properly interpreted, may be seen not simply as a distortion of the 'typical' case, but as a clarification, just as the addition by a computer of 'extreme' colors to a remote scanning image does not distort but 'enhances' the photograph by improving the visibility of the phenomena we are interested in" (1994:257–58). Development is always contested, but not always transparently so. In *Weapons of the Weak*, James Scott shows that the "normal" quiescence of the subaltern in public politics often masks a rich repertoire of ideologies and practices of resistance to the dominant order. Similarly, Ferguson argues that by constructing "poor Basotho" as "subsistence peasants" in "need" of development, official development discourse not only abstracted Lesotho from its political economy of dependency on South Africa, but also rendered agentless those who in their day-to-day struggles are in fact "doing development." In Kerala, democratic institutions bequeathed by the Indian nationalist movement, together with local patterns of conflict and mobilization, have conspired to bring the masses into the open—*before* the development of capitalism. This historical sequencing has enhanced the visibility of subordinate-class politics in contesting and making development.

Redistributive Development in Kerala

Kerala is best known to students of the subcontinent for its history of sustained social mobilization. Since the last decade of the nineteenth century Kerala has been the site of a nearly continuous succession of social movements: a social-religious reform movement in the early part of the century; nationalist, agrarian, and prodemocracy movements in the 1930s and 1940s; a series of rural and industrial labor movements (from 1930 to 1975); and most recently various new social movements including a statewide campaign for decentralization orchestrated by state reformers and nongovernmental organizations (NGOs). These high levels of social mobilization have been directly tied to what is widely known in development circles as the "Kerala model", namely levels of social development unparalleled in low-income societies. A question that has received far less attention yet carries important lessons about the dynamics of the double transition is the impact that lower-class mobilization and incorporation have had on the state's economic and political development.

The relationship between lower-class mobilization and Kerala's achievements on the social front is well documented. Under the impetus of a broad-based working-class movement organized by the Communist Party, successive governments in Kerala have pursued what is arguably the most successful strategy of redistributive development outside the socialist world. Direct redistributive measures have included the most far-reaching land reforms on the subcontinent and labor market interventions that, combined with extensive unionization, have pushed both rural and informal sector wages well above regional levels. Social welfare and entitlement programs have provided the general population with more equitable access to basic goods including education, health service and subsidized food than in any other state in India.[3] Even the more conservative estimates show that since the mid-1970s, the percentage of the population living below the poverty line, once the highest in India, has fallen by at least half (EPW Foundation 1993).

On all indicators of the physical quality of life Kerala far surpasses any Indian state and compares favorably with the more developed nations of Asia. The 1991 Census puts the level of literacy at 90.6 percent (87 percent for women), compared to a national average of 52.1 percent (39 percent for women). With 5.9 science and technology personnel for every thousand inhabitants—well over twice the national average of 2.4 and highest among all states—Kerala clearly has the most broad-based and high-end human capital resources in the country (CMIE 1991:tab. 2.22). On the health front Kerala's record is equally impressive. At thirteen per thousand live births in 1994, the infant mortality rate is decades ahead of the all-India figure of 73. Life expectancy in 1992 had reached over 71 years (69 for men and 73.5 for women) compared to 62 in India (GOK, State Planning Board, *Economic Review* 1995). Despite an average per capita income ten times lower than Brazil's, the average Keralite can expect to live four years longer than the average Brazilian. Dramatic improvements in primary health care and education—particularly in the levels of female literacy—have driven what is arguably the most rapid demographic transition on record (Bhat and Rajan 1990). From a ten-year population growth rate of 26.3 percent in 1971, Kerala plummeted to a rate of 14 percent in 1991, well below the national rate of 23.5 percent (GOI, Census of India 1991). Thus, despite per capita income levels that are well below averages in India and other low-income countries, Kerala

---

[3] The Kerala "model" of social development has received extensive documentation and commentary. For the earliest study see United Nations 1975. Comprehensive studies include Franke and Chasin 1989, Kannan 1988, Dreze and Sen 1995, and Ramachandran 1996. On land reforms, see Herring 1983, 1991a; Paulini 1979; and M. Oommen 1990. On wage increases in rural and informal sectors, see Krishnan 1991 and Kannan 1990b, and on the effectiveness of poverty alleviation programs, Kannan 1995. The January 1991 issue of *Monthly Review* is also largely devoted to a discussion of the Kerala model. For the most recent comparison with India, see Dreze and Sen 1995.

TABLE 1. Kerala: Basic socioeconomic indicators compared.

	Kerala	India	LICs[a]	U.S.A.	S. Korea	Brazil
Population (in millions)	31	916	1,050	263	45	159
Per capita GNP (in U.S. dollars)	292	340	290	26,980	11,450	3,640
Adult literacy (%)	91 (1991)	52 (1991)	54	99	97	83
Life expectancy	71 (1991)	62	56	77	72	67
Infant mortality (per 1,000 live births)	13	73 (1994)	89	8	10	44
Birthrate (per 1,000)	17	29 (1994)	40	16	16	24

Sources: Kerala and India figures from GOK, *Economic Review* 1996. Birthrate figures from United Nations Development Programme 1994. All other figures from World Bank 1997.

Note: All figures are for 1995, unless indicated otherwise.

[a]Low-income Countries as defined by World Bank, excluding China and India.

has achieved levels of social and human development that approximate those of the first world (table 1).

Kerala's rapid social development has a complicated relationship to economic growth. On the one hand there is a general consensus, represented most prominently in Jean Dreze and Amartya Sen's work (1989, 1995), that dramatic improvements in the quality of life of the poor are the direct result of effective public action and not economic growth. But what effect has social and redistributive development, driven by state intervention and lower-class mobilization, had on economic growth? A case can be made that a zero-sum tradeoff has been at work. Through the 1970s and 1980s the state's economic performance, as measured in growth rates, was sluggish at best. Per capita income levels that were 92 percent of the national level in the 1960s fell to 74 percent in the second half of the 1980s (GOK, State Planning Board 1991a:1). Many commentators have come to the conclusion that the Kerala "model" is no longer viable, and some have drawn a direct link between labor militancy and the state's poor economic performance. Social expenditures, rigid labor markets, and high wages have fettered economic productivity and depressed private investment.[4]

---

[4] One of the first statements of this view is J. Alexander 1972. More recently Raj 1991, Paul 1990, Sankaranarayanan and Bhai 1994, and Thampy 1990 have drawn a direct relationship between labor militancy and industrial stagnation. With respect to agriculture, the most nu-

Militant trade unionism has triggered the flight of traditional industries and produced a virtual boycott by national capital. In agriculture, wage militancy and labor legislation has precipitated a crisis of profitability. Between 1961 and 1989 industry limped along at an annual growth rate of 3.48 percent, with agriculture actually experiencing a negative growth rate of 0.43 percent (GOK, State Planning Board 1991a:2). Unemployment has also steadily increased and is by far the highest in India (Oommen 1992). Moreover redistribution without growth has produced a severe fiscal crisis, compounded by one of the highest tax burdens in India.[5]

Once hailed by the World Bank as a "third path" of development, Kerala for many now epitomizes the inherent contradictions of labor militancy and welfarism in a capitalist economy. In a classic rendition of the zero-sum model of class relations under capitalism, the lesson drawn is that the political and administrative interventions that have benefited wage earners have come at the expense of capital accumulation in a private-property economy. The implication of such arguments captures what has become a central, if rarely openly stated, maxim of the development literature: in the early stages of development, substantive democracy (in which subordinate classes secure redistributive gains) is fundamentally incompatible with market-led growth.

There is no gainsaying that the empowerment of the working class in Kerala—and specifically its capacity to capture a share of the social surplus—precipitated a crisis of accumulation. But the class conflicts underlying this crisis have proven to be neither immutable nor irreconcilable. Zero-sum views, whether Marxist or neoclassical, are informed by a reductionist view of economic interests that fails to account for the independent impact of *political* factors on the character of class relations. In keeping with the new literature on comparative political economy (Evans and Stephens 1988), I argue that the actual modalities and outcomes of the trade-off between social consumption and private investment are not given, but are shaped and mediated by political configurations and institutional structures. In Kerala, working-class mobilization and redistributive

---

anced and sophisticated version of this argument is to be found in Ronald Herring's work (1989, 1991a, 1991b). For case studies of both agriculture and industry see the special Kerala issues of *Economic and Political Weekly*, September 1–8 and September 15, 1990. Tharamangalam 1998 provides the most recent critique of the Kerala model.
[5] Of all major states, only Tamil Nadu had a higher tax-to-income ratio in 1991–92 (GOK, *Kerala Budget in Brief* 1997–98:39). For an exhaustive analysis of Kerala's fiscal crisis, see K. George (1993), who argues that while high social expenditures have contributed to the problem, the crisis in large part stems from a pattern of central funding that has penalized states emphasizing social services.

state intervention did not simply shift the balance in favor of labor at the expense of capital. Mobilization and intervention transformed the political structure of class relations, laying the institutional groundwork for regulating class conflicts across virtually all sectors, and in some instances even creating the basis for coordinating quasicorporatist bargains between capital and labor. The immediate effects of distributive conflicts are readily observable. Of lesser transparency but greater significance to long-term developmental prospects are the transformations in social structure and state-society relations that social conflicts engender. Not only have subordinate classes been politically and economically incorporated, but the deepening of democratic institutions coupled with the strategic role of a reformist Communist Party and an interventionist state have made it possible to negotiate and organize limited but significant positive-sum class compromises.

Economic Transformations

In discussing the economic changes that have taken place in Kerala since Independence, I must sketch out two historically linked but nonetheless distinct stages. The first has been a transition *to* capitalism in the classic form of an agrarian transition marked by the dissolution of precapitalist social and property structures. The second has been a transition *within* capitalism, away from labor-squeezing (despotic) forms of organizing capitalist production toward more mediated (hegemonic) but still contested labor-capital relations.[6] In contrast to linear and teleological models of economic transition, the distinction here centers on the politics of transitions and their social effects, an argument I develop more fully in the next chapter.

Over the past six decades Kerala has experienced the most far-reaching and comprehensive agrarian transition in South Asia. Under the organizational impetus of a cadre-based Communist Party, an agrarian movement of tenants and landless laborers secured the passage and effective implementation of land reforms and labor legislation in the 1970s, which marked the dissolution of the two defining institutions of the precapitalist agrarian economy: unfree (attached) labor and rentier landlordism. The sustained mobilization of the rural poor also successfully challenged the myriad forms of social domination of the traditional caste-based social system. As I argue in Chapter 2, this transition had two basic effects. First, it created the essential social preconditions for capitalism by commodify-

---

[6] The terms are Burawoy's (1985) and are further developed in Chapter 1.

ing land and labor. Second, in destroying traditional patron-client forms of political and social authority and drawing the state into agrarian relations, the agrarian movement extended the scope of public legality and broadened the base of political participation. As a result of this institutional deepening and social inclusion, Kerala's democratic polity has developed a far greater capacity for aggregating interests and channeling lower-class demands than has the fragmented, elite-dominated, and patronage-driven Indian democracy.

The second transition has been an ongoing and highly contested transition within capitalism, the significance of which becomes apparent only when contrasted to the national picture. Although labor in India is now mostly performed for wages, the social character of labor continues to bear the heavy imprint of precapitalist social institutions, including the segmentations of the caste system, pervasive clientalistic dependencies, and myriad other social vulnerabilities. In the virtual absence of state protection, workers in the so-called unorganized sector (the Indian terminology for informal sector), which accounts for an estimated 90 percent of the work force, are thus especially vulnerable to the "whip of the market." Playing on Polanyi's famous construction (1944), one might call this capitalism without countervailing forces. And under these social conditions (labor is always a social relation, never just a commodity), the organization of production continues to be dominated by labor-squeezing strategies.

In Kerala, the social logic of despotic capitalism has been compromised. Class mobilization, social protection, and extended citizenship have weakened the social vulnerabilities that underwrote despotic capitalism. But if the old is dying, the new has yet to fully develop. The midwife of capitalism was also its political antithesis. Because precapitalist institutions were dismantled from below through highly politicized social struggles, the birth of capitalism, and specifically the commodification of land and labor, produced strong and organized countervailing forces. The dominance of lower-class politics (trade unionism, welfare entitlements, and social legislation) in Kerala's post-Independence history has cushioned the whip of the market and imposed severe limits on capital's ability to squeeze labor. The power of organized labor has also created significant barriers to accumulation, and capital has responded, both in agriculture and industry, through disinvestment, flight (the search for more docile forms of labor), and even efforts to revive mercantile forms of production. It is the crisis of this early stage of capitalist production that gave rise to the zero-sum view that class mobilization in Kerala has become incompatible with capitalist growth.

To argue, as many have, that labor militancy and state intervention have simply run up against the structural limits of a private-property economy is reductionist because it fails to recognize the independent effect of political and institutional developments. The class struggles that spelled the demise of the precapitalist social order and curtailed despotic capitalism didn't simply leverage the bargaining capacity of labor at the expense of capital. These struggles, waged in the electoral arena as well as in civil society, fundamentally transformed Kerala's social structure as well as the nature of state-society relations. Over time, the dynamic interplay of class mobilization and state intervention had a mutually reinforcing effect. On the one hand, class interests crystallized within a democratic and legal order, making the trade-off between wages and profits more transparent and hence more negotiable. On the other hand, a half-century of repeated struggles forged a wide range of geographical and sectoral institutions that were capable of effectively reconciling, within limits, social consumption and private investment. Though the time frame has been telescoped and the outcome remains uncertain, this movement from an unregulated and despotic organization of production characterized by endemic conflict to a more regulated and negotiated organization of production characterized by class compromise closely parallels the movement from despotic to hegemonic production regimes in the West (Burawoy 1985).

As we shall see, these compromises have been uneven and in some cases remain precarious. In the final analysis, the economic outcomes of such compromises in a dependent subnational state might very well be dictated by exogenous factors. Nonetheless, two general findings will be highlighted. First, to a degree that no other state in India even approximates, the relationship between capital and labor in Kerala has been subjected to rational-legal modes of mediation; the state has displaced society as the central arena of distributive conflict. Second, the extent to which organized workers in both industry and agriculture have made explicit and strategic concessions to capital (both farmers and industrialists) in an effort to stimulate productive investments suggests that even in the absence of an already expanding economy, working-class mobilization can indeed be the basis for a positive-sum coordination of class interests.

The State and the Communist Party

To understand the dynamics of Kerala's finished and ongoing transitions is to understand the trajectory of class mobilization in Kerala. A first period, roughly 1930–57, saw the convergence of three independent social movements of caste, class, and nation under the organizational umbrella of the Communist Party. How a cohesive class emerged from these social movements is an issue I explore in detail in Chapter 2. The rest of this book focuses on subsequent developments and specifically the sequential phases of organized class struggle (1957–75) and class compromise (1975 onward). Two political and institutional forces have critically shaped the evolution from militancy to democratic corporatism. The first is the hegemonic role of the Communist Party in first forging a "working class" out of disparate class elements and then, having exhausted the politics of class struggle, orchestrating class compromises. The second is the role of the state in mediating conflicting interests.

Whether expressed in periodic legislative victories, the strength of the trade union movement, or in its ability to shape state policies, the working class has been the most cohesive and dominant political force in Kerala since the late 1930s.[7] In 1957, the Communist Party of India (CPI) won the state's first legislative elections, becoming the first democratically elected communist government in the world. The party's victory at the polls was the culmination of two decades of social struggles. Many historical contingencies gave these struggles their cumulative trajectory, but so did political action. Much as in Gramsci's discussion of the "modern prince" (1971), the Communists established their ideological hegemony by acting through a "dispersed will," tapping into existing points of cultural and economic resistance to precapitalist institutions. The resulting political project became the formation of a class that in its very existence was the negation of the traditional, hierarchical, ascriptive social order. Creating these new solidarities involved forging political and social ties that bridged religious (Hindu and Muslim) and caste communities, and in some cases, as in the grand agrarian alliance of tenants in the north and landless laborers in the south, overcame significantly different material interests. Though articulated in the language of revolutionary socialism, the practical and unifying message was not so much socialism itself as the means to achieving it, namely a mass-based democracy, the immediate task of which was the political defeat of the ancien régime.[8] The contingent character of this process is reflected in the simple fact that it stands

---

[7] Outside West Bengal, Kerala is the only state in India in which an explicitly class-based party has emerged as the central political player.

[8] Writing in 1953, party theoretician and future chief minister E. M. S. Namboodiripad theorized the two-step transition to socialism as the "struggle for the present, new bourgeois-democratic revolution and for the future, proletarian socialist revolution," adding that "although in its social character the first step taken is still fundamentally bourgeois-democratic, and although its objective demand is to clear the path for the development of capitalism, yet

out as certainly the most, and possibly the only, successful instance of lower-class organization in postcolonial India.

Since the 1957 Communist ministry, the party's electoral fortunes have been mixed. Its electoral support peaked in 1960, when it won 39.14 percent of the popular vote. But in 1965 the Party split into the CPI and the CPI(M)—"M" for Marxist. The split was occasioned by the decision of the CPI to favor a broad alliance with the national bourgeoisie in keeping with the new Soviet line of supporting Nehru. The CPI(M) (hereafter CPM) categorically rejected cooperation with the Congress Party and in midterm legislative elections that same year established itself as the dominant Communist party by winning 21 percent of the popular vote, compared to 8.1 percent for the CPI. In Kerala's multiparty system, no party has ever established electoral dominance. The popular vote has generally been split equally between Congress-led and CPM-led coalitions, with the outcome generally decided by narrow margins. The result has been an almost unbroken alternation in power of the two fronts.[9] With the support of the CPI and small left-of-center parties, CPM-led fronts governed in 1967–69, 1979–81, and 1987–91, and returned to power in the 1996 legislative elections by capturing 44.3 percent of the popular vote and eighty of 140 seats.[10] The presence of large Christian and Muslim communities (21 and 18 percent of the population respectively), both of which sponsor their own parties and support the Congress front, has always worked against the formation of a broader working-class electoral block. In this respect, the working class in Kerala has not enjoyed as hegemonic a position as, for example, the Swedish labor movement (Esping-Andersen 1990). Nonetheless, there are two broad senses in which Gramsci (1971) discusses hegemonic politics that bear directly on the social character and strategic capacity of the labor movement in Kerala.

The first relates to the ideological project that drew together a labor movement from a broad section of lower-class elements that included small peasants, agricultural laborers, and workers in the plantation, manufacturing, and government-service sectors. On the one hand, because the movement was born from the convergence of the economic struggles of peasants and workers as well as the social justice struggles of the caste-re-

---

it no longer belongs to the old type of revolution led by the bourgeoisie" (quoted in Lieten 1982:27).

[9] In a determined effort to keep the CPM out of power, Congress backed a CPI-led government for seven years in the 1970s. The CPI has since always aligned itself with the CPM.

[10] The combined vote of the CPI and CPM totaled 28.3 percent. Because the Communists ran candidates in only eighty-four of 140 electoral districts as part of their electoral adjustments with Left Democratic Front partners, this figure underrepresents Communist support.

form and nationalist movements, it has taken a more encompassing form than traditional labor movements. In this respect, Kerala's agrarian and labor movements bear a striking resemblance to the "social movement unionism" that Seidman (1994) argues drove democratization from below in Brazil and South Africa. On the other hand, the coordinating role of the Communist Party, organizationally cemented in the tight integration of its union and party leadership, has made it possible to continuously scale up industry and sector-level struggles into a broader political program of expanding social and economic rights. This programmatic thrust, to cite a well-known example, is what has differentiated the Swedish working class from its British counterpart. As comparative studies of the relationship between labor movements and welfare states have shown, the crucial difference lies in the organizational-political form of working-class mobilization (Stephens 1979; Esping-Andersen 1991). As a disciplined and ideologically coherent political formation, the CPM has given the often spontaneous actions of the working class a degree of cohesion and continuity. Local struggles, be they on the shop floor or in the paddy fields, have been translated into statewide demands for state protection and regulation. Most significantly, the success of the CPM in penetrating the informal sector has provided organized labor with a broad social base cutting across the traditional urban-rural and skill-unskilled divisions, in stark contrast to a national labor scene in which unionization has largely been confined to the organized economy.

Second, as a party doctrinally suspicious of the transformative capacity of the "bourgeois state," the CPM, in pragmatically embracing the parliamentary route (made official after a failed insurrectionary phase in 1948), was not deterred from committing its resources to organizing from below. This social-movement dynamic was somewhat fortuitously strengthened by the party's exclusion from power in all but three years of the 1960–80 period. As a democratic oppositional force with broad-based if not majority support, the Communists busied themselves with the task of occupying the trenches of civil society, building mass-based organizations, ratcheting up demands, and cultivating a noisy but effective politics of contention. In this manner, the Communists in Kerala (much as their Italian counterparts) have established a strong presence in many intermediate institutions, including the cooperative movement, local governments (panchayats and municipalities), cultural organizations, and the educational system.[11] In addition to its officially sponsored mass organizations, Com-

---

[11] The CPM directly controls a number of press organs as well as the state's largest mass organizations for students (Student Federation of India, SFI), youth (Democratic Youth Feder-

munist activists have also been instrumental in building the Kerala Sastra Sahitya Parishad (KSSP), a "people's science movement" that has promoted popular education, environmentalism, and decentralized planning and development and is widely considered to be one of the most successful mass-based NGOs in India. Thus even when out of power the CPM and its offshoots have been able to shape the political agenda and influence public policy debates through parliamentary opposition, agitation, and entrenchment in civil society. Moreover, working- and middle-class support for the welfare state—secured on the strength of universal entitlements—has created a dominant political culture in which Congress governments have continued and even extended social-welfare policies initiated by Left Front governments.[12] No major piece of social or labor legislation has ever been reversed. Thus, despite its inability to widen its electoral base, the CPM has established itself as—to use the party's own terminology—the "leading force" in the state. It is this secure position that makes the CPM hegemonic in Gramsci's second sense of the term, namely the capacity to act strategically, to move beyond the immediate defense of class interests (economism) and "concretely coordinate" with other classes. This capacity is represented in the shift from the politics of class struggle and redistribution to the politics of class compromise and growth that dates from the mid-1980s.

Of the many determinants of class politics, the character of the state stands out as one of the most important (Katznelson and Zolberg 1986). Though the impetus came from below, a democratic state provided first the spaces, and then the levers, of class transformation. The Kerala state has not only provided the bureaucratic and legal instruments through which precapitalist social institutions have been dismantled, it has also effectively institutionalized the interests of the working class. Large segments of Kerala's working class, including the bulk of landless laborers, enjoy a wide array of statutory benefits, shop-floor rights, and social in-

---

ation of India, DYFI) and women (All-India Democratic Women's Association, AIDWA). If one includes the party's peasant organizations and its labor federation the Congress of Indian Trade Unions (CITU), the total membership in these organizations was 4.7 million in 1987. This compares to a figure of just over one million in 1978 (S. Sen 1990:33).

[12] To give a few examples: both the land reform of 1970 and the Kerala Agricultural Workers Act of 1974 were implemented by Congress-led coalitions. The Public Distribution System has been extended by every government. The high turnover rate in the ruling-party coalition has had no discernible impact on social expenditures. Since the first Communist ministry of 1957, the outlay for social services in all five-year plans has varied only marginally from a low of 19.6 percent (fourth plan) to a high of 22.6 percent (third plan) (GOK, State Planning Board 1992).

surance schemes. The mobilizational clout of labor has been inscribed in the laws, institutions, and political practices of the state. Welfare entitlements, wage legislation, market regulation, and other forms of political-administrative intervention have not only substantially insulated wage earners from the more debilitating effects of market forces but have also leveraged the bargaining capacity of workers. If these institutionalized linkages to labor have given the state a pronounced redistributive bias, they have also, somewhat paradoxically, positioned the state to play a critical role in coordinating class interests.

There are, however, clearly limits to pursuing a redistributive strategy of development in a private-property economy. The contradictions of the welfare state, commonly referred to in Kerala's public discourse as the "sustainability" problem, have thrust the question of growth to the forefront of the political debate. Redistributive politics have reached the point of diminishing returns. The lesson "of the contemporary crisis of the Kerala Model," in the words of T. M. Thomas Isaac, one of the CPM's leading new theoreticians, "is that in the absence of an expansion of the production base, in the long run, it is not possible to maintain or expand the redistributive gains" (Thomas Isaac and Kumar 1991:2703).

This point brings us back to the substantive concern of this book. In the past decade or so, the organized working class, as represented primarily by the CPM and its unions, has undergone a fundamental political reorientation, forsaking the politics of class struggle for the politics of class compromise. As they are now taking shape, these compromises bear important similarities to the societal pacts characteristic of European social democracies: in exchange for its political and institutional power to maintain a social wage, labor has made explicit concessions to capital by relaxing some of its historical control over production in the explicit hope of stimulating productive investments. The actual shape, modalities, and viability of these compromises, which vary dramatically across sectors in the balance of power between capital and labor, will be the focus of Chapters 3 and 4 for agriculture, and Chapters 6 and 7 for industry. Behind these variations, however, lie two constants—the mobilizational and strategic capacity of a programmatic and pragmatic left-wing party, and a state that has achieved a degree of authoritative power, secured on the strength of a redistributive form of embedded autonomy (Evans 1995), which is unparalleled in the subcontinent.

Disaggregating the State and Democracy

In exploring the role of the state in development, the bulk of the literature has focused on the national state and has treated the state as a discrete unit of analysis. Such a focus works well for the study of economic development and indeed has produced a particularly rich analytical taxonomy for scrutinizing the state's actions. The study of state-society relations calls for a different approach. The modern state may indeed represent a particularly concentrated form of power, but the exercise of that power is ultimately a relational phenomena, and the actual effect of state forms of power can only be fully explored at their many points of contact with society. As state-in-society perspectives have argued, we must disaggregate the state, recognizing not only the multiple arenas of state-society interaction, but also that state authority and state capacity are neither monolithic nor uniform, but rather uneven and contested (Migdal, Kohli, and Shue 1994).

Nowhere is this more true than in the study of redistribution and democratization. In many respects the transformative capacities required of states to achieve significant redistributive or equity-enhancing reforms are far greater than those required for economic reform (Evans and Rueschemeyer 1985; Kohli 1987). Similarly, the focus on formal state institutions and elite actors that has characterized much of the recent literature on democratization underplays the jagged and compromised nature of state authority in much of the Third World and loses sight of the fact that in all too many developing democracies "the components of democratic legality and, hence, of publicness and citizenship, fade away at the frontiers of various regions and class, gender and ethnic relations" (O'Donnell 1993:1361).

India provides a particularly telling illustration of the limitations of using the nation-state as a unit of analysis. As a set of apparatuses and institutions, the Indian state has enjoyed a comparatively long and successful history of nation-building and by Third World standards is characterized by a fairly cohesive and consolidated administrative structure. Nonetheless, the actual degree of logistical and authoritative state capacity varies significantly across provincial boundaries. As Dreze and Sen (1989, 1995) and Kohli (1987) have shown, differences in the extent and quality of public intervention across states in India have produced radically different levels of social development and redistribution, ranging from the dramatic leveling of disparities in Kerala, and to a lesser extent West Bengal, to the extremes of deprivation associated with Bihar and

Uttar Pradesh.[13] That Kerala has had far more success in pursuing equity-enhancing reforms than the nation as a whole, despite sharing identical organizational features and roughly comparable financial resources, points to the need to explore local state-society relations far more carefully.

The same point holds for the study of democracy. Conventional analyses that rely on formalistic definitions of democracy and political practices have failed to recognize the degrees of democracy within India. The basic procedural infrastructure of Indian democracy—specifically the constitution, the separation of powers, and regular and open elections at both the national and state levels—holds constant across the subcontinent. But if democracy is ultimately about the *effective* exercise of citizenship rights, then democratization in India has been highly uneven. At one extreme, one might point to the neofeudal politics of Bihar and Uttar Pradesh, India's two most populous states. Public legality in this region is compromised by the pervasive exercise of traditional forms of authority and social control. Patron-client dependencies severely limit civic association and local power brokers subvert the autonomous political spaces provided by electoral competition.[14] The contrast with Kerala is palpable and telling. The oft-repeated view in the political science literature is that Kerala is a "problem" state, beset by a proliferation of political parties and unions, unstable governments, overly politicized institutions, and seemingly endemic contestation. This view confuses (as theorists of political development are wont to do) democracy with order. Class-based mobilization in Kerala has not only severed the more debilitating forms of clientelism but, in conjunction with state intervention, has extended the reach of public legality. The covert forms of "everyday resistance" that define subaltern politics (Scott 1985) have taken front stage, playing out in multiple civic arenas and in substantively contested elections that animate political life from the village up. Needless to say, this has made for messy and noisy politics. But if "high-density citizenship" is the mark of democracy, then Kerala indeed scores high. The pronounced character of class conflict notwith-

[13] Dreze and Gazdar summarize the difference dramatically: "a new-born girl can expect to live *20 years longer* if she is born in Kerala rather than Uttar Pradesh. And the probability that she will die before the age of one is more than six times as high in Uttar Pradesh as in Kerala" (1996:40). Somewhere in between the low-performing Hindi-belt states and Kerala, one might point to the case of Tamil Nadu where a tradition of charismatic neopatrimonial politics, erected on the base of Dravidian cultural nationalism, has produced a stable, and by north Indian standards, moderately effective form of redistributive populism.

[14] Dreze and Gazdar draw a direct connection between the lack of local democracy in Uttar Pradesh and its dismal track record in social development (1996:100).

standing, violence has been rare and fairly contained. Kerala has experienced none of the so-called caste atrocities so common in rural India, and despite the presence of sizable minority communities it has witnessed only rare cases of communal (interfaith) rioting (Varshney forthcoming). Most notably, the resurgence in Indian national politics of communalism and its exclusions has had a negligible impact.[15] Civic peace has also been accompanied by effective and accountable government. Notoriously short-lived multiparty governments (normally a prescription for paralysis and pork) have had great success in legislating and implementing a wide range of institutional reforms and social programs. The programmatic and encompassing nature of public action marks the extent to which citizenship in Kerala, much as in the European case, has evolved beyond civic and political rights to include social rights (Marshall 1992).

The larger lesson here is that democracies are about more than just formal rights and institutions, constitutional procedures, and competitive elections. An authentic and consolidated democracy, as O'Donnell has argued, is one in which democratic practices have spread throughout society "creating a rich fabric of democratic institutions and authorities" (1988:288). Thus we must look beyond the conventional macroinstitutional concerns of the political scientist, and in particular the rarified "democratic" state, and investigate the intermediate- and local-level institutions and consultative arenas where "everyday" forms of democracy either flourish or flounder. We need, in other words, a sociology of democracy, one that specifically recognizes the dynamic affinity between a dense civil society and an institutionalized democracy (Putnam 1993).

A Note on Methods

This book is concerned with exploring a number of concrete outcomes such as levels of growth and redistribution in postcolonial Kerala. For this I have relied on a wide range of published and unpublished government documents to examine various economic indices, patterns of finance and investment, and levels of labor militancy and poverty. The Indian government has long been very active in collecting a wide range of statistics. By standards of the developing world, the quality of this data is certainly quite good. As much as possible, however, I have tried to use multiple in-

---

[15] The BJP (the Hindu-chauvinist party) has yet to establish a noticeable presence in Kerala's electoral politics. In the most recent municipal elections, the BJP captured only three out of 1,200 panchayats (village councils), and only one out of twenty-six municipalities.

dicators of a given variable, and where possible I have collected corroborating qualitative evidence.

But this book is even more specifically concerned with dynamic processes that cannot readily be captured with quantitative data. To examine and understand phenomena such as democratization, class compromise, and "stateness," I have relied on a combination of documents, interviews, and informal observation. Documents include official papers and reports and minutes from unions, political parties, the Labour Department, and local state bodies. I was also fortunate enough to stumble onto some key private documents, most notably the notes of a union leader who had regularly attended state-level negotiations on agricultural affairs for over thirty years. My richest source of data comes from 177 interviews conducted between November 1991 and December 1992, and in the summer of 1997. I interviewed state officials, party activists, unionists, farmers, laborers, and journalists. I also conducted a number of structured sets of interviews with nonrandom samples of informants. In the case of agriculture, in two separate villages I interviewed fifty-four farmers, laborers, and local officials in order to develop a full picture of local agrarian conditions. I also interviewed eleven CEOs in major industrial concerns to assess changes in Kerala's labor relations. Because I was concerned with actually disaggregating the state and exploring the points of interface between the state and society, I targeted specific sectors and traced them down through multiple levels. One illustration will suffice. The process of wage determination in agriculture in Kerala is organized both at the state level, through enabling legislation and organized concertations, and at the district and village levels, through formal and informal negotiations. To explore this process, I followed it from the capital down to the village. Having chosen two panchayats in two different districts (the choices are explained later), I systematically interviewed union officials, Labour Department officers, and farmer representatives at all three levels. Finally, because I was specifically interested in the process of negotiation and forging compromises, wherever and whenever possible I attended meetings and rallies where contested issues were taken up. In all, I attended seven different meetings of state-level industrial relations committees (IRCs), and a dozen meetings at the district or local level.

1

Classes and States in the Making of Development

As a dynamic social process, development is driven by the conflicts among organized social actors. Outcomes are varied and indeterminate. But they are not infinite and random. Insofar as my concern in this book is specifically with a case of democratic capitalism, which in this last decade of the twentieth century is indeed the modal shape that "development" has taken (with, of course, many permutations), it is possible to identify some patterns and make some causal claims. The key pattern I emphasize is the interplay of the processes of state formation and class mobilization in shaping the consolidation of a particular form of capitalism. Explaining why Kerala has evolved a social-democratic form of capitalism, and in doing so has diverged dramatically from the rest of India despite sharing the same basic political and economic structures, is my principal task here.

The most influential perspectives on development have always posited ideal or even necessary trajectories of development consisting of discrete stages of economic, social, and political change. Of course, the different social sciences all argue for the primacy of their respective domains. The lack of consensus notwithstanding, a common and recurrent assumption has been the difficulty, and for some even the inherent impossibility, of simultaneously securing the conditions for capitalism and mass democracy. In the political science literature this has taken the form of arguing, following Huntington's classic statement (1968), that economic transformation unleashes new patterns of social mobilization which, when left unchecked, threaten political stability and effective governance. In the economic literature, the view that economic reform must preceed social reform reflects the belief that growth and redistribution, at least during the

22

early stages of development, is a zero-sum game.[1] In either scenario, delaying the political and economic incorporation of subordinate classes becomes an implicit precondition for successful development. Democracy becomes viable only when institutions of modern governance have had sufficient time to take root. Equity concerns can be addressed only when the pie, enlarged by self-sustaining accumulation, is sufficiently large. This thinking has taken its most explicit and influential form in the so-called shock therapy versions of structural adjustment, in which politics and popular demands are viewed as inimical to successful implementation of market reforms. But rather than treating growth, democracy, and equity as discrete stages or issues, with corresponding policy arenas and calculable trade-offs, there are compelling historical and comparative reasons for arguing that they are inseparable and dynamically condition each other in shaping developmental trajectories.

Karl Polanyi (1944) was arguably the first to draw attention to the fact that the transition to a market economy—the "great transformation"—was made possible by social interventions that minimized the havoc that the commodification of land and labor threatened to wreak on the social fabric. Polanyi also drew an intriguing correlation between socially unmediated transitions and political outcomes. Where countervailing forces failed to manage the social impact of laissez-faire capitalism, Polanyi argued the ensuing political and social crises produced fascism. Barrington Moore (1966) has made a similar but more agent-centered claim, arguing that the political outcomes of the twentieth century hinged largely on how rural classes responded to the challenge of commercialization and whether, in the absence of a strong bourgeoisie, peasants were mobilized for reaction (resulting in fascist dictatorship) or revolution (resulting in communist dictatorship). More recently, Gregory Luebbert (1991) has shown that political outcomes of interwar Europe—fascism, liberalism, and social democracy—were determined by the relative success with which interwar regimes were able to reconcile liberal economic policies with the political challenge of accommodating working-class mobilization. Differences aside, these comparative and historical perspectives challenge the teleology of development theory by drawing attention to the fact that in Europe modernity has taken different paths, many of which produced calamitous dead ends, and all of which were profoundly shaped by

[1] Development economics has often parted company with standard neoclassical assumptions. The "basic needs" approach of the 1970s, the work of institutionalists, and the recent work on endogenous theories of growth have all questioned the primacy and effectiveness of market forces. For neoliberals however, the innate superiority of market allocations over political or bureaucratic allocations remains an article of faith.

the state-society dynamics through which the social conflicts of the "great transformation" were played out. The common denominator of all these scenarios has been the circumstances under which the masses entered politics.

If the European path was more checkered than the revisionism of development theory suggests, the circumstances of postcolonial development have only further blurred the stages. The differences separating the structural and historical circumstances of development in the post–World War II period from the early developers are far too great and varied to allow for generalization, but three sets of analytical issues can be highlighted.

The first concerns the interplay of market forces and social structures. Capitalist development in European was autocentric in the sense that it was driven primarily by domestic social relations and was characterized by dynamic internal linkages between the agrarian and industrial sectors, and between consumption and capital goods sectors. In the developing world, economic transformation originated in large part outside the national social structure. With some sectors more closely linked to the world economy than to the domestic economy, and with foreign capital playing the dominant role, the result has been what dependency theorists call disarticulated development: uneven economic transformation in which different sectors and even different modes of production coexist without being dynamically integrated. And because industrial growth has generally been slower than the pace of marketization (East Asia being the exception), precapitalist classes have been exposed to the competitive pressures of market economies (often losing access to their traditional means of subsistence) without being absorbed into the modern sectors of the economy. If the highly varied experience of late-developing countries could be generalized, one might say that economic modernization has not kept pace with the rate of social dislocation, creating particularly acute distributional conflicts.

A second wrench that has been thrown into the sequential logic of development is what might be called *compressed democratization*. The rise of democracy in Europe was fraught with conflict, but was nonetheless incremental. As Marshall (1992) has famously argued, citizenship in Europe evolved through three relatively discrete stages of civic, political, and social extension of rights, each stage in effect representing a higher level of working-class incorporation. In the developing world, in contrast, historical and geopolitical forces have preempted a graduated trajectory of democratic incorporation. The antinomies of capitalism and democracy were sharply posed from the very moment of decolonization. First, if the bourgeoisie in Europe was instrumental in promoting democracy (Moore

1966), the dynamics of dependent development, state-led industrialization, and resilient rural bases of social power have produced Third World bourgeoisies with a far more ambiguous relationship to democracy. Second, the extractive and despotic logic of colonial rule reinforced state power, as well as the power of local intermediaries (chiefs, landlords, caciques), at the expense of civil society. These institutional legacies severely limited the development of autonomous associational life in the postcolonial period. Third, whereas political incorporation in Europe consisted of gradually extending the franchise downward through the social structure more often than not in response to working-class mobilization, political participation in the developing world has often been introduced against the backdrop of "unformed" class structures in which authority is still very much vested in local strongmen. This difference in large part would appear to explain the pervasive fragmentation and clientalism of democratic political competition in postcolonial societies. In sum, because democratic institutions in the developing world have only partially evolved out of domestic struggles between classes, and between civil society and state, they are not well adapted to the challenge of managing class-based demands. Thus even when, as in the case of India, democracy has proven capable of accommodating a wide range of interests and of maintaining a modicum of stability, it has proven wholly incapable of promoting redistributive reforms and hence of organizing class compromise.

The third factor that has complicated the challenge of managing the double transition in much of the periphery is that it has taken place against a backdrop of ongoing nation- and state-building. The transition to full-blown industrial capitalism in western Europe followed after and was indeed crucially facilitated by the formation of centralized and rationalized nation-states. In much of the developing world, by contrast, state-building and nation-building remain contested processes and, as the state-society literature has emphasized, have proven to be endemic sources of conflict.

In sum, rapid but disarticulated integration into the world economy, compressed democracy, and the unfinished business of state-building have prevented even a semblance of sequenced phases of development. States in the developing world are thus faced with the simultaneous challenge of consolidating their own power and sovereignty, coping with the social dislocations of encroaching market forces, and answering to or otherwise managing a rapid proliferation of newly organized and mobilized citizen demands. The outcomes have been anything but uniform, ranging at one end from instances of total state disintegration (some African countries), the fragmentation of the polity and the pulverization of civil society (Latin America), crises of overload and governability (India), the resurgence of subnationalities and ethnic conflict (eastern Europe and South Asia), and, at the other end, the imposition of authoritarian but developmentally effective state domination (East Asia).

Thus it becomes clear that any understanding of development must embrace a comprehensive view that recognizes the complex interaction of structures, institutions, and social processes. We can begin disentangling this complex picture by recognizing that the dynamics and impact of economic transitions, far from being self-propelled, are critically mediated and shaped by the interface of state structures and social forces. Taking a cue from classical political economy, I maintain that states and social structures are "mutually constitutive" and, more specifically, that there is a dynamic relationship between class formation and the evolution of the modern state. These dynamics can prove to be stagnant and even disintegrative.[2] Or, as in the case of the "developmental state," they can be mutually and functionally reinforcing. Such a symbiosis is not, however, given through some inexorable process of systems integration. It is instead the stuff of politics and represents the consolidation—as do all institutions—of a specific balance of forces. Dissecting the developmental state requires focusing on the complex configuration of institutions and political practices that mediate the relationship between societal interests and state actions.

Developing States in Comparative-Historical Perspective

The idea that the modern state and capitalism are mutually constitutive has a long history. Its most classic expression is found in Max Weber's work, especially in his emphasis on rationalization—rule-bound behavior grounded in universalistic law—as undergirding both modern bureaucracy and capitalist enterprise. Weber pointed to an "elective affinity" between the rise of the modern bureaucratic state and the emergence of rational economic activity as embodied in the modern enterprise and institutionalized in the exchange relations of the market ([ca. 1927] 1981). That is, the modern state provided the predictability, impartiality and regularity of execution of laws and rules required for the expansion of a cap-

---

[2] See, for example, Bratton's argument that there has been a mutual "disengagement" of state and society in Africa (1994), and Stepan's depiction of the simultaneous weakening of state and civil society under Argentinean bureaucratic authoritarianism (1985).

italist economy. More ambitiously, Gramsci's writings on hegemony draw attention to the modern state's role in "coordinating" the interests of the dominant class with those of subordinate groups, thus actively organizing consent to capitalism. Neo-Marxist theories of the state (Offe 1984; O'Connor 1973) have adopted a similar, although somewhat more functionalist, view. The state and capitalism are viewed as not only mutually reinforcing but systemically integrated, with the state providing the institutional basis for the accumulation of capital (including the reproduction of labor power) and also securing capitalism's long-term viability by redressing its social contradictions through administrative interventions. This form of a hegemonic politics of production, in which the state plays an integral role in securing the material and social conditions of capitalism and regulating the labor-capital relationship, can be contrasted with a despotic politics of production in which the relationship between capital and labor goes unmediated by the state (Burawoy 1985).

The systemic character of modern capitalism is not, however, to be confused with its genesis (Cohen 1982). That state and society in advanced capitalist societies are interlinked in a positive-sum relationship is not the result of functional necessity. The "rationalization" of economic activity and political authority is historically specific, inextricably tied to the emergence of a capitalist class society and to the forging of class compromises. To theorize capitalism as an integrated "system" in which the political and the economic are institutionally separated but functionally coordinated, and in which the state plays the critical role of legitimating capitalism by organizing a redistribution of privately appropriated social surplus, is in fact to theorize the particular class history of European capitalism. Two distinct episodes of class formation gave birth to hegemonic capitalism.

The first was the rise of the bourgeoisie, symbiotically tied to the modern nation-state. As Weber writes, it is "out of this alliance of the state with capital, dictated by necessity [war-making], [that] arose the national citizen class, the bourgeoisie in the modern sense of the word. Hence it is the closed national state which afforded to capitalism its chance for development" (cited in Callaghy 1988:70). The ascendancy of this class as bearer of new relations of production *and* champion of liberal democracy was predicated however, as Moore (1966) has shown, on the political defeat of the ancien régime. Where the national bourgeoisie did triumph over landed elites and the monarchy, the establishment of representative institutions marked the formal integration of capitalism and democracy.

But formal democracy alone does not provide the basis for organized coordination of class interests. In the second episode, the substantive integration of capitalism and democracy followed from the mobilization of the working class and the extension of universal suffrage (Rueschemeyer, Stephens, and Stephens 1992). The terms under which working classes were incorporated in turn gave rise to different kinds of welfare states, with varying capacities for coordinating accumulation and redistribution—that is, for organizing class compromise. The differences between social-democratic, liberal, and corporatist welfare states are significant, and have been tied to working-class mobilizational and cross-class coalitional histories (Esping-Andersen 1991). So the functional integration of the modern bureaucratic state and capitalism can only be understood as the outcome of historically concrete class struggles and their interaction with state forms.

Developing states are often viewed as Leviathans. From a strictly formal and technical point of view, they often enjoy material and organizational resources that far surpass what European states had enjoyed at comparable levels of socioeconomic development. The process of state formation in Europe, when successful, was a slow and incremental one of marshalling and centralizing resources from society (Mann 1984). In the nineteenth century, the state rapidly expanded its powers by bargaining for more resources from ordinary producers and capital in exchange for providing new services and expanding representation (Tilly 1984). Though the need for state expansion was driven by interstate competition, the terms of expansion were internally negotiated. The historical roots of the postcolonial state are instead marked by a disjuncture: having in many instances inherited the formidable machinery of the extractive colonial state, it possesses bureaucratic apparatuses and coercive resources that were transferred from states at higher levels of formation; this is the sense in which Alavi (1982) has characterized the postcolonial state as "overdeveloped."[3] But with the exception of the East Asian newly industrialized countries (NICs), most postcolonial states have failed to translate formal infrastructural capabilities into authoritative power. State-building has followed a tortuous and contested path of compromising with and accommodating traditional strongmen and local notables (Migdal 1988). In reinforcing the power of precapitalist elites, these accommodations have more often than not crippled the capacity of states to pursue the ambitious mandates of postcolonial nationalism. Indeed, rather than building the synergistic and developmentally functional relationships with society asso-

---

[3] Of the more notable effects of this disjuncture has been the role of the military. Whereas the centralization of coercive capabilities—technologies and men—in Europe was achieved through a gradual process of negotiation and compromise with society, modern military institutions in the developing world are external impositions, and continue to be funded with little internal negotiation or accountability (Tilly 1992: chap. 7).

ciated with the "developmental state," many postcolonial states have at best become, in Callaghy's term, "lame Leviathans" (1988), or at worst, predatory apparatuses. Because the range of outcomes has been so wide, monocausal explanations of rational choice theory are not very helpful. Instead, explanations must be sought in the historical specificity of institution-building and state-society engagements (Migdal, Kohli, and Shue 1994).

Migdal (1988) begins with the proposition that the relationship between state and society is one of conflict, pitting the traditional mechanisms of social control that prevail in precapitalist societies against the centralized bureaucratic-legal authority of the state. Rather than the conventional smorgasbord of diffuse "primordial loyalties" readily swept away by state action, traditional society is a weblike constellation of overlapping forms of social power in which "the overall sum of authority may be high . . . but the exercising of that authority may be fragmented" (28). These forms of social control, concretely rooted in "strategies of survival," present a formidable barrier to the state's ability to effectively "penetrate society, regulate social relationships, extract resources, and appropriate or use resources in determined ways" (4). Pressed by the political exigencies of staying in power, state authorities in Third World countries are invariably led to seek accommodations with traditional strongmen. The political imperative of striking such compromises—given the state's inability to mobilize independent sources of support—forms the basis of the politics of patronage. Patronage regimes in turn strengthen the authority of strongmen, elevating them to the position of power brokers mediating between the state and local clienteles and thus further limiting the state's ability to orchestrate institutional and social reforms. Much of the literature on the developing state, spanning the full range of political regimes from democratic India (Frankel 1978) to authoritarian Brazil (Hagopian 1994), has pointed to the role of traditional oligarchies in frustrating the efforts of political elites to build state capacity.

The key contribution of the state-society literature is to have challenged the tendency within development theory to reify the state by according it the monolithic and unitary qualities associated with such labels as "capitalist," "rent-seeking," or "dependent" (Migdal 1994). Instead we need to recognize that there are multiple arenas—material, organizational, and symbolic—of engagement and contestation between state and society. Depending on the actual configuration of forces, including strategic alignments, states might have varying degrees of success, if any, in forging national identities, imposing the rule of law, or instituting property reforms. The point here is that in contrast to reductionist perspectives, it becomes possible both to acknowledge the independent significance of state actions and to recognize that the social structures over which they preside are difficult to transform. Despite its developmental incapacity, Migdal's "weak" state remains an independent actor, with a logic and interests of its own. The accommodations it makes are born of political calculations made necessary by the trade-offs between securing political stability (exercising power through strongmen) and extending state power (displacing strongmen).

Rethinking the Developmental State

In differentiating developmental from nondevelopmental states, the analytic usefulness of Weber's ideal type of bureaucratic rationalization is well established. Actual state capacity, however, is intimately tied to a state's autonomy, that is, the ability of state agencies to surmount particularistic interests and secure collective goals. And unlike bureaucratic capacity, the value of which can be scaled on a continuum that runs from the polar extremes of patrimonial arbitrariness to rule-bound rationality, the value of autonomy has proven to be treacherously two-sided. Autonomy has been conventionally identified with insulation and indeed has most recently been given pride of place in neoliberal calls for shielding technocratic decision making from politics. But insulation without connectedness is a poisoned gift (Evans 1995). What makes the modern state unique as an organization is its ability to coordinate and structure social cooperation, to marshall and channel resources—material and organizational—within society (Mann 1984). If the modern state is to make good on its bureaucratic capabilities, it must target discrete groups that are defined in terms of their instrumentality for achieving specific economic or social ends. The autonomy of the state as such must be complemented by what Evans (1995) calls its "embeddedness," that is, the extent and quality of its concrete ties to society. For it is only through such concrete ties that "the institutionalized channels for the continual negotiation and re-negotiation of goals and policies" (Evans 1992:164) necessary for deploying an effective strategy of state-led development can be secured.

The concept of embeddedness is particularly useful because it allows us to distinguish state-society ties that are mutually reinforcing and instrumental to securing development objectives from those that degenerate into the rent-seeking of rational choice theory or the self-defeating accommodations of Migdal's weak state. All states are enmeshed in patterns of authority, power, and influence. Only close empirical analysis can disentangle those patterns characterized by clientalism from those that approach the ideal-typical universalism of rational-legal states.

In the past decade, the East Asian states, specifically Taiwan and South Korea,[4] have become the benchmark for developmental capacity. The literature on developmental states has focused the spotlight on the role that strategic state interventions have played in nurturing and directing the growth of the market in the particular circumstances of late development.[5] The success of these interventions derives from the nature of the specific institutional configurations through which the planning and "disciplining" functions of state managers and the entrepreneurial activities of private groups have synergistically combined. The merit of this literature is to have recognized first that the state can indeed be a critical and independent actor, and to then to have rigorously examined specific linkages that translate state power into measurable developmental outcomes. As a set of analytical insights, the literature on the East Asian state has provided an important rebuttal to neoliberal and dependency accounts of development. To treat these states as modular developmental states, however, as much of this literature has implicitly done, raises some thorny theoretical problems.

The first concerns the generalizability of the model. The East Asian "miracle" economies all evolved and prospered under rather extraordinary geopolitical and historical circumstances. Cumings (1987) notes that both South Korea and Taiwan enjoyed the protection and tutelage of Japanese and then American hegemonic spheres of influence. The politics of the cold war facilitated export-led growth by creating exceptionally favorable economic conditions including high levels of direct aid, concessional lending, and preferential access to core markets. Even more critical was the interplay of external and internal forces in laying the groundwork for the ascendancy of a powerful and autonomous state (Koo 1987); in both cases, the preconditions for state intervention and capitalist development were established through massive societal dislocations (war and/or colonialization) and structural reforms imposed by occupation forces. Extensive land reforms implemented in Taiwan by the invading Leninist

---

[4] Because Hong Kong and Singapore are city-states and have no agrarian hinterland, they are excluded from the present discussion.
[5] For a review of this literature see Onis 1991. Key works include Evans 1979 on Brazil, Johnson 1982 on Japan, Amsden 1989 on Korea, Gold 1986 on Taiwan, Stepan 1978 on Peru, Bardhan 1984 on India, and Lubeck 1992 on Malaysia. Key comparative works include Wade 1990 and Deyo 1987 on the Asian NICs, Haggard 1990 on East Asia and Latin America, and Evans 1995 on Brazil, India, and Korea.

state-party apparatus of the Kuomintang and in Korea by the Japanese colonial state and then the U.S. military dissolved precapitalist institutions and paved the way for peasant-based capitalist agriculture. In the case of South Korea, Amsden ties the consolidation of state power to the weakness of all social classes: the landed aristocracy had been emasculated by land reform and the peasantry atomized into smallholders, the working class was too small, and the capitalists were too dependent on the state (1989:52). Gold (1986) emphasizes the Leninist-militarist structure of the Kuomintang and its reliance on violence in the Taiwanese state's successful subjugation of a society in disarray. As Castells succinctly notes, "the dominant classes were either destroyed, disorganized, or made totally subordinate to the state" (1992:65). In sum, a prostrate society offered little resistance to the rapid consolidation of state power.

If the economic decoupling from Japan and the geopolitical reconfiguration of World War II in the Pacific conspired to tilt the balance of power toward the state in East Asia (Koo 1987), history also provided the building blocks for rapid bureaucratization. The Korean state had a long history of meritocratic recruitment and inherited a robust and extensive administrative structure from Japanese colonial rule (Kohli 1994). The steel frame of the Taiwanese state was provided by the discipline of a battle-hardened military organization in exile. In both cases, moreover, external military and economic support coupled with powerful legitimating ideologies born of the anticommunist "politics of survival" (Castells 1992:53) provided a coherent nationalist mandate for rapid development and afforded state elites a high degree of discretion. With respect to both autonomy and capacity, any analytical appreciation of the institutional features of the East Asian developmental states must be qualified by the observation that they emerged from a particularly fortuitous convergence of internal and external factors.

A final qualification to the prototype status of the East Asian state is the danger of conflating development with growth. The East Asian developmental state is first and foremost a *capitalist* developmental state characterized by its engagement with an emerging and state-fashioned entrepreneurial class. Different forms of embeddedness can produce synergies that are just as certainly developmental but not necessarily oriented toward growth. The almost exclusive focus on industrial development that has preoccupied the literature on the state has diverted attention from analyzing redistributive outcomes, including successful cases of pregrowth "support-led" social development (Dreze and Sen 1989). It has also downplayed the fact that many postcolonial states have had to answer to very different political imperatives. Herring notes that, given the legacies of colonialism, "the peripheral developmental state was more likely to legitimate itself, and perhaps to view its success, in terms of non-wealth-maximizing desiderata: eradication of poverty and social indignities, balanced regional growth to bring up backward areas, and so on" (1999:3).

East Asian states faced no such constraints. The single-minded determination with which state elites pursued growth was predicated on the political and ideological capacity to virtually ignore popular demands.[6] The political exclusion of the working class not only streamlined planners' range of policy concerns but also facilitated wage-repressive strategies of economic competition. Thus institutional successes in "governing" the market were critically tied to highly effective modes of labor regulation (Deyo 1987). Repressive capacity also proved instrumental in whipping potential entrepreneurial elements into shape. Direct repression neutralized the greatest threat to national economic policy, capital flight. In 1961, South Korea's military government threw profiteers in jail, passed legislation prohibiting "illicit wealth accumulation" (exporting profits), and threatened violators with confiscation. Having set the rules, the state then initiated partnerships (Amsden 1989:72). Business elites in Taiwan have been even more tightly controlled (Gold 1986). Capital was initially coerced, rather than invited, to participate in the national economic development project. The East Asian developmental state is a rare genus indeed. It has operated largely independently of the political pressures, distributional coalitions, populist impulses, and dominant class interests that have, as a rule, frustrated the realization of Weber's ideal-typical modern bureaucratic state.

Whereas the institutions regulating state-market and state-society relations in East Asia were forged largely from above, at the behest of singularly autonomous states, corresponding institutions in most of the developing world have evolved through a much more politicized and contested process of pact-making, concessions, and political deals, which compromised both the autonomy and capacity of the state. There is an irony here that stands neoliberalism on its head. If the market-augmenting strategies of midwifery and husbandry (Evans 1995) that characterized the East Asian state's carefully nurtured and synergistic relationship with business

---

[6] The political exclusion of the working class did not, however, rule out effective redistribution, as in the Latin American case. The redistributive and social successes of the East Asian NICs were not secured politically, but rather through extremely favorable material conditions (Haggard 1990; Dreze and Sen 1989). Initial conditions of asset distribution in agriculture secured comparatively equitable income distribution in rural areas. And the sheer magnitude of growth achieved through export-led industrialization guaranteed real income growth despite wages that lagged behind productivity.

ultimately prevailed over more regulatory and direct forms of intervention, it is precisely because state managers initially enjoyed the untrammeled capacity to discipline capital (and labor) and preempt the formation and hardening of distributive coalitions. The state could, in other words, act as the executive committee of a bourgeoisie that it cajoled into existence. In contrast, the heavy-handed interventions of dirigiste developing states (which ultimately fostered the formation of rent-seeking interests) can be traced to the difficulties state builders faced in removing precapitalist barriers to integrated national markets, a project that was complicated by the separate and often antagonistic social origins of political and economic elites (Chaudhry 1993).

In emphasizing the sociohistorical determinants of state capacity in East Asia the point is not to suggest that institutional forms derive from underlying political and societal factors. As comparative studies of the East Asian economies highlight, there is actually great variation in the institutional character of public-private partnerships which explains divergences in the pattern of development.[7] Moreover, the study of these forms is critical to our understanding of how markets can be nurtured, even engineered, by strategic state interventions (Evans 1995). But institutions are the sums of historical vectors, as indeed the literature on developmental states recognizes but often underplays. In the case of the Asian NICs, the linkages, policy tools, pilot agencies, public-private partnerships, and corporatist arrangements that underwrote state stewardship of the economy were the product of a very specific state-society balance. As we have seen, societal disruptions coupled with external geopolitical dynamics converged to create a weak society and a comparatively uncluttered path to state domination.

The final point about the developmental state that must be raised concerns its sustainability. Well before the financial crisis of 1997, the political and institutional arrangements of the East Asian accumulation project were being increasingly tested by new social conflicts. In South Korea in particular, rapid industrialization had underwritten the formation of a large, cohesive, and increasingly militant industrial working class. Politically and institutionally, East Asian embeddedness was predicated on exclusionary mechanisms of rule that stifled the emergence of intermediary political forms (for example, independent judiciaries and political parties) and stunted the growth of civil society. If the class specificity of its embed-

---

[7] The contrast between the family-based small-enterprise structure of Taiwan and the dominance of the vertically integrated multidivisional cheabols (conglomerate) in Korea is the most obvious example (Castells 1992).

dedness, that is, its ties to business elites, served the project of accumulation well, it has also made the prospect of developing more inclusive forms of political representation that much more difficult (Evans 1995:227–34).[8]

The social conflicts that emerged from authoritarian development have, in fact, driven significant political reforms across a wide range of cases. Most notably, in Brazil and South Africa, the absence of legitimate channels for expressing grievances and institutional mechanisms for organizing accommodations pushed what were shop-floor-centered and economistic unions into broader and more political alliances (Seidman 1994). Though pressures from below have resulted in democratic reforms, the degree of democratic "deepening" remains an open question (O'Donnell 1993). Whether these countries will be able to grant broader and more substantive political representation to subordinate classes while sustaining the conditions for economic growth in an increasingly competitive global economy emerges as the most pressing question of the decade to come (Onis 1991; Przeworski 1995). At the moment, it is clear that weak and fragmented civil societies and poorly developed democratic institutions—both exacerbated by structural adjustment policies—do not augur well for democratic consolidation (O'Donnell 1993; Chaudhry 1993).

The dilemmas of the "double transition" call for a broader test of a state's developmental capacity. The relative neglect of the political dimension of the developmental state has provided us with a one-dimensional view of late development. Because the question of development has been phrased in terms of growth—and this is as true of institutionalist perspectives as of Marxist development theories—insufficient attention has been paid to the social and political problems associated with the emergence of a market economy. Our understanding and definition of the developmental state must be broadened. As White notes, "The democratic developmental state will need to have a broad writ with at least three basic socioeconomic functions: regulative, infrastructural and redistributive. It will also need sufficient political authority and administrative capacity to manage the social and political conflicts arising both from the persistence of 'primordial ties' and from the tensions inherent in a successful growth process" (1995:31).

---

[8] The general strike of January 1997 in South Korea, described as the largest ever, is a case in point. Workers struck to protest the new labor legislation aimed at increasing management's prerogative and curtailing the growth of independent unions. The legislation was debated only within the ruling party and passed in a closed session of parliament (*Le Monde Diplomatique*, Paris, February 1997).

The case of Kerala provides an example of one such alternative scenario of state-society engagement. Through an iterative process of class mobilization and state intervention played out within formal democratic institutions, state embeddedness has taken the form of a mutually reinforcing project of social-redistributive transformation. The net effect has been the consolidation of a *democratic developmental state* marked by incorporation of the subordinate classes.

Class, State, and Politics in the Transition to Capitalism

In recent years, stage-based and evolutionary theories of development have come under increasing attack. The very concept of "transition," which implies discrete stages with identifiable contours, has lost much of its attraction. Thus Stark and Bruszt write that "in contrast to the transition problematic . . . we see social change not as transition from one order to another but as transformation—rearrangements, reconfigurations, and recombinations that yield new interweavings of multiple social logics that are a modern society" (1998:7). It is indeed critical to emphasize that there are multiple paths to economic modernity, and multiple outcomes. The transformation from command or state-dominated economies to market economies, which has been the focus of the recent literature on economic change, represents, however, a different problem from the debate that was at the heart of classical political economy and sociology, namely the transition to capitalism. What differentiates these two debates is the centrality of labor, and in particular the "agrarian question." In eastern Europe and, to a lesser extent, parts of Latin America, the most basic precondition for capitalism, the existence of formally free labor, has been secured. The transition to capitalism, as Marx and Weber, and later Polanyi, argued, was about the transformation of labor into a commodity. "Capitalism" notes Katznelson, "is unthinkable without proletarianization" (1986:14). In this sense, the use of the term "precapitalist" (with its implicit notion of transition) is justified in that it serves to emphasize that in much of the developing world the commodification of labor (and land) remains unfinished. Market transformations, then, must not be confused with the "great transformation." In this book the concern is with the latter, and the processual dynamic of transformation, rather than the teleology of transition, is emphasized in order to highlight the centrality of social change and hence the multiplicity of outcomes.

Of the many rebuttals to the deterministic readings of agentless economic transformation—recently given new life in breathless accounts of the irresistible forces of globalization—Robert Brenner's remains the most compelling. His basic argument can be easily summarized. In the Smithian (classical) as well as what Brenner (1977) labels neo-Smithian (world-system and dependency) theories of genesis, capitalism is equated with the expansion of markets. As trade expands, increased demand stimulates specialization of labor and more productive patterns of investment. Brenner rejects this causal sequence by arguing that production for the market does not necessarily require the commodification of land and labor. Precapitalist agrarian economies can respond to new market opportunities without reorganizing production. Indeed, as Brenner and others point out, capitalist economic development is just one possible outcome of the expansion of market forces. Increased exposure to commercial pressures and competitive product markets is just as likely to lead to the extension of repressive labor systems (for example, the second serfdom in fifteenth-century eastern Europe). Only with the qualitative transformation in the relations of production—the relations among classes that govern the deployment of land and labor—and specifically the emergence of a capitalist mode of surplus extraction does production for the market assume the dynamic, self-sustaining, and systemic qualities associated with modern capitalism. To quote Brenner: "Economic development can only be fully understood as the outcome of the emergence of new class relations more favorable to new organizations of production, technical innovations, and increasing levels of productive investment" (1985:18).

There are two critical points in Brenner's argument for making the case that economic change is driven by sociopolitical transformations. Precapitalist societies encompass a wide range of political and cultural formations, but analytically, and in opposition to capitalism, they are distinguished by the fact that land, labor, and capital are not commodities and cannot as such be optimally combined into a capitalistic organization of production. The use of labor and land in precapitalist societies is socially and politically embedded, regulated by a complex tapestry of customary rights, overlapping and negotiable claims, and forms of social domination. For economic sociologists it is, of course, a truism that all economic activities, including those of advanced capitalist societies, are governed by nonmarket mechanisms including social ties and networks. The fact that economic exchange is always socially embedded—that is, governed in part by nonmarket forces—is not, however, the same as arguing that existing social and political relations preclude reorganizing and recombining labor and land in response to new market opportunities. The second point is that any set of institutionalized social relationships congeals a distribution of power—and specifically the power to appropriate surplus—which privileged, vested, or dominant interest groups or classes will naturally seek to reproduce. These social relations in turn determine whether surplus is reinvested primarily in consumption (kinship systems), coercion (tributary systems), or production (capitalism), to use Wolf's classifications (1982).

The resiliency of precapitalist economic institutions must, as such, be located in their social and political relations. If there is a logic to any economic system, it is to be found in the full constellation of forms of domination—ideological, institutional, coercive—through which the social order underpinning the production system is reproduced. More generally, then, we rejoin Migdal here by noting that the "solidity" of precapitalist institutions, even in the face of powerful market forces or a modernizing state, resides largely in the internal coherence of its configuration of political and social power. Elites have an obvious interest in maintaining the social structures through which their privileges are secured and, in doing so, divert surpluses into the reproduction, through coercion or persuasion, of those structures. And, in the absence of viable alternatives, and given the reciprocities (however asymmetrical) and subsistence guarantees that characterize precapitalist systems, subordinate groups have little short-term incentive to challenge the system. Precapitalist institutions do not dissolve under the irresistible logic of capital; they are politically destroyed or transformed, and under only the most exceptional of circumstances. It is for this reason, as Mouzelis has noted, that the neglect of the political "is particularly limiting in the analysis of peripheral capitalism, where all too often it is struggles over the means of domination and coercion, rather than struggles over the means of production, that seem to be central for understanding overall societal transformations" (1988:39).

The state looms large in reproducing social order. It must also then, as Marx insisted, play a critical role in the process of primitive accumulation, a point that has been elaborated in comparative studies of European agrarian transitions. The relationship of the state to agrarian structures in the developing world has proven to be just as critical to economic transformation. In East Asia, as we have seen, highly autonomous states orchestrated wholesale transformations in the agrarian social structure, implementing land reforms, developing rural infrastructure, stimulating technological innovations, providing critical inputs, and, most dramatically, redirecting surpluses from agriculture to industry (Amsden 1985; Burmeister 1990). The centrality of the state is highlighted by the fact that primitive accumulation has been engineered from above in countries that were both formally capitalist (Taiwan) and communist (China) (Ka and

Selden 1986). At the other end of the spectrum, weak and neopatrimonial African states have largely failed in their endeavors to transform the countryside (Boone 1994). In Latin America, a peasant household and subsistence-oriented rural economy alongside a capital-intensive largeholder sector has been actively reproduced by states politically beholden to landed elites. And in India, as we shall see in greater detail later, the ties of the ruling Congress Party to dominant landed castes explains the general incapacity of a populist state to restructure agrarian relations.

As important as it is to recognize the role of the state in shaping agrarian transitions, it is just as critical to acknowledge that modern states are also *effects* of agrarian transformations. "One of the basic axioms of historical materialism," Anderson reminds us, "[is] that secular struggle between classes is ultimately resolved at the *political*—not at the economic or cultural—level of society. In other words, it is the construction and destruction of States which seal the basic shifts in the relations of production, so long as classes subsist" (1974:11). In the most influential statement of this idea, Moore (1966) argues that the political character of the modern state results from the outcome of struggles that oppose lords and peasants. Where landlords successfully preserved themselves, the outcome was fascism. Where peasants ultimately triumphed, the outcome was communist dictatorship. Where landlords were defeated by an ascendent bourgeoisie, or transformed themselves in tacit alliance with a strong bourgeoisie, the outcome was democracy. The ambiguous case is India, where Moore argues that an aborted transition has produced a genuine but extremely weak democratic state, incapable of addressing the problems of economic backwardness.

We can now draw an important conclusion. Any understanding of the conditions that favor the emergence of a state capable of pursuing transformative projects must begin with an analysis of the historical circumstances of agrarian transitions. Not only is every modern state a product of such transitions, but its character and, most important, its links to society are critically structured by the dynamics of the transition, be they internally or externally driven. Most critically, the prospects for political and economic modernization are directly tied to the emasculation or transformation of landed elites, as much a precondition for democracy and capitalism as for the expansion of the modern state.[9] As we shall see in

---

[9] Evans makes this point forcefully: "The degree to which the state apparatus was decoupled from landed elites is even more important to the developmental success of the major East Asian NICs than is the relative autonomy of the state vis-à-vis the industrial bourgeoisie" (1987:214).

the next chapter, a completed agrarian transition is precisely what distinguishes Kerala from the rest of India.

Capitalism and Economic Development: The Transition Within

At the most rudimentary level, those who view capitalism as a social system of production identify the wage labor form as its defining characteristic. Hence the attention paid to the historical process of primitive accumulation, by which precapitalist producers are separated from the means of production and transformed into an army of wage laborers with nothing but their labor to sell. The demise of precapitalist institutions, while conventionally equated with the genesis of capitalism, should not, however, be equated with capitalist economic development. The wage labor form is widespread in much of the developing world, yet the "reproduction of capital on an ever-expanding scale" that characterizes *systemic* capitalism remains elusive. Brenner captures this distinction succinctly: "The differencia specifica of modern economic growth . . . is not, per se, the spread of international trade, nor the rise of cooperation, nor the growth of manufacture, nor the extension of machinofacture—although all of these things do, of course, contribute to economic growth. What distinguishes modern economic growth is something more general and abstract: it is the presence in the economy of a *systematic* and *continuous* tendency or drive to transform in the direction of greater efficiency" (1986:24).

The paradox of economic development in the developing world—and especially in India—is the existence of capitalist social forms, which are the result of primitive accumulation, in the absence of systemic capitalism. Thus is necessary to explore the problematic of a second transformation *within* what is conventionally called capitalism.

The dispossession of workers from their instruments of production frees up land and labor and makes combination, cooperation, and specialization possible, yet it does not of itself generate the drive for innovation. Profit, competition, and even accumulation do not necessarily revolutionize the system of production. To understand this paradox we must return to Marx's classic distinction between absolute and relative forms of surplus value. The former is taken to express any combination of means by which surplus is obtained by squeezing labor. Most characteristically, this would involve some form of extraeconomic coercion, hence its association with precapitalist structures. But absolute surplus can also be extracted from workers, as in Marx's classical example, by extending the workday, or, much more commonly, pushing down wages. The point is that absolute surplus extraction is a zero-sum game. The capitalist's gain is exactly the worker's loss. The extraction of relative surplus value, however, relies on increasing productivity. While the trade-off in exchange values remains a zero-sum game, the increased output per unit of labor power produces a greater total output of use values (Burawoy 1985:28).

The classical political economists drew a categorical distinction between unfree and free labor. But free labor in both senses of the term, that is, free from the means of subsistence and free to sell itself, is historically constituted, and, as Miles (1987) reminds us, there are degrees of unfree labor. Labor may be bought and sold, but the contractual character of this relationship should not obscure the inherently asymmetrical social and political relations that often underlie the exchange, especially in contexts where "low intensity citizenship" (O'Donnell 1993) prevails. Even in the most competitive capitalist markets, labor may be commodified, but it is never just a commodity. It is constituted by and through social relations among classes, and thus can achieve varying degrees of self-realization. Wages— the value of labor—are never simply a function of supply and demand but reflect the balance of power between capital and labor, a balance that is shaped by institutional and organizational forces (state intervention, collective bargaining) as well as cultural and ideological ones (moral conceptions of a "fair" wage). The social conditions under which labor is made available to the market thus directly shapes the logic of surplus extraction and hence accumulation.

In a despotic regime (to use Burawoy's terminology [1985]) workers no longer have access to the means of subsistence, lack collective organization, and enjoy few, if any, protections from either state, guild, or community. They are thus completely exposed to the "dull compulsion of economic forces" and dependent on the market for survival. But if workers are "freed" from the instruments of production and must secure their livelihoods in the market, they are not free from extraeconomic forms of control. In contrast to fully commodified labor (free in the double sense), labor's absolute subjection to the market under despotic capitalism works *through* the social subjugations of gender, caste, race, ethnicity, and region. In the absence of effective social protection or self-organization, this extreme social vulnerability and exposure to market forces (compounded by large labor surpluses) favors despotic forms of authority in both the labor market and the workplace. In turn, these social relations make labor-squeezing strategies of profitability far more attractive than productivity-based strategies.

The politically unorganized and socially vulnerable character of labor

under despotic capitalism stands in contrast to the class-formed and socially protected character labor assumes under hegemonic (dynamic) capitalism. I emphasize this distinction within capitalism because it explains
India's arrested capitalist transformation. In agriculture and the so-called
unorganized (informal) sector of industry, as I explore in detail throughout
this book, the predominance of labor-squeezing has less to do with the
forms of direct coercion that characterize precapitalist economics than with
the social vulnerability of labor. Outside the organized factory sector and
white collar employment, the bulk of the wage-earning class is suspended
between a declining traditional economy with its guarantees of subsistence
and a young democracy in which forms of social domination such as caste
and clientelism persist. Underpinning the "unity of the reproduction of
labor power and the process of production" (Burawoy 1985:126) that
characterizes despotic capitalism is the double political and social disen-
franchisement (no customary rights, no social rights) of labor.

The advent of hegemonic capitalism is marked by what Polanyi referred to as the re-embedding of markets in society and more specifically
the expansion of social citizenship associated with the welfare state. As
the state and labor organizations emerge to actively institutionalize social
limits to the whip of the market, the reproduction of labor is decoupled
from social vulnerabilities. It is precisely in this sense that I will argue
that class mobilization and democratization in Kerala have severely curtailed the purview of despotic capitalism. Unionization and the building
of what is by Third World standards a developed welfare state has socialized the costs of labor reproduction and leveraged the bargaining capacity of labor. The transition to hegemonic capitalism remains unfinished,
however. Precisely because the period of despotic capitalism was cut
short and because democratization and the extension of social citizenship
rights were, by historical standards, premature, capital remains in a sense
underdeveloped and social democracy overdeveloped. The resulting economic crisis has, however, set the stage for the crystallization of the politics of class compromise and heightened the imperative of effective state
coordination of class interests.

Democracy and Class Compromise

The advanced or hegemonic stage of capitalism is predicated on the active
organization of class compromise. Such a compromise necessarily rests on
a material base, in which labor is guaranteed a share of the social surplus

in return for its support of private-property capitalism (Przeworski 1985). But class compromise is first and foremost political. The political economy literature on advanced capitalist economies generally takes for granted (crisis tendencies notwithstanding) that some sort of fairly stable compromise between private profits and redistribution has been worked out. For the developing world, such arrangements are generally assumed to be impossible, either because the material base is too narrow and distributional inequalities too severe to allow for class coordination, or, in a Huntingtonian vein, because reconciling such antagonistic interests is simply beyond the institutional carrying capacity of the system. The case of Kerala defies both assumptions. Across both agriculture and industry and against the backdrop of a very precarious economic situation, a stable class compromise has emerged. Making this case amounts to making a claim about the autonomy of the political: under certain historical circumstances class politics and democratic institutions, quite independently of economics, can be the basis for reconciling, within limits, the logic of accumulation and the democratic imperative of redistribution.

Classical political theorists were inclined to see democracy and capitalism as inherently at odds. The extension of the vote to the propertyless would inevitably threaten private property. Thus James Madison spoke of a "permanent animosity between opinion and property." Yet, much as democracy under capitalism can be a source of acute tension, democracy is also the very means through which class compromise can be forged. This view originates from the recognition that class interests under capitalism can be reconciled, or in Gramsci's expression, "concretely coordinated" (the compromise is concrete in the sense that it rests on a material base). The working class consents to capitalism—specifically to the prerogative of capitalists to organize production and to make investment decisions—because, as Przeworski puts it, "Current realization of material interests of capitalists is a necessary condition for the future realization of material interests of any group under capitalism" (1985:139).

Those material interests are not static because under capitalist conditions of production (relative surplus extraction) cooperation produces positive-sum gains. Yet while the private appropriation of surplus is a precondition of capitalist growth, there is no structural guarantee under a private-property economy that surpluses (wages withheld in the present) will be productively invested (Przeworski 1985:139). Thus the consent of the working class is economically rational only if there is a reasonable probability that capitalists will indeed behave as capitalists. And it is precisely democracy that provides the means—the "rules of the game," structured

iterations, bargaining procedures, transparencies, and mechanisms of interest aggregation—through which the terms of a positive-sum trade-off, a
necessarily delicate balance between current and future wages, can be secured. Political democracy is the historically specific form under which the
struggle over the social surplus can be institutionalized under capitalism.
Burawoy provides the most succinct formulation: "The combination of
capitalism and democracy is a compromise in which those who don't own
the means of production consent to private property while those who do
own the means of production consent to political institutions that organize an uncertain but limited redistribution of resources" (1989:71).

Market forces do not produce socially optimal outcomes, and economic forecasting, including the long- and short-term trade-offs of current wage levels, is imprecise at best. The terms of class compromise cannot as such be read from market signals. As Przeworski (following
Gramsci) argues, class compromise must be politically organized and institutionally secured. There must be not only clearly defined and organized class interests, but also institutions and political processes through
which the terms of class compromise, which are in continuous flux, can
be negotiated.

Two problems are involved here. As Marx recognized, but never adequately problematized, capitalism atomizes actors. In a competitive environment in which workers must compete for jobs and for the highest
wages, particularistic interests, all other things being equal will prevail
over collective interests. The (anarchic) laws of competition dictate a logic
of action for individual capitalists that if left unchecked would either destroy the market and/or provoke social tensions. As a first condition, then,
parties to a compromise must not only recognize their own class interests
as a class, but also not push their interests too far: "Each side agrees to
avoid striking the limits of the capitalist system: labor agrees not to demand wages that would be confiscatory (expropriate the expropriator)
while capital assures labor minimum wage below which labor withdraws
its 'consent' to exploitation" (Burawoy, 1989:70). This collective action
problem can only be resolved through the formation of organizations, political parties and unions for example, that have the "strategic" capacity to
restrain the pursuit of individual interests in favor of more solidaristic,
unified, and long-term interests.[10] This, in Przeworski's formulation, is essentially the question of class formation.

[10] Przeworski, citing Pizzorno, notes that organization "is the capacity to act on behalf of in-
dividuals even if such actions go against their individual interests, those interests that pit in-
dividuals in competition with one another" (1989:96).

The second problem is the "prisoner's dilemma": compromise becomes possible only if the cooperation of both parties can be secured (even the perception of the possibility of unilateral action from either will result in opportunistic behavior). To some extent this problem can be overcome through various direct or indirect forms of compulsion (as in forms of state corporatism) or penalties for withdrawal (making strikes or capital flight illegal). Most states, however, do not enjoy such power, and compliance must be elicited. And because the ends cannot be guaranteed (economic outcomes are by definition uncertain), consent must be forged through the process itself. Class compromise as such can only be democratically organized. In the absence of procedurally and representationally legitimate means of negotiation, the prospect of uncertain outcomes will result in short-term interest maximization, opportunistic rather than cooperative behavior.

The range of political configurations that can support class compromise is broad. In the United States class compromise is decentralized, negotiated primarily at the level of the firm (Burawoy 1985). Such a system has created a dual economy, in which only the unionized and monopoly sector segment of the working class has benefited from positive-sum trade-offs. Under European social-democratic regimes, class compromise is more centralized, enforced through state-mediated social pacts. In the United States the capacity of the state to mediate social contradictions is weak; in Europe it is much stronger.

This variation draws us back to the basic insight in Przeworski's work, which is to have theoretically established the link between class formation and class compromise. The conditions under which a class coalesces politically will in large part determine the possibility and shape of class compromise. Przeworski's line of reasoning here neatly parallels the cross-national empirical findings of the "working-class power" approach to explaining the rise of the welfare state. These comparative studies have pointed to organizational characteristics such as the degree of union centralization, party-union linkages, and class coalitions as shaping the success of the working class in securing welfare measures. And what is the welfare state if it is not the form that institutionalized class compromise has taken under advanced capitalism? Working-class mobilization can thus be tied to both the material basis (the welfare state) and the institutional-political basis (mass-based democracy) of class compromise. From these connections, then, we can conclude that the state actively intervenes to redress the social contradictions of capitalism—and hence secure its long-term viability as a system of production—not out of structural necessity, but as a direct result of the political power of organized and mobilized workers. Moreover, insofar as working-class demands are actively processed through democratic channels (the "legitimation" function) the state develops the institutional and political resources to forge class compromises, or as Gramsci puts it, to "form stable equilibria." State and society become highly (and functionally) integrated.

Because of the overwhelming weight attached to economic factors and an elite-centered view of politics, the relationship between class mobilization and political institutions—so central to the development of advanced capitalist states—has received little independent attention in the study of developing countries.[11] The persistence of dualistic economic structures in the developing world has generally fragmented subordinate-class interests. But classes are formed as an *effect* of political struggles (Przeworski 1985), and these struggles are shaped as much by existing institutional configurations as they are by the structural properties of the economy. For the developing world, a case can be made that the effect of political processes on class formation has been even more significant than in the European case. As we have seen, the institutional character of the postcolonial state is as much the legacy of the extractive logic of colonial capitalism as it is the product of internal state-society engagements. If state formation in Europe was symbiotically tied to class dynamics, and in particular to the rise of the bourgeoisie, the process of state formation in the developing world has taken a more independent path, with the result that the state in many cases remains "overdeveloped" with respect to local class forces. In most African states, for example, weak bases of political support at the time of independence gave life to the politics of clientalism and tribalism. Thus even where agricultural commercialization has been strong, class interests, and especially those of the peasantry, have remained fractured. As Bates notes, "The politics of the pork barrel supplant the politics of class action" (1981:118). In India, early democratization and the comparatively advanced institutional differentiation of the state have in particular heigthened the role of politics in shaping class. Thus Kohli points to the "variability in the class content of political power" across Indian states and argues forcefully that "only when we focus simultaneously on class and institutional variables—on the relationship of state to society—can we understand how the relative power of the lower classes can increase within the framework of a democratic-capitalist model of development" (1987). In the absence of such a perspective, the anomalous urban-rural alliance of

---

[11] Exceptions include Rueschemeyer, Stephens, and Stephens 1992 and Collier and Collier 1991.

lower classes that crystallized into a sustained political movement in the Kerala of the 1940s (see Chapter 2) is unintelligible.

Institutions are not the neutral arbiters of pluralist theory. They actively shape the manner in which interests are organized and hence determine patterns of collective action (Skocpol 1985). Class mobilization in turn has a dynamic impact on institutional developments. Political institutions do not emerge from a teleological process of modernization, but are rather the outcome of a wide range of social conflicts, of which class conflicts have been the most salient in the making of the modern state. This dialectic of political institutionalization and class mobilization can be highlighted by comparing Kerala to India.

Class Mobilization and the State in Kerala and India

In many respects India is axiomatic of Migdal's strong society/weak state dichotomy (1988). India's independence movement resulted in a democratic but not a bourgeois revolution. It was led by an amorphous urban middle class that cultivated ties with a wide range of rural interests. Though the movement successfully challenged British rule, it largely stopped short of challenging the social power of traditional elites. Calls for radical reform notwithstanding, the persistence of local power bases rooted in the control of land thwarted efforts to reform agrarian relations. Lacking a clearly defined social base, and operating in what was a fragmented social order, the Congress Party ruled through local notables from the dominant landowning castes, mobilizing "popular participation in the wider electoral process through a complex pyramiding of vertical factional alliances" (Frankel 1978:25).

Because they were enmeshed in a matrix of patronage networks, Kohli concludes that these "party-class linkages increasingly made the Congress more a part of a tacit alliance of domination than a potential force for social transformation. Not only was the deliberate politicization of the Indian lower classes thus set back, but the capacity of the Congress to force changes upon the propertied was further diminished" (1987:64). Theorists ranging from neomodernization to neo-Marxist persuasions have across the board pointed to the increasing subordination of the state to a cacophony of societal demands. Lloyd and Susan Rudolph thus speak of a crisis of "demand overload" (1987) and Bardhan characterizes the Indian polity as a "flabby and heterogeneous dominant coalition pre-occupied in a spree of anarchical grabbing at public resources" (1984:70). Efforts by state elites to build ruling coalitions out of these fractious forces have only exacerbated the role of the "brokerage system" (Brass 1994:110–11) in building political support. One is reminded of Gramsci's distinction between a state that rules and one that leads.

The price of this (fragmented pact of domination) has been not only an erosion of the Indian state's once considerable autonomy and its developmental capacity but also an increasingly acute crisis of authority. Once held up as a paradigm of effective institution-building in the developing world (Huntington 1968), the Congress Party has succumbed to a slow but steady process of what has come to be described as the "deinstitutionalization" of the party, and of Indian politics in general (Kohli 1990; Brass 1994; Kothari 1991; Rudolph and Rudolph 1987). As Kaviraj has put it, "[D]emocratic government functioned smoothly in the early years after 1947 precisely because it was not taking place in a democratic society; as democratic society has slowly emerged, with the spread of a real sense of political equality, it has made the functioning of democratic government more difficult" (cited in Bardhan 1997:18).

The political forces that have stepped into this vacuum are, however, as fractious as ever. Higher rates of political mobilization have been marked by a proliferation of exclusionary identities. A plethora of religious, caste-based, and regional parties now vie for power on the basis of competing populisms and opportunistic coalition-building. Governing coalitions are cemented through tactical dispensations of patronage rather than programmatic policy. In the absence of organized, encompassing links to society, politics has become an increasingly desolidarizing affair, as reflected in the widely documented "criminalization" of politics,[12] an explosion in cases of organized corruption circles (often spanning multiple parties), and most dramatically in the upsurge of sectarian and caste violence, a trend that has even spread to the once communalism-free southern states. Disaggregative politics and the widely perceived delegitimation of the state (its developmental and secular credentials are in question) has led Kothari (1991) to observe that the state has become disembodied from society, relying increasingly on administrative power and coercion rather than on democratic participation. Thus, though it would be a mistake to underestimate the solidity of parliamentary institutions in India,[13] it has become

---

[12] To cite one example: "According to the Chief Election Commissioner, 180 of Uttar Pradesh's Members of the Legislative Assembly (MLAs) have criminal cases pending against them, at least 52 of which involve 'heinous crimes' such as rape and murder" (Dreze and Gazdar 1996:108).
[13] The delegitimation of the state should not be confused with the delegitimation of democracy, especially one as federal as India's. And because Indian democracy has a demonstrated

increasingly difficult for the state to juggle conflicting interests and ultimately provide the most basic of state functions, lawfulness and social
predictability, much less developmental goods.

If Kerala has traveled down a very different path, the causes are to be
sought in the full complexity and contingencies of its history, and in particular its agrarian history of class formation examined in the next chapter. Suffice it here to highlight the critical moment of 1957 when the dynamics of political class formation culminated in the electoral victory of
the Communist Party in the state's first legislative elections. If national liberation and the advent of democratic pluralism under the auspices of the
Congress Party produced an unfinished revolution (Moore 1966), the
democratic and nationalist mantle in Kerala was donned by the CPI and
produced a full-scale assault on the ancien régime. The installation of a
class-based ministry marked a political trajectory that parted decisively
from the national path. Class mobilization, actively and programmatically
framed by an indigenized Leninist party committed to the parliamentary
route, produced a logic of interest aggregation that broke the hold of
Migdal's fragmented forms of social control. Instead of the hyperpluralistic and vertically organized patronage pyramids of the Indian polity, the
predominance of the politics of class in Kerala facilitated the crystallization of "fundamental" interests (cast primarily in an encompassing language of social justice) organized principally around transformative agendas of redistribution and social citizenship.

The formation of lower-class interests was accompanied by the extension of the state's bureaucratic and regulatory reach. At the most abstract
level, one could, following Polanyi, summarize these developments as the
"countervailing" forces that must necessarily accompany the "great transformation." Certainly lower-class mobilization and state intervention
have imposed social limits on capital. But the story at hand is neither so
neat nor so even. In disentangling the effects of social forces on economic
development in Kerala, three analytically distinct moments of transformation, crisis, and compromise can be identified.

The first has been the most trenchant. Agrarian mobilization and state
reforms have swept away most of the institutions of the precapitalist social structure, in particular landlordism, the attached labor system, and
caste domination. Second, there are clear signs that sustained labor mobilization in agriculture and industry, coupled with the growth of the welfare
state and the expansion of social rights, has begun to eat away at the logic

---

capacity for managing conflicts within the dominant coalition, it is unlikely to be threatened
by any of the dominant class factions (see Bardhan 1988:216).

of despotic capitalism. It has in other words become increasingly difficult in Kerala for capital to expand simply by squeezing labor. But this second transition within capitalism remains unfinished and highly contested. Labor's political clout, marked by the redistributive bias of the state, has increased its share of the social surplus and its capacity to exercise control over the labor process, but it has also triggered a crisis of accumulation. This crisis would lend credence to theories of development that implicitly assume the incompatibility of substantive democracy (in which lower-class demands are organized) and capitalist development, if it were not for the emergence, since roughly the mid-1970s, of the organized forms of class compromise that I document in this book.

How these compromises will affect Kerala's long-term economic development remains an open-ended question, especially given the state's limited macroeconomic powers and Kerala's dependency on both national and global markets. What stands out nonetheless is that the two basic preconditions for forging the class compromises that characterize democratic capitalism are in place. The first is the crystallization of class interests and their representation through encompassing organizations, specifically the CPM but more broadly through the hegemony of working-class politics. The second is the existence of strong democratic institutions through which class compromises are actually negotiated. Though class compromise is not possible without these organizational and institutional prerequisites, it is, in the final analysis, about political processes. Thus across regions and sectors within Kerala, differences in the level of lower-class organization, the composition and mobility of capital, and the degree of state penetration have shaped the specific terms and modalities of class compromise. These variations notwithstanding, the argument of this book is that class mobilization and conflict, rather than precipitating a crisis of governance or producing a zero-sum economic stalemate, has actually furthered the functional integration of political and socioeconomic life, and specifically increased the state's capacity to manage the contradictions associated with development. The state in Kerala can thus be described as "developmental" not only because of its achievements on the social and redistributive fronts, but also because it has acquired the capacity to concretely coordinate class interests. As a subnational and democratic state it lacks the full repertoire of market-augmenting tools of the East Asian NICs, but within these limits it does possess significant authoritative and organizational means for reconciling the social imperatives of welfare with the economic imperatives of growth. And this, in a democratic society, is the key to promoting sustainable economic development.

I

Agriculture

Just what does modernization mean for the peasantry beyond the simple and brutal fact that sooner or later they are its victims?

Barrington Moore, *Social Origins of Dictatorship and Democracy*, 1966

In the relatively short span of half a century, the agrarian landscape in Kerala has undergone a profound transformation. A largely subsistence-oriented rural economy in which rice was the principal crop has become a highly commercialized economy in which cash crops, primarily rubber and coconut, now account for three-quarters of the cultivated area. The importance of agriculture to the state's economy has declined rapidly. In 1991, only 37.8 percent of the population in Kerala earned its livelihood from agriculture, the lowest percentage of any major Indian state and well below the national average of 66.5 percent (Kurien 1994:29). Most dramatic has been the change in class relations. The class of upper-caste land-lords—the *jenmies*—that once wielded almost absolute economic and social power in the countryside has all but disappeared. A labor system characterized by patron-client relations of material and social dependency that were firmly embedded in local caste structures has been replaced by contractual wage relations governed by market forces and labor legislation.

The demise of the traditional labor system and the commercialization of agriculture in Kerala bear all the structural traits of a classic agrarian transition. Yet as the next three chapters show in detail, behind the linearity and inexorability suggested by terms such as "transition" and "commercialization" lie complex and sometimes contradictory processes. There are three dimensions of Kerala's agrarian transformation that stand out.

First, the most important institutional reforms that have marked the transformation—comprehensive land reforms introduced in 1970 that abolished landlordism, and state interventions that codified labor relations—resulted directly from a communist-led mobilization of agricultural

51

laborers and cultivators, which not only produced successful electoral plu-
ralities but also democratized local agrarian institutions. The historical
conditions under which the broad-based agrarian coalition was formed
and sustained is examined in the next chapter.

Second, in contrast to most agrarian transitions that are either openly or
quietly violent, with poor peasants and the landless inevitably paying the
costs of transition, Kerala's transformation has been a comparatively pain-
less one, especially by the standards of the subcontinent. Though driven
by open and organized forms of class struggle and taking place against a
backdrop of severe poverty, the transformation has produced few of the
revolutionary or reactionary excesses that always seem to accompany
agrarian radicalism. How potentially explosive class conflicts were successfully institutionalized and managed is the subject of Chapter 3.

Third, though the transformation in Kerala has been marked by the decline of the traditional moral economy and its guarantees of subsistence,
by the disappearance of traditional rural occupations, by the multiplica-
tion of marginal landholdings, and by high levels of landlessness, it has
created few of the wrenching dislocations that normally accompany such
changes. Poverty levels in rural areas have in fact fallen dramatically, and
on all indicators of social development Kerala continues to rank well
above all other Indian states. The explanation, moreover, does not lie in
economic growth per se, which stagnated during much of the period under
study and has only picked up recently. Instead, as we shall see in Chapter
4, state interventions as well as organized class compromises combined to
produce a *socially mediated transition.*

2

Tenants and Laborers in Kerala's
Agrarian Transformation

The sheer size, diversity, and unevenness of agrarian social structures in India defy generalization. Areas of mechanized capitalist farming coexist with large expanses of small peasant production and redoubts of semifeudalism. A district in which landed upper castes rule supreme and command private armies can share one border with a district in which the middle peasantry prospers and another in which armed Maoist groups champion the cause of the landless, attacking landlords and state officials with impunity. But to situate the case of Kerala, some generalizations are necessary.

Agrarian change in postcolonial India has been dominated by two related developments. The first has been the role of the state in successfully promoting the green revolution, during which India has become self-sufficient in food grain production. The second has been the formation, from the ranks of locally dominant cultivating castes, of a class of middle and large capitalist farmers who have come to play an increasingly powerful role in Indian politics. These developments notwithstanding, many scholars of rural India would concur with Bharadwaj's influential argument that a significant increase in production for the market has not been accompanied by a commensurate development of capitalist relations of production (1985:7). Land reforms undertaken in the 1950s did abolish parasitic landlordism by breaking up the large Zamindari holdings of the colonial period, but the principal beneficiaries were smaller landlords and the larger tenants (Patnaik 1986:782). The social power of dominant landed castes went largely unscathed. As a result, the economic position of subordinate rural groups, most notably landless laborers and poor tenants, continues to be shaped by precapitalist social institutions (Kurien

53

1992). Because land ownership in the Indian countryside is closely inter-
twined with local forms of political and social domination, relations of
surplus appropriation range from the semifeudal, with pronounced elements of coercion (Bhaduri 1983), to various forms of extramarket exchange relations (Rudra 1985). In some areas, transparently "unfree"
forms of labor, including attached and bonded labor, are widespread.[1]
More commonly, labor and land are embedded in local institutions. In a
context of severe scarcities and pronounced inequalities in the distribution
of material and social resources (including access to state patronage),
labor is "tied" into dependent and clientalistic relations with landowners
through the village-level "interlocking" of factor markets for land, credit
and labor (Bardhan 1984b; Rudra 1985).

To be sure, there are important areas of dynamic capitalist farming in
India, including large mechanized farms and small but surplus-producing
family farms. But also in many parts of rural India landed elites generate
agrarian surpluses by squeezing labor and tenants (or marginal peasants),
through their control of markets, inputs, and sheer social power rather
than by organizing or investing in production itself. The persistence of
such landed social power has, despite significant technical innovations and
state interventions, slowed the capitalist transformation of agriculture.
Even with the green revolution, annual growth in agriculture has averaged
only 2.3 percent since 1960 (CMIE 1994b:tab. 13.7).

India's competitive democracy has provided a far more propitious environment for the expression of rural interests than is true of most agrarian
societies (Varshney 1995). Since the late 1960s, democracy has slowly but
surely percolated down, eroding the basis of traditional Brahmanical authority and emasculating the vote-banks of local notables that once under-
girded the Congress Party's hegemony. New social alignments have in turn
increased political competition and the mobilization of new social groups.
Nonetheless, the dominant strategy of rural mobilization continues to be
one of undifferentiated sectoral politics couched in the populist discourse
of *bharat* (Hindi for India) versus India and dominated by rich farmers.
Agrarian populism has been constructed through multiple exclusions of
caste, class, and gender (Gupta 1998). The successful independent mobilization of the rural poor has been the exception rather than the norm. The
predominance of personalized clientalism, notes Bardhan, "fragments the
labor market, fractures the formation of class consciousness and emascu-

---

[1] For case studies see Gough 1981, Breman 1985 and Ramachandran 1990. For a classifica-
tion of types of unfree labor see Nagesh 1981.

lates class organization" (1984b:187). The commercialization and semi-proletarianization of Indian agriculture has produced conflict and protest, but outside of Kerala, and to a lesser extent West Bengal, there have been no cases of sustained mobilization by the rural poor.[2] Though the number of landless laborers in India has increased both in absolute and relative terms, organized agrarian protest has generally taken the form of commodity reform movements (Paige 1975) and has been led by India's new class of intermediate-caste capitalist farmers.[3]

The dominant political parties in India continue to rely on clientalistic factional alliances anchored in propertied groups or various forms of populism organized around regional, communal, or caste-based identities. None has openly challenged the economic and political power of landed elites. Competitive democratic politics and the expansion of secular-bureaucratic state power have certainly eroded the legitimacy of Brahmanical social authority, but caste inequalities and the control over land continue to dictate the logic of political mobilization. "In routine politics," Brass summarizes, "the low castes who form the bulk of the landless are coopted by the factional and party leaders of the dominant castes in village, district and state politics. When they attempt to mobilize for political agitations for higher wages against the landed castes, however, they generally meet strong resistance and their movements usually fail, except in states such as Kerala and West Bengal at times when the ruling communist parties there support their demands" (1994:334).

Having secured its political base through accommodations with landed elites, the state has failed to effectively impose its authority over local forms of social control. The scope of public legality remains severely curtailed and local institutions—panchayats (village councils), credit cooper-

---

[2] With respect to agricultural laborers, the district of Thanjavur in Tamil Nadu is the only exception (Gopal Iyer and Vidyasagar 1986).

[3] The size and contours of this class are highly disputed. Lloyd and Susan Rudolph reject the polarization thesis by arguing that rural politics have become increasingly centrist, dominated by a large class of nonexploiting "self-employed and self-funded" "bullock capitalists" (1987:340) operating holdings between 2.5 and fifteen acres and accounting for 34 percent of agrarian households and 51 percent of the cultivated area (337). More disaggregated studies paint a picture of a much more internally differentiated middle strata, including a large number of cultivator-owners who remain dependent on wage labor and/or renting-in land (Harriss 1992:212; Bardhan 1984:172). Structural definitions of this middle class notwithstanding, what remains beyond dispute is the large share of rural households whose landholdings are insufficient for self-reproduction. In 1982, 66.6 percent of rural households fell below the marginal ownership category of 2.5 acres. Together they accounted for 12.2 percent of total land ownership, less than the 14.3-percent share of the top one percent of households (Kurien 1992:321).

atives, government offices—remain firmly in the hands of local elites. The persistence of what Mamdani (1996) in the African context has called decentralized despotism takes many forms, ranging from the clientalistic networks of political bosses, the social control of traditional caste or community leaders, and in the extreme case of Bihar the existence of privatized forms of violence (the infamous landlord *senas*). More generally, the circumscribed nature of public legality has limited the effective exercise of political and civic rights. In this respect, the local, if not the national, arena of political life in India is characterized (much as in Latin America) by the concentration and blurring of public and social authority, producing what O'Donnell (1993) calls low-intensity citizenship.

As a result, rather than giving expression to the class interests of the rural poor, agrarian politics in India have been dominated by the distributive demands of propertied classes (procurement prices, input subsidies, loan "holidays"). These have not only eclipsed demands for and effective implementation of agrarian reforms including tenancy reform and land redistribution,[4] but have also undermined the political saliency and effectiveness of social development and poverty-alleviating interventions. The social costs of what Dreze and Sen (1995) have called "public inertia" have been truly staggering. After fifty years of independence and planned intervention, and despite a small decline in the percentage of rural households living in poverty, the absolute number of rural poor, estimated at 245 million in 1993–94, is as high as it has ever been. And on basic indicators of the physical quality of life such as infant mortality and illiteracy, India finds itself in the same range as subsaharan Africa (Dreze and Sen 1995:30–31). This failure of state authority coupled with persistent poverty has fed a growing cycle of rural unrest and violence marked most dramatically by the increasing incidence of caste violence between laborers and landlords (Januzzi 1994).

The Indian countryside has undergone dramatic transformations in the postcolonial period. The most important of these has been the rise and consolidation of a class of rich and middle capitalist farmers. This class represents somewhat of a paradox. On the one hand, it has been the carrier of notable "capitalist tendencies" by consolidating land and modernizing agricultural production (Patnaik 1986). On the other hand, it has secured many of its economic privileges through extramarket means and local po-

---

[4] Though official government documents continue to acknowledge the relationship among failed agrarian reforms, persistent poverty, and rural violence, by the 1980s land reforms and strategies for transforming agrarian institutions had been all but expunged from the policy debates within the government of India (Jannuzi 1994:175).

litical domination. It has captured the bulk of state investments in agriculture and at the same time has successfully resisted state efforts at taxation or price controls, thus in effect blocking the classic developmental strategy of fueling industrialization with agrarian surpluses. The upshot of all this is that the rural poor—small and marginal landholders, tenants, and the landless—continue to suffer from an arrested agrarian transition. Any economic opportunities created by the commercialization of agriculture have largely been offset by demographic pressures, concentration of land at the top and fragmentation at the bottom, inflationary pressures, segmented labor markets, and the class bias of public investments. Wage growth has been stagnant, and the bulk of the peasantry has seen the green revolution pass them by. What Barrington Moore wrote of agriculture under colonial rule still tragically rings true: "The Indian peasant was suffering many of the pains of primitive capitalist accumulation, while Indian society reaped none of the benefits" (1966:360).

Explaining Kerala's Agrarian Transformation

When summarized, the story of Kerala's agrarian transformation has a certain logic and linearity. Agrarian class conflicts in the 1930 and 1940s produced an agrarian movement that captured power in Kerala's first elections in 1957. A radical peasant-labor alliance and the state then combined to dismantle the seigneurial regime through land reforms and labor legislation. But successful collective action on the part of rural actors, especially those with highly insecure property rights (or none), has been the historical exception rather than the rule (Bates 1981; Scott 1985). The strains of the traditional agrarian economy in Kerala did not simply throw up a unified revolutionary rural class. The agrarian coalition that emerged in the 1950s was born in the interstices of caste and nation, but took its final form by combining what were in fact two axes of class conflict. In the southern part of the state, Travancore, agrarian protest took root among lower-caste field laborers and rapidly took the form of a classical trade union struggle for collective bargaining rights and legislated regulation of work conditions and wages. In the northern part of the state, Malabar, the central issue was land, not labor, and the central players tenants, not laborers. That these two movements converged as part of a broad-based "antifeudal" project, suggests, as E. P. Thompson might have put it, that Kerala's working class ("tilling" is actually the better adjective) was not made, but made itself.

It made itself through a political process marked by historical opportunities and strategic moments, and was shaped by an institutional context, the most important dimension of which was the character of the state. If a historical contingency approach to class formation (Katznelson and Zolberg 1986) helps explain the making of Kerala's subordinate classes, it is also critical to understanding subsequent developments. If classes are indeed the *effects* of political struggles (Przeworski 1985), then it follows that they are constantly being made and unmade. With the successful implementation of land reforms in 1970, the solidarities that bound the antifeudal agrarian coalition unraveled as the interests of tenants-turned-proprietors and their erstwhile allies, agricultural laborers, parted ways and produced new antagonisms—resulting in a new cycle of organized conflicts that, many have argued, precipitated a crisis of agrarian accumulation. In the 1980s, however, this "class stalemate" (to use Herring's description [1991b]) gave way to a highly organized form of class compromise, underwriting new forms of capitalist development. In Chapters 3 and 4 I explore the conditions under which conflicts were institutionalized and compromises hammered out. I focus specifically on Kerala's two principal rice-growing regions of Kuttanad (formerly in Travancore) and Palghat (formerly in Malabar) and find that though the sequencing of conflict and compromise was similar, the actual terms and mechanisms through which the interests of laborers and farmers have now been reconciled are quite different. These differences can be traced back to the historical circumstances, examined in this chapter, under which classes were mobilized and formed in each region.

The Crisis of the Traditional Social Order

Until its unification along linguistic lines in 1956, the modern state of Kerala was divided into two distinct regions. The southern part of the state consisted of two princely states, Travancore and Cochin, which enjoyed significant autonomy under British rule. In the case of Travancore, by far the larger of the two,[5] the state successfully centralized power at the expense of landlords and nurtured the rise of a commercializing landed elite.

---

[5] Because Cochin and Travancore largely resembled each other and the former was five times smaller in area, the discussion here will focus only on Travancore. In 1941, Travancore had a population of 6.1 million, compared to 1.4 million in Cochin and 3.9 million in Malabar (Jeffrey 1992:26).

The northern part of the state, Malabar, was a remote and often neglected outpost of the Madras presidency under direct colonial rule, in which social and economic power was concentrated in the hands of a notoriously parasitic class of Brahman landlords. Though distinct in their agrarian structures and their relationship to the colonial state, Travancore and Malabar had in common a Malayalam-speaking population and what is generally considered to have been the most rigid caste structure in colonial India.

The famous Hindu reformer, Swami Vivekananda, after having visited the state called it a "veritable lunatic asylum." Intercaste codes of conduct, speech, dress, and ritualized deference were strictly enforced, and so pervasive that they extended to the Christian and Muslim communities. These were not, moreover, simply status markers. Caste distinctions codified an elaborate division of labor, property, and even space. Only in Kerala could ritual pollution be communicated over a distance. Untouchables were considered to be "unseeable." The 1860 account of the wife of a church missionary provides a vivid picture:

[A] Nair may approach but not touch a Nambudiri Brahmin; a Chogan Irava must remain thirty-six paces off, and a Poolayen slave ninety-six steps distant. A Chogan must remain twelve steps away from a Nair, and a Poolayen sixty-six steps off, and a Pariar some distance farther still. A Syrian Christian may touch a Nair (though this is not allowed in some parts of the country) but the latter may not walk with each other. Poolians and Pariars, who are the lowest of all, may approach but not touch, much less may they eat with each other. (quoted in Jeffrey 1976:14)

Ascribed occupations were rigidly enforced and most lower-caste groups were denied the right to hold property and public office. Property-owning castes and communities, in order of social rank, consisted of "clean" caste (sarvana) Namboodiripads (Brahmans); Nairs belonging to both the Kshatriya (warrior) varna and the Sudra varna of cultivators; Syrian Christians; and the upper strata of the Muslim community who also doubled as Kerala's traders. Below the Nairs and just outside the sarvana order was Kerala's largest caste, the Ezhavas (often spelled "Irava") and related castes. Ezhavas were primarily engaged in manual occupations as field laborers, coconut-tree climbers, and toddy tappers (toddy is a fermented coconut drink), though some were tenants and even small peasant proprietors. At the bottom of the social order were the untouchable castes—Pulayas, Parayars, and Cherumars—reduced to performing the "unclean" work of agricultural labor as either attached workers or slaves.[6] The shared material conditions and social indignities of these lower castes would eventually provide a common base for mobilization. The social closure intrinsic in caste identities, however, militated against any spontaneous solidarity. Ezhavas were treated by caste Hindus as untouchables, and they themselves considered caste groups below them to be polluted (Ramachandran 1996:276).

The first challenge to the traditional social order in the semiautonomous princely states of Travancore and Cochin came in the form of socioreligious reform movements (Tharakan 1998; Jeffrey 1992; T. Oommen 1985). The commercialization of the economy in the mid-nineteenth century (see below) had created prosperous segments within all the major religious and caste communities. These elites formed associations, dedicated to the social reform and uplift of their communities, that built schools and hospitals and sponsored cultural and social programs. By the 1890s, Nairs, Ezhavas, and Christians were petitioning the government for access to government jobs and the opening of more schools.[7] Even the untouchable Pulayas, whose status as slaves had only been revoked in 1855, organized to demand the right to travel public roads. By the 1920s Travancore society was in full ebullition. Brahmanical authority was under fire, and an increasingly pluralistic and politically competitive public arena had spawned the emergence of an educated, articulate, and sophisticated group of political entrepreneurs.

Mobilization occurred along community lines in Travancore and took the form of constitutional agitation (as opposed to the peasant uprisings of Malabar) because of the unique character of the state. On the one hand, the Travancore state was patrimonial and deeply conservative, a theological state commanded by divine rulers who viewed themselves as guardians of Hindu orthodoxy and the caste order. On the other hand, Travancore's early exposure to the world economy as an exporter of cash crops, its early successes in centralizing power against chieftains, and its semisovereign status produced modernizing impulses. Having undergone a process of administrative rationalization under pressure from the British in the 1850s, and enjoying a significant degree of autonomy from landed elites,

---

[6] In 1847 the Travancore government still owned 15,000 untouchable slaves whom it leased to farmers (Jeffrey 1976:24). Slaves could be legally killed, and in Malabar were often included in land transactions.

[7] The maharajah's state perfectly replicated Travancore's caste structure. The upper ranks of the government were exclusively reserved for Brahmans, and Nairs populated the lower levels of administration. Syrian Christians and "polluting castes" were excluded from government employment (Jeffrey 1976:9).

this paternalistic state became what the British secretary of state of India in 1867 called a "model native state." In its efforts to promote public health and education, as well as manage food distribution in times of shortages, the state of Travancore significantly outperformed colonial India and other princely states (Tharakan 1998).[8] That the princely state had expanded its scope of activities beyond the law-and-order and rev-enue-collection functions of its Malabar counterpart explains why orga-nized contention first took the form of entitlement agitations that focused on enlarging the role of the state and increasing access to state jobs.[9] And it was because the state played such a direct and visible role in reproduc-ing caste inequalities and exclusions that distributive demands would be organized around discrete communities.

A very different state and agrarian structure in Malabar produced fun-damentally different social tensions. Direct British rule in this peripheral area of the Madras presidency had the effect of rigidifying a particularly oppressive form of high-caste landlordism. Rack-rented tenants, most often Muslims, repeatedly rebelled only to be violently repressed by the colonial state. By the 1930s, however, agrarian protest had assumed a broader social base, encompassing prosperous (mostly Nair) tenants, and the small tenant-cultivators who constituted the bulk of the peasantry. Be-cause of the close nexus between landed elites and the colonial state, de-mands for reform converged with the independence movement and Mal-abar became a stronghold of the nationalist struggle. But despite the fact that peasant agitations were clearly targeted against an oppressive, sur-plus-extracting class, what bound the diverse social elements of the move-ment together was not so much economic grievances as opposition to the increainsgly illegitimate social character of landlordism.

In Malabar, as in Travancore, political mobilization thus first centered on the social grievances of parochial communities. These movements were dominated by upwardly mobile elite interests and fell short of articulating a transformative project. In neither region did broader class-based de-

---

[8] It has been argued that modern Kerala's noted capacity for public action and its high levels of social development are an extension of the historical character of Travancore's state-soci-ety relations (G. Sen 1992). But such an observation fails to explain the transition from the Brahmanical paternalism of Travancore (which in many ways has its contemporary counter-part in the clientalistic welfarism of the Indian state) to the class-based and more universalis-tic character of Kerala's modern welfare state. Nor can it explain how the gap between Mal-abar and Travancore, which on all social development indicators was pronounced in the nineteenth century, was so dramatically closed in the post-1957 period (Krishnan and Kabir 1992).

[9] In 1941, Travancore and Cochin together had 85,000 public officials, compared to only four or five thousand in Malabar (Jeffrey 1992:82).

mands emerge until later. In Travancore, mobilization was particularly segmented, closely resembling the dynamic of sanskritization noted by Srinivas (1967). Caste associations were dedicated to elevating the status of their communities by, in effect, emulating the ritual and social practices of higher-status communities. In Malabar, peasant leaders limited their protests to the more pernicious aspects of the traditional agrarian system and pressed only for tenancy reform, not for a fundamental redefinition of property relations.

Nonetheless, the impact of these reform movements was profound. E. M. S Namboodiripad, first chief minister of Kerala and the Communist Party's most accomplished scholar, has observed: "It is a historical fact that the first form in which the peasant masses rose in struggle against feudalism was the form of caste organizations" (1967:122). Identities that had been the basis of hierarchy and acquiesence were politicized, creating the first breach in the cultural and ideological hegemony of the Brahmanical order. "God helps those who help themselves" was the slogan championed by the Sri Narayana Dharma Paripalana (SNDP), the social reform association of the Ezhavas. In promoting education and self-respect, the movements forged new solidarities and created new bases of collective action. The competition among communities not only produced an extraordinary effervescence of associative life but also established the modular forms of collective action that sustain social movements (Tarrow 1994). The major associations developed community resources by funding schools and hospitals and pioneering the basic organizational practices of registering members, collecting funds, and holding public meetings. They sponsored cultural and social activities such as reading rooms and community newspapers that would later become staples of Communist Party organizing. They also developed new protest tactics, in a first stage presenting mass petitions to the government and holding mass meetings. By the 1930s, social boycotts, picketing of government offices, and protest marches (*jathas*) were standard movement practices.[10] Most notably, the Vaikom temple-entry movement of 1924–25, which sought to desegregate worship, drew the Indian National Congress and Gandhi into local politics and popularized civil disobedience tactics. At the broadest level these caste reform movements inaugurated a new kind of public politics, one in which communities actively pressed demands on the state and began to ar-

[10] The *jatha*, as Jeffrey notes, was a symbolically powerful form of protest as it "implicitly attacked many of the principles of deference and acceptance which were long established in old Kerala. Walking from place to place constituted an assault on the discrete localities which helped to maintain the old social system" (1992:121).

ticulate conceptions of citizenship and entitlement. Finally, they provided the training grounds for an entire generation of organizers and social activists, many of whom would become the leaders and the cadres of the Communist Party.

Travancore: The Mobilization of a Rural Proletariat

The distinctiveness of Travancore's agrarian history can largely be traced to its history of state formation. With the help of the British, the principality began annexing the lands of local Nair chieftains at the end of the eighteenth century. In order to curb the power of conquered *jenmies* (Hindu landlords), the state took control of land and gave tenants fixity of tenure. The removal of rent-extracting intermediaries and the imposition of relatively low state taxes saw the owner-cultivators of Travancore prosper (Varghese 1970:30–31). With the Pattom Declaration of 1865, these state tenants were given full proprietary rights and land was declared a tradable commodity. This newly endowed class was not, however, one of middle peasants in the classic sense of the term. The pattern of land-ownership conformed closely to the caste structure. Of the 191,823 "cultivators" enumerated in the 1875 census, 98,330 were Nairs and 54,770 were Syrian Christians (Jeffrey 1976:29). Because of their social status, neither of these groups directly participated in cultivation, depending rather on the maintenance of a repressive labor regime.

Spurred by colonial export markets for primary commodities and by state support, capitalist farming progressed rapidly in the early part of the twentieth century (Varghese 1970). By 1920, fully 46 percent of the cultivated land was under cash crops, and public reclamation projects of low-lying, waterlogged lands and leasing-in arrangements in the region of Kuttanad (Kerala's "grain basket") had helped accelerate the consolidation of large-scale commercial rice farming.[11] The extension and intensification of paddy cultivation that followed from the increase of paddy prices during the two world wars, as well as the introduction of mechanized pumping and further reclamations, increased the demand for casual labor (Jose 1977). Coupled with demographic pressures, these economic changes gave

[11] In the Travancore-Cochin area, medium and small holdings (below five acres) accounted for 94.8 percent of all holdings and 57.1 percent of the total area. The balance of the area was thus held by just 5 percent of cultivators (GOK, *Economic Review* 1959:5). It was these large landowners (mostly Syrian Christians who had successfully reclaimed land) who most forcefully resisted the mobilization of laborers.

rise to a large rural proletariat (Kannan 1988). Between 1911 and 1951, census figures for Travancore show that agricultural laborers increased from 229,800 to 1,488,600, or from 12.6 percent of the agricultural population to 34.6 percent (Varghese 1970:128 and tab. 3.1) The commodification of rural labor was only partial, however, as the labor process itself remained firmly embedded in despotic social structures and casual labor coexisted with various forms of unfree and tied labor (Tharamangalam 1981:chap. 4).

That the more extreme forms of labor attachment could survive despite the casualization of the labor force is a testament to the sheer social power of landed elites as well as the agronomic particularities of rice cultivation in Kuttanad. Because most of the cultivated area in Kuttanad lies at sea level and is crisscrossed by backwaters and rivers, paddy cultivation requires the constant maintenance of embankments (bunds) and carefully calibrated watering and dewatering operations. Attached labor provided an effective means of securing the necessary labor inputs and minimizing supervision costs. Multiple forms of dependency that included fear of eviction, debt bondage, and culturally enforced servility effectively tied lower-caste workers to their landlords.[12] Increased scales of operation and mechanization of pumping did make the use of casual labor increasingly attractive for planting, weeding, and harvesting operations. But even this labor market remained firmly embedded in social relations of domination. A ban on leasing prevented the lowest untouchable castes of Pulayas and Parayas from becoming tenants, and laws of pollution prohibited their entry into trades or crafts that required contact with upper castes (A. George 1987). Caste gradations of pollution enforced labor-market segmentation even among field workers. Thus the job of collecting clay to replenish embankments—a "polluting" job by definition—was reserved exclusively for Pulayas and Parayas. And both attached and casual workers were subjected to a wage structure that was differentiated according to caste, with untouchables receiving lower wages than clean-caste workers for the same work (T. Oommen 1985:221–22). With no access to other employment, these groups, although formally free, were in effect tied to

---

[12] Labor attachment extended to the whole family and was hereditary. The ties of dependence were embedded in exchanges of gifts and other ceremonial practices that emphasized the laborers' loyalty and allegiance. Even contemporary observers are inclined to romanticizing: "The attached labourer identified himself so much with his field and his master that the passing moods of his face often reflected the state of the crop. He was ready if need arose to make the supreme sacrifice in order to save the crop or to serve his master" (Pillai and Panikar 1965:121).

the land and constituted a captive and largely quiescent army of reserve labor.

There is no better illustration of the organizational successes and opportunism of the Communists than the circumstances under which the agricultural laborers of Kuttanad were mobilized. Agrarian radicalism emerged in Kuttanad in the 1940s largely because of the region's proximity to the town of Alleppey. The heart of Travancore's coir industry, Alleppey's factories had been successfully unionized by the Kerala Congress Socialist Party (KCSP)—the left breakaway faction of the Congress Party and the forerunner of the CPI. In 1938 this small but militant working class lent its support to the Travancore State Congress's prodemocracy movement by launching a general strike. The political success of the strike convinced the KCSP to draw on its seasoned Alleppey cadres to extend its organizational reach into the countryside. The success of these efforts was facilitated by existing networks and solidarities, as most of Alleppey's workers were Ezhavas, many having in fact migrated from Kuttanad.

The first agricultural union—the Thiruvithamkoor Karshaka Thozhilali Union (TKTV—Travancore Agricultural Labourers Union)—was formed in 1941, the same year in which the CPI formally came into existence, and the first organized strikes took place in 1943–44. Specific demands centered on a wide range of issues including wages, form of payment (cash vs. in-kind), and working hours, but, even more important, strike actions were strategically targeted to expose the abuses of landlordism and the attached labor system. Propaganda campaigns denouncing the injustices of the caste system were launched through the popular media of theater and folk songs. Alex George argues that this direct assault on the social authority of landlordism was so effective that it precipitated the demise of the attached labor system (1987:A147). Just how far the politicization of rural laborers developed in the short span of half a decade is manifest in their participation, alongside coir factory and boat workers, in the CPI-led Punnapra-Vayalar uprising against the maharajah's Travancore government in 1946, which, although violently repressed, marked the baptism by fire of an urban-rural working class alliance (Paulini 1979:193).

With Independence in 1947 came a critical turning point in the form and trajectory of agrarian mobilization in Travancore. A shift in the balance of power from state to society creates new opportunities for the mobilization of subordinate groups (Rueschemeyer, Stephens, and Stephens and 1992). Formal democratic institutions and procedures provided new spaces in which lower-class organizations could form and created new incentives and rewards for mobilization. The Communist Party and its organizations, banned and driven underground following the Punnapra-Vayalar uprising, could now operate without fear of state repression. An agrarian movement characterized by localized protests aimed at exposing the social indignities and abuses of landlordism was rapidly transformed into a wage earners' trade union movement demanding programmatic concessions from the state. In 1951, the TKTU issued a charter of demands and launched a mass agitation involving thousands of laborers, the first in all of India. A shaky coalition government responded by brokering an agreement that included a 50 percent wage increase for women, a half hour lunch break, and the reduction of the work day to eight hours. The writ of the state remained limited, however, and landlords actively resisted the agreement. Confrontations escalated between 1950 and 1957: union records indicate that there were 4,279 disputes, 1,873 of which resulted in organized agitations (KSKTU 1991). A strike in 1954 over labor's share of the harvest involved 200,000 workers (Pillai and Pannikar 1965:128). Under pressure from the unions, the government appointed the first Minimum Wages Committee for agricultural laborers in India. Though the notification (to use the Indian terminology) of a minimum wage would have to wait for the advent of the Communist ministry in 1957, trade unionism had successfully established the legitimacy and necessity of regulatory action aimed at curbing the arbitrary power of landlords and opened the gate for state efforts to impose administrative-legal authority over the traditional prerogatives of landed elites.

Malabar: Tenancy Reform Movement

In the Brahmanical creation myth of Kerala, the god Parasurma created the Kerala Brahmans, the Namboodiripads, as a special race of rulers upon whom he conferred ownership of all the land. If ever there was a caricature of a parasitic feudal ruling class, it was the Malabar Namboodiripad landlords, the *jenmies*. Ritually pure, the Namboodiripads had no direct contact with actual cultivation, and sat atop a complex tenure system of Nair "superior" tenants (*kanamdars*) who enjoyed rights of perpetual tenancy and subleased their land to "inferior" tenants (*verumpattamdars*), mostly Ezhavas and Muslims. As in most premarket systems, the prerogatives of the lords were tempered by the customary rights and privileges of tenancy holders, including fixed rents and protection from eviction.

When the British wrested control of Malabar from the Muslim overlord, Tipu Sultan, in 1792, they saw the *jenmies* as the perfect intermediaries for organizing indirect rule. In a pattern that was a precursor to British colonial rule in Africa, the revenue settlements took the Brahmanical creation myth rather literally and conferred absolute ownership rights on the *jenmies*. Varghese calculates that in 1861 the *jenmies* represented less than 2 percent of the total agricultural population. "To these janmies, constituting an insignificant minority of the agricultural population, belonged practically every right and interest connected with land in Malabar" (1970:39). Indivisible rights of property, backed by the colonial courts, undermined customary tenancy arrangements and triggered a crisis in the traditional moral economy (Herring 1996). The *kanamdars* were reduced to twelve-year mortgagees, and the *verumpattamdars* to tenants-at-will (Sathyamurthy 1985:145). Given this new writ, the *jenmies* "began to shed their pretensions as the customary benefactors of actual cultivators" (Varghese 1970:29). Throughout the eighteenth century, the condition of tenant cultivators went from bad to worse as *jenmies* resorted to evictions and illegal exactions in the pursuit of higher rents. In 1900 a British land revenue official pointedly summed up the situation by noting that "South Malabar has earned the unenviable reputation of being the most rack-rented country on the face of the earth" (quoted in Varghese 1970:81).

Resistance first came from the ranks of Muslim cultivators, the Mappilas. Various forms of social banditry in the nineteenth century escalated into what one commentator has called the first modern peasant revolt in India (Gough 1968–69:725). In 1921, armed Mappila rebels attacked and killed an estimated six hundred Hindu landlords and British collaborators and took control of the entire interior area of south Malabar. Isolated from the nationalist movement and repudiated by the Congress Party, the revolt was brutally repressed. Over 45,404 rebels were arrested and 3,989 (the official figure) were killed (Panikkar 1989:163). That the first large-scale challenge to the *jenmi*–colonial state nexus came from a community that was outside the Hindu caste order is telling. The quiescence of the lower-caste Hindu peasantry during this episode of agrarian upheaval, despite economic circumstances that were no less dire, points to the independent effects of cultural subordination. As Scott has warned, however, the "onstage" conformity of subordinate groups often masks counterhegemonic discourses of justice and equality (1985). If open resistance is the exception to the rule in peasant societies, this has less to do with conformity to elite ideologies than with viable opportunities for collective action. The catalyst to the Mappila rebellion was the launching of the national Khalifat movement, an anticolonial, Congress Party–led protest against the treatment of Turkey by European powers. As Muslim leaders in Malabar took on the Khalifat cause, the simmering grievances of the Mappila peasantry were quickly and powerfully focused against Hindu landlords and their colonial guardians. Similarly, changes in what social movement theorists call the political opportunity structure would soon provide the Hindu peasantry with the framing ideologies and strategic leverage for organized resistance.

The leading edge of protest was the relatively privileged and prosperous community of Nairs. As an educated caste that had developed both commercial and professional elites, the Nairs were increasingly resentful of the caste indignities they suffered (Namboodiripads could enter into "informal" marriages with Nair women) at the hands of a Brahman caste which they viewed as increasingly degenerate and parasitic. Challenging *jenmi* dominance, superior Nair tenants (*kanamdars*), with the support of a Congress Party that they largely dominated, began a comprehensive campaign of protests and lobbying for more secure rights of tenancy. In the short period of eight years, the *kanamdars'* tenants association (the Malabar Kudiyan Sangham) established about a hundred local chapters, which became the organizational backbone of subsequent Communist-led mobilizations. A colonial state sensitized to the need for agrarian reform by the Mappila revolt (Herring 1996) passed the Malabar Tenancy Act in 1930. Though the Act secured the rights of *kanam* tenancy holders and reaffirmed the basic rights of *jenmies*, it did precious little in practice for the actual cultivators—the *verumpattamdars* and the small cultivating *kanamdars* (Sathyamurthy 1985:154). The realignment of the Nairs on the side of the propertied interests polarized the agrarian structure and transferred the leadership of the agrarian movement to the lower strata of the peasantry (Namboodiripad 1985:185). Moreover, the Act marked the opening chapter in what Herring has dubbed the "ratchet effect strategy" that would drive and sustain agrarian mobilization for the next four decades. State concessions, however minimal, provided opportunities for expanding the agrarian coalition both by creating incentives to mobilize around effective enforcement of legal provisions and by fueling demands to extend reform to lower strata of the peasantry (Herring 1996:25).

Social realignments in the countryside were reflected and amplified in political shifts. Support for the Malabar Tenancy Act marked the limits of the Congress Party's support for agrarian reform. The socialist wing in the party, however, recognized the strategic possibilities of tying the struggle against British imperialism to agrarian radicalism and formed the Kerala Congress Socialist Party (KCSP) in 1934. Drawing on a core of seasoned cadres from the Congress Party's civil disobedience campaigns, the KCSP organized the Kerala Karshaka Sangham (KKS—Kerala Farmers' Association), rapidly absorbing into its fold existing local peasant unions. As was

the case in Travancore, the socialists built on both the ideological and organizational repertoires of contention of the caste reform and nationalist
movements. *Jathas* (marches) created ties among movements, activists,
and regions. A salt march in 1930 was followed by two temple-entry
marches in 1931 and 1932 and a hunger march to Madras in 1936. In
1938 a "united front against imperialism" of Congressmen and Socialists
marched from Calicut in Malabar to Travancore, and a second march
brought peasants from all over Malabar to a mass peasant conference in
Calicut. In contrast to the "Sunday Congress" —as the party was derisively called because its leaders only ventured out into the countryside on
Sundays—the Socialists entrenched themselves in Malabar's villages. In
the words of Namboodiripad, "[t]he primary units of the organization,
the village committees, carefully planned multifarious activities . . . Night
schools for the education of the illiterate and the semi-literate; reading
rooms and libraries where the literate could enhance their fund of knowledge; the staging of dramas and other forms of culture which combined
entertainment with political education; the running of manuscript maga-
zines and other forms of developing the talent of the rising generation"
(1994:30).[13]

These organizational efforts had a profound transformative effect on
agrarian relations of class and caste. Movement demands remained
couched in the language of reform, targeting the "excesses" and "abuses"
of feudalism, but these were more and more tied to class identities. At the
first all-Malabar peasant meeting in 1936, Vishnu Bharateeyan, a KKS
leader, declared in his opening speech that "there are only two castes, two
religions and two classes—the haves and the have nots" (D. Menon
1994:134). The meeting passed two major resolutions: one demanding an
end to feudal exactions and one calling for the abolition of the customs
and speech of subordination. These actions, notes Menon, "marked a
major shift from the objectives of caste associations and the activities of
Gandhian Congressmen which had stressed self-help and self-betterment
over the need to question inequality" (1994:134). As the confrontational
character of the movement escalated, the right faction in the Congress
Party denounced its tactics as anti-Gandhian and all but surrendered the
organizational initiative in Malabar to the Left. In 1939, KCSP cadres se-
cretly joined the underground Communist Party (the CPI officially came
into existence in Kerala two years later) and broke with the Congress

---

[13] Between 1891 and 1921, literacy rates in Malabar had actually fallen from 12.9 percent to
12.7 percent. From 1931 to 1951, during the height of Communist activity, literacy levels
jumped from 14.2 percent to 31.3 percent (see figures in Ramachandran 1996:257).

Party the following year. When at a 1946 peasant conference the Communists declared that "the aim of the present movement is to end the feudal lord-janmi system and establish the ownership of the cultivator over the land" (Menon 1994:100), it was clear that the agrarian question in Malabar had moved irretrievably beyond the class-accomodationist line of the national Congress Party.

After an abortive insurrectionary period in 1948, the Communists quickly embraced a strategy of combining extraparliamentary struggles with representations to the government by its elected officials. The KKS pressed for and secured important reforms with the 1954 amendment of the Malabar Tenancy Act, whereby lower tenants were granted greater security from eviction and rents were subjected to regulation. Politically, the amendment was significant because it marked another advance in the Left's "ratchet politics" and vindicated the Communist Party's new strategic line of supporting parliamentary struggles. Far from slowing the momentum of the movement, the amendment provided the party with new leverage and the movement with new resources. The reforms fell short of actually dismantling landlordism but did provide poor tenants with a measure of increased independence from landlords and a degree of political maneuverability comparable to that of the middle peasants so often associated with agrarian revolutions (Wolf 1969). Moreover, in response to the new enactments, the KKS adopted an entirely new organizational agenda of securing implementation (Paulini 1979:225). The Communist Party's vigorous push to implement the laws paid political dividends when it won a majority in the Malabar district board elections of 1954—the first time that the movement became institutionally linked to the state.[14]

Forging the Agrarian Coalition

The grand agrarian coalition that propelled the CPI to electoral victory in 1957 was forged from very different agrarian structures and movements. In Travancore, the nineteenth-century land reforms had all but eradicated rentier landlordism and created a class of peasant proprietors and large

[14] "As a result of this victory, the district board administration began to function under the leadership of the communist party, and to serve as the kindergarten in which the communist cadres learnt the ABC of responsible government and effective administration" (Fic 1970:43–44).

capitalist farmers. In 1958, 77 percent of the total cultivated area in Travancore belonged to owner-cultivators. In contrast, 85 percent of the cultivated area in Malabar was held by tenants (Varghese 1970:164–65). The commodification of land in Travancore did not, however, spell the end of the social and political forms of domination associated with the traditional caste-based division of labor. Travancore's capitalist farmers, especially those who had successfully consolidated large holdings through purchases or reclamations, continued to rely on a highly repressive labor regime to secure reliable and cheap supplies of labor. Much as Barrington Moore's thesis on labor-repressive agriculture (1966) would predict, these rural elites, who had one foot in a capitalist economy and the other in a precapitalist social order, stubbornly resisted social and democratic reforms that threatened to loosen their control over labor.

The resilience of the repressive side of precapitalist social institutions in the face of the casualization of the labor force only aggravated class tensions. On the one hand, agricultural laborers remained largely subservient to the social and political power of the propertied classes. On the other hand, the commercialization of agriculture eroded many of the subsistence and insurance mechanisms of traditional patron-client relations, exposing laborers to the vicissitudes of the market. The social conflicts that Travancore's agrarian structure engendered thus set rural proletarians—wage earners exposed to the laws of the market—against a labor regime regimented by caste hierarchies.

In Malabar, the colonial state-*jenmi* nexus had, if anything, strengthened the feudal property structure as well as the political power of landlords. Backed by the coercive and legal apparatuses of the colonial state, surplus extraction remained firmly rooted in rental monopolies of a parasitic landed oligarchy, resulting in a weak impulse toward commercialization. The erosion of traditional mechanisms of security that resulted from the imposition of absolute property rights, coupled with the absence of any economic dynamism, produced an increasingly impoverished and disaffected peasantry. In his study of agrarian transitions, Moore concludes that "the landed upper classes either helped to make the bourgeois revolution or were destroyed by it" (1966:7); in Malabar, the landlords, politically dependent on a defunct colonial regime and economically wedded to a stagnant feudal economy, were destroyed by it.

The incapacity of landed elites and the state to respond to the social contradictions of Malabar's agrarian structure created, in the context of the nationalist struggle, an opening for change to come from below. Agrarian discontent first took the form of inchoate and sporadic uprisings and later, during the independence struggle, a tenancy reform movement that was the most organized peasant movement in India of its time. Given a landed class with neither the political nor social wherewithal to make concessions, and urban middle classes that, through the Congress Party, sided with landed interests, it is hardly surprising that peasant discontent took the form of agrarian communism.

The crisis of Kerala's traditional agrarian structure did not produce uniform points of resistance or a homogenous transformative class, for the structural bases of class mobilization in Malabar and Travancore were dramatically different. The tenants of Malabar sought more secure property rights and less onerous rents, while agricultural laborers in Travancore, along with their class allies in the coastal towns, struggled for the right to exert collective control over wages and conditions of work.[15] This difference bears emphasis since, as we shall see, conflicts between tenants and laborers would surface in the early 1970s. But in the 1950s the two classes shared a common interest, and a common opportunity to dismantle through the ballot box the institutions that supported an increasingly illegitimate traditional social order. Capitalizing on this moment required a strategic actor—the CPI—which drew together disparate voices of protest into a coherent antifeudal ideological project.

What distinguished the CPI from the Congress Party was that in both its ideology and its organization the CPI was more resonant with emerging forms of popular contestation. The "collective will"[16] expressed by the CPI first took shape as a radical doctrine of caste equality, which the party, in piecemeal fashion (driven more by events and concrete struggles than theoretical insight), translated into a class agenda. Speaking of the early days of the KCSP in Malabar, the Communist leader K. P. Gopalan noted, "We had socialist aims without knowing anything about socialism" (D. Menon 1994:147). The social and, in particular, educational resources developed by the caste reform movement served as the building blocks of class consciousness and action. Reading rooms became incubators of a new secular culture transcending caste and religion. The party newspaper, *Prabhatham*, launched in 1936, provided news of union activities, peasant struggles, factory conditions, "a new world populated only by the working masses and the exploiting classes" (1994:146). As the "proclaimer of

---

[15] When the all-Kerala Karshaka Sangham (KKS—peasant association) was formed in 1956, following the formation of the state of Kerala, out of a total of 134,000 members 116,537 were from Malabar and only 17,463 from Travancore-Cochin (T. Oommen 1985:90).

[16] "The modern Prince," writes Gramsci, "can only be an organism, a complex element of society in which a collective will, which has already been recognized and has to some extent asserted itself in action, begins to take concrete form" (1971:129).

an intellectual and moral reform" (Gramsci's words) the CPI also under-took a wide range of cultural activities, substituting itself for landed elites as the patron of the arts. Temple festivals became venues for political meetings. Theatrical troops toured the countryside, presenting plays that popularized Marxist ideas, exposed caste injustices, and celebrated revolutionary heroism. A new generation of socialist novelists launched the "progressive literature" genre, writing popular works with such titles as "From the Gutter," "Drink of Blood," and "Victory to the Revolution." The party's active role in the revival of Malayalee culture was underscored politically by its championing of the cause of a united Kerala, a position it had first embraced in 1942 when the Congress Party still refused to interfere in the "internal affairs" of the princely states.

Agrarian protests in the 1930s were aimed not at the system but at its excesses, and were framed by an "inchoate sense of moral economy" (D. Menon 1994:135). The party concretized the ideological project when it attacked property as the material expression of the injustices of the caste-dominated order. In 1946 the Communists specifically linked the social reform movement to the question of economic equality. "Land reform was the new slogan, and it was presented as the panacea for 'material, social and cultural progress' " (1994:180). In Travancore, the party transformed broad-based but diffuse demands for social change into an antifeudal and prodemocracy class struggle organized primarily on the strength of a growing urban and rural trade union movement. In 1936, the Travancore Labour Association had sponsored "a massive condolence meeting when the British Emperor passed away" (Govindan 1986:55); exactly ten years later, workers and field laborers took up arms in the Punnapra-Vayalar revolt to overthrow a despotic government.

If, as sociologists have argued, social movements have transformative effects, they stem less from immediate movement successes than from the cumulative effects of what Hirschman (1984) has called the "conservation and mutation of social energy." More specifically, movement repertoires of contention, once established, become "learned conventions of collective action [that] are a part of society's public culture" (Tarrow 1994:18). Innovations of organization, protest, and cultural media are to a certain extent fungible, especially when the movements are linked by dense networks of activists. As we have seen, the movement forms that were pioneered by the caste reform movement and the nationalist movement—*jathas*, petitions, civil disobedience, cultural self-assertion through education and social services—were adopted to great effect by class-based movements. The contestatory logic of these movements was so powerful that by the late 1930s political and social agitation had become "respectable and commonplace" (Jeffrey 1992:124) and was part of the repertoire of every major community. By delegitimating traditional forms of social and political authority and undermining the most abject forms of servility, these reform movements weakened cultural dependencies and opened the door to horizontal mobilizations. The agrarian transformation in Kerala thus began not with a struggle over the means of production, but with a struggle against the means of domination.

While community, peasant (tenant and laborer), and national movements shared a modular repertoire, they were not necessarily convergent politically. If caste reform movements created the initial challenge to the privileges and prerogatives of Brahmans, they also strengthened identities and created associations that often cut across the grain of emerging class solidarities. The nationalist movement provided a point of resistance to colonial power, but it also provided, in its reformist vein, the basis for elite-dominated class accommodations that submerged agrarian discontent. And the interests of tenants in Malabar and landless laborers in Travancore were not given, but had to be constructed. If these movements converged to create more broad-based and sustainable forms of mobilization, they did so because they were politically and organizationally articulated by a disciplined and ideologically cohesive Communist Party, whose cadres, somewhat ironically, exemplified the selfless dedication of the Gandhian *sanyasi*. With their organizational flexibility and autonomy, the Communists made the most of "ratchet politics" and optimized the trade-offs (despite repeatedly flirting with disaster) between insurrection and parliamentarism. But most important, Communist success was rooted in its ideological project. "Ideology," David Apter writes, "dignifies discontent, identifies a target for grievances and forms an umbrella over the discrete grievances of overlapping groups" (cited in Tarrow 1994: 22). It was the party's capacity to capitalize on popular idioms of moral outrage and social justice in creating class-based solidarities that underwrote the formation of a class of the agrarian poor.

The Demise of Landlordism

The advent of the 1957 Communist ministry marked the first time that a non-Congress party came to power in an Indian state, no minor feat given the popularity of Nehru and the hegemonic aura enjoyed by the Congress Party as the party of national liberation. It also marked the ascendancy, through the ballot box, of the poor and propertyless, social classes that in a few short decades had gone from complete social and economic subordination to political power. Communist control of the state, however, galvanized the fractious forces of the ancien régime, bringing together the Christian church, upper-caste Hindus, landlords, plantation owners, and merchants, all organized under the umbrella of the Congress Party. In what had all the unmistakable characteristics of a seignorial reaction, these forces launched a "liberation struggle" that combined open protest, lockouts by land owners, and intimidation of Communist supporters. Kerala was on the brink of civil war when Nehru dismissed the ministry in 1959 and imposed president's rule, a first in India.[17]

Though brief, the Communists' tenure in power (1957–59) propelled agrarian class struggles to a new level. The Ministry gave legitimacy to and set into motion, if not into law, the basic components of agricultural reform that were to dominate the state's politics for the next two decades. Most notably, the land reform act passed by the legislature enjoyed popular support, and despite being ultimately struck down by the center, created an irresistible political momentum. The ministry also changed the balance of power in agrarian relations by notifying minimum wages for agricultural laborers and creating an Industrial Relations Committee (IRC), charged with mediating conflicts. Threatened by the state's challenge to their traditional authority, the landlords of Kuttanad organized a farmers' association (Upper Kuttanad Karshaka Sangham), raised private armies, and became key players in the "liberation struggle."

The dismissal of the government gave new life to the factions within the party that advocated the primacy of class struggle over parliamentarism.[18] The party redoubled its mobilizational efforts, and by the 1960s the agricultural laborers' movement in Kuttanad was at its height. At stake was control over the labor process and the labor market in a labor-surplus economy. In 1961, the TKTU was able to mobilize over 100,000 laborers who struck for twenty days in support of wage demands (Pillai and Panikar 1965:128). When the union's collective bargaining leverage was threatened by the use of casual migrant workers, it countered by restrict-

---

[17] Indian government officials were quoted in the press as saying that they were "fully alive to the dangers of allowing the Communist party to establish itself firmly in power in Kerala and [of] spreading itself out" (Jeffrey 1992:4). Kerala became widely know as the "Yenan of India," after the province that was the beachhead of Chinese Communism.

[18] Though renewing its commitment to parliamentary democracy, the Amritsar Congress of the CPI in 1958 declared that "the Kerala experience has also shown that the verdict of the ballot box in favor of popular forces is not necessarily respected by the vested interests. It has to be defended by mass actions" (quoted in Leiten 1982:19).

ing the right to harvesting operations to local workers (Tharamangalam 1981:86). And when ploughmen were threatened by mechanization, they successfully agitated for a ban against the use of tractors. By the late 1960s the state had institutionalized the bargaining rights of unions not only by codifying gains on wages and work conditions, but also by extending the role of the Kuttanad Industrial Relations Committee. Between 1960–61 and 1968–69 the real wages of male agricultural laborers rose 42 percent (Kannan 1988:258).

But the Communists' greatest success in sustaining the momentum of class mobilization came on the land issue. After the central government scuttled the Kerala Agrarian Relations Bill of 1959, legislation passed by Congress-led governments amounted to little more than efforts at counter-reform (Paulini 1979; T. Oommen 1985). Parliamentary efforts to bring about important changes in property relations are notoriously difficult (Herring 1983); provisions that survive judicial review and backroom deal-making are often emasculated through the maneuverings of vested interests (illegal evictions, falsified property records, or dispersal of assets).[19] That land reform in Kerala ultimately escaped this fate is a testament to the organizational efforts of the Communists and their allies. The tortured legislative history of Kerala's land reforms, rather than demobilizing the movement, proved to be a catalyst of continuous debate, struggle, and conflict. In protesting reformist bills, the CPI and the KKS repeatedly organized marches, satyagrahas, picketing, hunger strikes by the leadership and even a "Land Reforms Act Burning Day" during which copies of the 1963 Act were publicly torched (T. Oommen 1985:114). In organizing support from below for more radical land reform, the party organized a farmer's protection force to protect tenants against evictions, recruited and trained para-military units to counter the landlords' private armies, and launched agitations at the local level to identify surplus land and formalize oral tenancy agreements.

Though the party split in 1965 over the question of extending support to the Congress Party, the new CPM retained most of the CPI's cadre base and led a left coalition to power in 1967. The new ministry lost little time in passing the Kerala Land Reforms Amendment Act (KLRAA), which in the new national climate of Indira Gandhi's pro-poor populism escaped the center's scalpel. When the CPI (the smaller and "right Communist"

[19] Commenting on the disempowerment of the poor in northeastern Brazil, Nancy Scheper-Hughes notes that "foot-dragging, lies and false compliance are not only the tactics of the oppressed and the weapons of the weak as James Scott's (1985) analysis would seem to imply; they are also of strategic importance to politicians and bureaucrats . . . hostile to the demands of the poor and popular classes" (1992:514).

party) withdrew from the government, the minstry fell, leaving the task of implementation of the Act to a Congress-led coalition with a CPI chief minister.

The implementation of KLRAA has received extensive commentary. There are differing views as to who benefited the most and how far the reforms actually went (a debate made difficult by the absence of reliable prereform data), but there is wide agreement on a few salient points. The reforms were by far the most extensive in India and are routinely referred to in central government documents as a model of effective implementation. As Herring has noted, the Act itself was carefully patterned after the recommendations of the 1949 Congress Agrarian Reforms Committee Report.[20] In reviewing its main provisions he concludes that "the conceptualization was explicitly anti-feudal and pro-capitalist, not socialist" (1980:A59). The reforms had two broad objectives which reflected the specific interests of tenants and agricultural laborers: conferring ownership rights on tenants and redistributing surplus land. On the first count the reforms have been extremely successful. By October 1980, over 3.6 million applications for transfer of ownership rights had been received from tenants, and about two-thirds of these were accepted. In all, government figures indicate that 2.4 million tenants became de jure property owners (Raj and Tharakan 1983:50).[21] Over two million acres representing 40 percent of the total cultivated land thus changed hands (Herring 1980: A61). Herring (1980) presents some data which suggests that larger tenant households benefited disproportionately from the reforms. However, he also carefully points out that each tenancy case yielded an average transfer of .8 acres, which, given the high productivity of land in Kerala, represents a substantial transfer of economic endowments. In the most recent review of the net impact of the reforms, M. A. Oommen notes that "Kerala enjoys the unique distinction among Indian states of having abolished feudal landlordism lock, stock and barrel" (1990:29).

The land ceiling legislation which limited the size of holdings, was only marginally effective. By 1991 only 63,045 acres of surplus land—less than

[20] A United Nations study concluded that from 1957 onward, "land reforms became almost the center piece of the programme for social and economic progress in the state. Though none of the measures proposed or adopted for the purpose since then have gone beyond the proposals made for the entire country in successive five-year plans, the main difference in Kerala, compared to other states in India, has been the political environment which has kept up sustained pressure on this issue" (1975:59).

[21] Herring points out that the government figures refer to cases, not tenants. His own estimate puts the figure of actual beneficiaries at 1.27 million (1980:A60).

1.2 percent of the net sown area—had been distributed (GOK, *Economic Review* 1991).[22] A number of factors contributed to emasculating the impact of ceilings. In an effort to protect the most productive area of the agricultural economy, the legislation exempted plantation lands. Anticipating the reforms, landlords had, moreover, divided their land among family members, or, in what amounted to a de facto form of land reform, had sold rights to tenants. Finally, with the lowest per capita area of cultivable land in India, and an average farm size that stands today at a minuscule .34 hectares, there was little room for fulfilling the movement's rallying slogan of "land to the tiller" to the satisfaction of both tenants and laborers. The land ceilings did, however, have the effect of limiting the amount of land that rich tenants were able to acquire.[23] And there was one redistributive provision that directly benefited laborers. The reform granted *kudikidappukars*—landless hutment dwellers—ownership of their huts and one-tenth of an acre of surrounding land. In this manner some 288,349 laborer households were granted homesteads (GOK, *Economic Review* 1991:255). Though small, the plots can sustain vegetable gardens and even a few coconut trees. Most important, home ownership brought an end to the threat of eviction as a source of landlord control. A government survey in 1983–84 (GOK, Department of Economics and Statistics 1985) found that only 7.8 percent of agricultural labor households were landless compared to 29.8 percent in the prereform period.[24]

The implementation of KLRAA marked the end of the poor peasant tenancy reform movement born in the mid-1930s. A large class of poor, rack-rented tenants was transformed into a class of independent property owners. The *jenmies*, who had reigned supreme for centuries over the countryside, watched as the economic base of their domination was simply legislated away, and with it, much of their social and political standing. Kerala's land reforms thus represented much more than the demise of feudal property structures. They produced a fundamental realignment of agrarian class forces, and dealt the final blow to the old order.

Examples of such thoroughgoing and successful legislated reforms, especially land reforms, are few and far between. There is no issue more ex-

---

[22] In comparative terms this was more than respectable. No other major Indian state has redistributed more than one percent of its cultivable area (see Mallick 1992:tab. 1).

[23] In 1985–86, large operational holdings (ten hectares and above) accounted for only 9.7 percent of the total cultivated area in Kerala (CMIE, *Basic Statistics*, 1993:tab. 7.9).

[24] The social welfare impact of these redistributive effects has been far-reaching. Kerala's high performance on the health and educational fronts has been tied to the land reforms, as has the dramatic demographic transition of the past two decades (Ratcliffe 1978; Zachariah 1984).

plosive in any agrarian society than the issue of property rights. The power of traditional elites, be they landlords, officials of the crown, soldiers, or clergymen, is intricately tied to the control over land. A transformation in property relations is a direct challenge to the power (and status) of these traditional elites. In the context of parliamentary democracy, land reforms thus entail imposing the authority of the state and its legalistically defined and bureaucratically enforced conception of property rights over the entrenched power, prestige, and traditional rights of landed elites. The resistance of vested interests aside, in redefining property rights the state must also confront the Herculean logistical and informational task of actually identifying owners, appropriating land, and rewarding targeted beneficiaries. Though class mobilization was the dynamic underlying the agrarian transition, the democratic state was the actual instrument.

That land reforms in Kerala were not only legislated but implemented (there were almost three million cases in which land was transferred) is a testament to the administrative capacities of the state. The transfer of land did not result from forcible appropriation, but took place through a legal and bureaucratic process that saw the arm of the administration and the courts reach into every village of the state and evaluate and act upon over five million applications. But for all the instrumental power the state displayed, the power to actually force the surrender of land by landlords came from below. Had the state not been linked organizationally and politically to poor peasants and agricultural laborers, by means of electoral pressure and direct action, implementation of the land reforms would have been stymied by the same forces that had ousted the 1957 Communist ministry. Two factors in particular provided the pressure from below that contributed to the success of the reforms.

The first and the most visible of the political factors was the large-scale direct action mobilizations that the CPM and its unions organized to force the hand of the government. On the first day KLRAA went into effect, a land-grab agitation was launched to encourage hutment dwellers to take possession of their land in anticipation of the legislation's *Kudikidappu* provision. Union leaders had concluded that the proposed bureaucratic process was too cumbersome, and that laborers should instead simply fence off their land. Two hundred thousand laborers are reported to have asserted their rights in this manner (T. Oommen 1985:127). In 1972, with the support of the celebrated Father Vadakkan (who had been one of the most prominent leaders of the 1957 reaction) a second statewide agitation was organized to pressure the government to speed up implementation of the Act. Surplus land was identified and occupied (by planting red flags), and district offices were picketed. According to CPM sources, over an eighty-day period 160,000 militants were arrested and 10,000 later sentenced (Nayanar 1982:150). In sum, the pressure of organized demands from below, as expressed in a competitive electoral framework, generated an irresistible political logic that no government could afford to ignore. The demand for land reforms had brought together the body of the agrarian poor into a highly mobilized and increasingly coherent political force, one that had already on two occasions carried the Communists to power. The CPI, which was part of the governing coalition in power when KLRAA was implemented, was in particular sensitive to accusations leveled by the opposition CPM that it had become a "bourgeois" party, and to fears that it was losing its already narrow mass base. Moreover, the organizing successes of the CPM had a ripple effect, as other political parties tried to ride the wave of agrarian discontent and organize their own farmers' unions.

A second factor was the democratization of local institutions. The entrenched presence of the party and its unions at the village level, coupled with the educational work conducted through the party's media organs and its local committees, secured active and informed popular participation. The party was able to exert constant, concerted pressure on local officials, making sure that surplus land was identified, petitions filed, and decisions followed up. Herring writes: "Officials in the land revenue administration were candid with me about the effect; without mass pressure and exposures of fraud and bureaucratic misbehavior, implementation might well have moved in the sluggish and corrupt manner typical of sub-continental reforms" (1991b:178).

Class Struggle after Land Reform

Land reform and the demise of landlordism marked the culmination of the Communist-led tenant reform movement. The agrarian question, however, was far from resolved. Agrarian mobilization, particularly in Malabar, had directly and explicitly challenged a distinctly feudal mode of surplus extraction defined by a set of proprietary rights deeply embedded in upper-caste social domination and the legal-coercive apparatus of the colonial state. The logic of the reforms accordingly emphasized the transfer of property rights from rent-collecting landlords to a class of small peasant proprietors. The reforms, in other words, addressed the question of land, but not of labor, of peasants, but not of proletarians.

The political coalition that had challenged landlordism rested on a politically sound but economically shaky rationale. In E. M. S. Namboodiri-pad's words, "the antifeudal slogan of the organized peasant movement attracted the agricultural workers also although the movement included rich peasants. The rights of landlords to evict the tenants, increase the rent and make other exactions and the accompanying social repression disturbed the agricultural workers as well as the peasants. In short, the slogan of 'End feudalism and distribute the land to the peasant', created a common target for agricultural workers as well as the peasantry" (quoted in Krishnaji 1986:401).

Somewhat more concretely, laborers were promised a share of the surplus traditionally extracted through rents. According to Herring, "The mechanism to recruit the *majority* of agriculturalists—the landless laborers and various insecure tenant or quasi-tenant strata hinged on a structural feature of landlordism: the rent fund (Wolf 1966). Tenants would get the land, but would share their windfall with laborers via higher wages" (1991a: chap.1, p. 22).

The alliance was thus predicated on a corporatist compromise which specifically anticipated that the increased productivity associated with capitalist property structures would create the material base (high profits and high wages) for class compromise. But if classes can be made, they can just as readily be unmade. The political logic of the CPI's broad-based multiclass agrarian coalition, which had proved so effective in challenging the landed ruling class, succumbed to its own internal class contradictions.

Kerala's former tenants, secure in their property rights and no longer subject to the burden of paying rents, could now look to the market for the realization of their newly acquired assets. Because most of Kerala's major crops, especially rice, require the use of hired-in labor, the search for profits brought farmers into direct conflict with agricultural laborers. These tensions were aggravated by the fact that the laborers had moral, if not proprietary, claims on the rent fund. The embourgeoisement of the peasantry, a phenomenon that has received extensive attention from scholars of agrarian Kerala,[25] thus produced new axes of conflict and new political alignments in the countryside.

The conflict between laborers and farmers was most pronounced in the south Malabar district of Palghat, the primary rice growing region of Malabar, where the land reforms had the greatest impact and where the green revolution and the completion of large public irrigation projects in the 1960s accelerated the commercialization of rice farming and increased the

[25] See for example Nossiter 1982; Herring 1989, 1991a; K. Alexander 1989; T. Oommen 1985; and Kannan 1988.

demand for casual labor. The casualization of the labor force in turn undermined the traditional attached-labor system (which had persisted up to this point in Palghat) and with it the security and customary arrangements laborers depended on. The exposure of the landless to market forces was compounded by demographic pressures. In the 1961–71 decade alone, the percentage of agricultural laborers in the total work force exploded from 17.4 to 30.7 percent.

Though laborers had long constituted the largest agricultural class in Malabar—43.9 percent of the agricultural population in 1951 (Varghese 1970:126–28)—the agrarian movement in Malabar, driven as it was by the logic of tenancy reform, had largely failed to take up the interests of laborers, whether attached or casual. Between 1958 and 1970, while real wages grew in Travancore, they fell in Malabar (Jose 1973:283). Only when cracks in the Communist's agrarian alliance emerged did the party organize a statewide independent laborer's union in 1968, the Kerala State Karshaka Thozhilali Union (KSKTU), and begin to take up separate agitations for Palghat laborers in 1970–71. And in a pattern that bears close similarities to the mobilization of agricultural laborers in Kuttanad in the 1940s, Palghat witnessed the sudden and explosive rise of a militant laborer movement.

Labor's demands centered on the question of wages and the traditional right of attached workers—soon to be legislatively redefined as "permanent" workers—to be given exclusive and essentially proprietary control over harvesting operations. The terrain of the struggle was the field, but the object of the struggle was the role of the state. In a labor market characterized by oversupply, farmers favored market mechanisms to both maintain low wages and discipline labor. The union was determined to impose social limits on the labor market by formalizing labor relations and establishing the right to bargain collectively.

In 1970, as the KSKTU organized peaceful protests, the government formed an industrial relations committee for Palghat district and notified an increase in the minimum wage over the protests of the Deseeya Karshaka Samajam (DKS), the newly formed Palghat farmers' association.[26] The government's determination to head off open confrontations was clear; it organized local conciliations, introduced the Kerala Agricultural Workers Bill in 1971, and even invoked the Defense of India Rules (national security laws) to statutorily settle differences in the share of the harvest paid to workers. As Herring's account describes in detail, the full ma-

---

[26] The following account is based on Herring 1991a, chap. 6, evocatively entitled: " 'A Paddy Field Is Not a Factory': The Farmer's Lament."

chinery of the government was deployed. The district collector, the police, the labor and revenue departments, and the courts all actively played a role in working out compromises. The major thrust of their efforts was to enforce the implementation of minimum wages and curb the use of outside workers in replacing striking workers. These combined interventions, Herring notes, had the effect of removing the "traditional farmer managerial prerogatives from their control" (1991a:6.6). The district collector banned the import of cheaper, more docile workers from the neighboring state of Tamil Nadu, and the high court prohibited the use of strikebreakers in disputes where farmers were deemed to be in violation of existing orders. The Labour Department in 1973 published a notification that "in cases where workers are actually in receipt of higher wages than the minimum wage fixed, they shall continue to get the benefit of the higher wage" (Herring 1991a:6.7). Despite these orders and various conciliation efforts, there were countless violent confrontations as farmers, and particularly the DKS, refused to give in. In 1973 the KSKTU launched a massive harvest strike involving over 150,000 laborers. The following year, the Kerala Agricultural Workers Act (KAWA), the most comprehensive legislation of its kind ever to be introduced in the subcontinent, was passed against the strenuous protests of the DKS. The last major struggle occurred in October 1974 when the KSKTU, in a tactic that had often been used in Kuttanad, marshalled all of its forces in a symbolic but powerful confrontation with a large farmer who had denied permanent workers the right to harvest. Some six hundred farmers and two thousand laborers affiliated with the DKS tried to break the harvest strike but were met by five thousand KSKTU militants (Herring 1991a:6.10). The confrontation led to the arrest of 180 DKS members and the death of a laborer.

In reviewing these events, two phenomena stand out. First was the speed and intensity with which the class contradictions following land reform came into focus and led to open class conflict. Although it is difficult to ascertain which strata of farmers actively resisted, it is clear that many were ex-tenants and former Communist sympathizers. When it was founded in 1970, the DKS had a membership of two thousand. By 1974 it had grown into a powerful body of 20,000 (Jose 1977:42). In 1970, the Palghat division of the KSKTU had only 11,000 members, compared to 17,000 in Alleppey district. Three years later there were 45,000 members in Palghat and 35,100 in Alleppey (Kannan 1988:249). Moreover, the confrontations involved thousands of activists on both sides and resulted in prolonged strikes, damaged crops, and a number of killings.

Second was the role of the state, which directly challenged the prerogatives of farmers and gave institutional expression to the interests of labor-

ers. It deployed its full legal and institutional machinery in an effort to
manage the conflict, extending its authority into every village of the district, and its role was clearly biased toward meeting the demands of agricultural laborers. Police intervention, which in rural India generally has a
pronounced landed-class bias (Brass 1994:59), was by all accounts even-
handed and in keeping with court rulings.

The state's actions cannot be attributed to the character of its regime.
The coalition in power—an unlikely and seemingly unmanageable coalition of the CPI, the Congress Party, the Muslim League, and smaller parties—was held together only by its opposition to the CPM. The left partners of the ruling coalition had all broken with the CPM over the latter's
advocacy of mass agitation during the United Front government of
1967–69. The pressure of mass mobilization and the inevitable polarization of class forces that it presaged dictated a response aimed at providing
at least institutional remedies to the emergent class conflict. Because no
state, and particularly a democratic one, can ultimately afford to deal with
the consequences of open class conflict, the state-as-institution prevailed
over the state-as-regime. Recalling the experience of the "liberation struggle" (an ultimately unsuccessful effort to stem the tide of agrarian reform)
and Kuttanad's agrarian struggles, the state acted decisively.

As explanation of Kerala's agrarian transformation it would be tempting
to conclude that both landlordism and the attached labor regime had become increasingly incompatible with the commercialization of agriculture
and ultimately succumbed to the logic of capital. Yet as the development
literature has so often documented, precapitalist social institutions display
extraordinary resilience. When confronted with the forces of the market
they are just as likely to adapt as to dissolve. In much of rural India, debt
bondage, labor tying, interlinked factor markets, and sharecropping have
all survived the commercialization of agriculture (albeit in altered form),
creating the hybrid modes of production that have so preoccupied students of the subcontinent.

The agrarian transformation in Kerala was driven from below. It resulted from the formation and alliance of two classes—tenants and wage
earners—that became the active agents of the dissolution of the precapitalist social structure. These classes were not, moreover, born of some inexorable process of market penetration resulting in polarization and differentiation. They were formed through concrete struggles and specifically
emerged at the confluence of three distinct social movements of peasants,
castes, and nation. The most lasting effect of these movements was to develop and popularize a form of contentious politics that directly chal-

lenged the social institutions of the traditional order. The resulting ideological and political ferment provided an opening for the emergence of
new actors and new solidarities. A Communist Party that was more the
product of spontaneous oppositions than theoretical insight, that was
born and incubated from the ground up, provided the organizational and
ideological frames within which the politics of class could congeal. Much
of its success was in its capacity for building mass organizations of tenants
and wage earners and linking these to a larger project of social and political transformation. But just as critically, the success of the party was in its
ability to insinuate itself into the very fabric of local institutions—panchayats, schools, reading rooms, cultural associations, and even temples—
and to produce a lived experience of class consciousness and class action.

Finally, near-continuous popular mobilization and open class struggles
from 1930 to 1974 were sustained because confrontations with the state
produced incremental but significant concessions that transformed the
rules of the game in favor of the lower classes. A democratic state provided the basis for new alliances and new channels for pressing demands.
The ballot box, industrial relations committees (IRCs), legislative enactments, and government committees all became new loci of class struggle in
which the power of the propertied was leveled. With each successful struggle, the authority of the state substituted itself for the authority of the traditional patron, further increasing the mobilizational capacity of the rural
poor.

The dynamics of Kerala's current agrarian structure can only be understood in light of the historical and political particularities of class formation. At first view, the story of Kerala's agrarian transformation reads very
much like the class-struggle dynamic Brenner (1985) develops in his account of the rise of capitalist agriculture in western Europe. As new classes
with new capacities emerged they successfully challenged the existing balance of class forces, paving the way for a transformation of the existing
social-property system.

Where Kerala parts company from Brenner's scenario is in the identity
of the protagonist. A bourgeois agrarian transition—one that saw the
emergence of both land and labor as commodities—was led not by a commercializing landed elite, but by tenants and landless laborers. The tenants
freed land and the laborers freed themselves from the clutches of precapitalist social institutions. The class consolidation of tenants signaled the
transition to private-property capitalism, marked politically by their embourgeoisement. The class consolidation of laborers, however, dictated
that the logic of the market, and specifically the full commodification of
labor, would be contested. In the classical scenario of primitive accumula-

tion, labor emerges as a commodity when it is separated from the means of production (land) and freed from extraeconomic control, only to be subjected to the whip of the market. More often than not, landless laborers have been the product of, rather than a player in, the emergence of capitalist agriculture. In Kerala, however, labor was the agent of its own transformation. And having liberated itself through political means from subordination to the precommodity form of labor, it had the subjectivity and capacity to resist its subordination to the commodity form.

The land reforms settled the "peasant question" by abolishing landlordism. But this only exposed a second set of contradictions, those pitting a class of small independent farmers against a large and increasingly uprooted class of rural proletarians. How this class conflict has in turn been resolved is the question to which we now turn.

3

The Institutionalization of
Class Conflict in Agriculture

It is difficult to imagine an agrarian society more prone to class conflict than Kerala in the 1970s. A large class of agricultural laborers (34.5 percent of the rural work force in 1971) depended for employment on a landholding class 85 percent of which owned less than one acre (CMIE 1991:tab. 7.8–1). Tight profit margins for farmers and scarce employment for laborers made for a trade-off between wages and profits that was both precarious and palpable. In 1970 the percentage of the rural population in Kerala below the poverty line was estimated at over 60 percent (EPW Foundation 1993). In contrast to the rest of the country, furthermore, Kerala's agricultural laborers were highly organized and, in the aftermath of the land reforms, determined to reap the rewards of a struggle they had so actively supported. The embourgeoisement of the peasantry and the mobilization of laborers triggered, as we have seen, widespread struggles in the early 1970s.

Over the past two decades, however, the countryside in Kerala has been uncharacteristically quiet. The confrontations of 1974 were the last large-scale organized conflicts, and the local strikes that routinely accompanied every harvesting season have become a rarity. Disputes over wages and work conditions reported to the Labour Department have declined precipitously; the process of wage determination that is examined in this chapter has in fact become so routinized that the labor commissioner in 1997 recommended that the department withdraw from its conciliation functions and concentrate instead on extending social protection to less organized sections of the work force such as quarry workers.

Comparative and historical insight suggest three plausible explanations for this decline in militancy. The first would be that structural changes in

87

the economy have removed the "objective conditions" for class conflict, either by absorbing much of the rural wage class in industry or by stimulating higher wages through increases in agricultural productivity. But the size of this class has, if anything, increased, and its improved material position is largely, as we shall see, the result of state intervention and institutionally driven real wage increases. Economic forces may be driving a "great transformation," but it is nonmarket forces, as Polanyi argued, that are making it socially sustainable.

A second explanation would be that organized agrarian militancy is rare to begin with and that instances of sustained agrarian mobilization, especially among agricultural laborers, are even rarer. The decline of militancy in Kerala, it could be argued, was in this sense a political inevitability, particularly in the postreform period when the embourgeoisement of the peasantry deprived agricultural laborers of a crucial ally. As we shall see, politics has certainly played a role in defusing agrarian radicalism (especially in the CPM's efforts to reconstruct the agrarian alliance), but it would be a mistake to equate a decline in overt militancy and conflict with political marginalization. Labor's quiescence has not been marked by a deterioration in its bargaining capacity or economic position. Quite the contrary. The KSKTU's membership has continued to grow, increasing from 47,700 in 1970 to over one million 1990, and its organized power is reflected in the active role it plays in negotiating and implementing wages. Thus the decline of overt class struggle does not reflect a shift in the balance of class forces, or the triumph of market forces.

A third explanation, which comes closest to the one developed here, would point to the role of the state and political actors in institutionalizing class conflict. In the East Asian scenario, conflict has been institutionalized from above, as powerful and authoritarian state/party machines have preempted agrarian radicalism through patronage and other strategic interventions such as land settlement schemes (Scott 1985; Hart 1989). In Latin America, the most significant effect of repeated agrarian "reforms" has been an increase in the state's role in regulating agriculture and in its capacity to diffuse rural protest (Grindle 1986). Even when the rural poor have found an independent voice, sustaining mobilization has proven difficult. In the most significant case, militant organizations of small peasants and landless laborers in Brazil with roots in both the church and the Communist Party came together under the corporatist umbrella of the Confederation of Agricultural Workers (CONTAG), and not only secured significant state concessions, including the extension of welfare benefits, but also played a critical role in the transition to democracy (Pereira 1997). But state support for the movement, which was critical to its success in the authoritarian period, proved to be its undoing under democracy. As the confederation became increasingly bureaucratic and dependent on state resources, including salaries for its leadership and guaranteed benefits for its membership, the defensive logic of trade unionism prevailed over the more encompassing logic of social-movement unionism. Having secured its place but surrendered its political autonomy, CONTAG was unable to push for a broader conception of agrarian reform, including land redistribution, in the 1988 constitution. This failure, concludes Pereira, marked the "the exclusion of the peasantry from Brazil's political transition" (1997:154).

Labor quiescence in Kerala can be attributed to neither political exclusion nor economic forces. It marks instead the institutionalization of class conflict, driven on the one hand by the active intervention of the state, and on the other by the conversion of the CPM to the politics of class compromise. But institutionalization in this case must not be confused with demobilization or co-optation. Some observers have noted that the CPM's willingness to regulate class conflict represents the abandonment of its "revolutionary" agenda (Tharamangalam 1981). But this observation misses two critical points. First, as Offe and Weisenthal (1985) argue, the inherent problems of collective action in sustaining working-class militancy underscores the need to secure institutional representation of working-class interests. Second, organized class compromise and consent to capitalism can have a material base (Przeworski 1985). As I will show in Chapter 4, the withdrawal of militancy in rural Kerala has been predicated first on institutionalizing labor's share of the surplus and second on regulating the pace and modalities of proletarianization.

The form of democratic corporatism that I describe here—an organized trade-off between wages and profits, between accumulation and social protection—must be fundamentally distinguished from state corporatism. The pluralistic traditions of the Indian state, and in particular its labor laws, have limited the capacity of the state to construct and ultimately control corporatist organizations. Even more critically, in the case of Kerala the logic of incorporation has been driven from below by dynamic and competitive class-centered mobilization. The state's role has been less significant in its direct interventions that in the extension of its rational-legal authority. The claims of labor have been institutionalized as general rights of social citizenship, not as revocable corporate privileges granted in exchange for political support. And, although peak-level government institutions have played a role in regulating the terms of conflict, it is the democratization of local arenas and the penetration of the rule of law into the fabric of agrarian relations that has allowed for genuine negotiation of class compromises.

The robustness of public legality and high degrees of citizenship do not derive simply from the formal attributes of parliamentary democracy, but rather from actual relations between state and society. Across the Indian political landscape there are pronounced degrees of democracy and state capacity and corresponding variations in the character of agrarian relations, particularly with respect to the "double freedom" of labor. Kerala marks one end of the spectrum, but even within Kerala the terrain is uneven. The effects of state power and the dynamics of class relations do not simply radiate outward from core institutions and structures. The consolidation of state authority and the development of organized class interests have provided the backdrop for institutionalizing class relations in Kerala, but the shaping effect of local mobilization on local institutions and alignments has determined the actual procedure and substance of class compromises.

I explore these dynamics by focusing on Kerala's two principal rice-growing regions, Palghat and Kuttanad.[1] Of Kerala's three major crops, rice provides the greatest challenge for managing the social costs of agrarian transformation. Unlike rubber and coconut, rice is a seasonal crop that requires intensive labor at peak periods (land preparation, planting, harvesting) and is thus particularly dependent on wage labor. As traditional rice-growing areas, Palghat and Kuttanad are highly proletarianized with the highest ratios of laborers to farmers in the state (3.5:1 and 3:1 respectively). The mechanization of rice farming, the conversion of land to less labor-intensive crops, and demographic pressures have severely strained the capacity of rice to support the rural population. To make matters worse, over the past two decades farm gate prices for paddy (unmilled rice) have declined continuously, making the terms of exchange between wages and profits particularly acute. Not surprisingly, the most pronounced and prolonged agrarian conflicts of the post-land-reform period have been in these two areas. But if the class structures and the material terms of conflict are comparable, their respective histories of agrarian mobilization are not. As part of Malabar, Palghat produced an agrarian movement dominated by tenants and centered on the question of land. In Kuttanad, as we have seen, the agrarian movement was one of

---

[1] Palghat is a district (one of fourteen), whereas Kuttanad is a continuous low-lying area that stretches across seven taluks (district subdivisions) located in Alleppey district and three taluks in Kottayam district. Together, Kuttanad and Palghat account for 584,000 agricultural laborers, more than one-quarter of the state total (GOI, Census 1991).

unfree laborers and centered on collective bargaining rights and social protection. Though the postreform period has been marked by convergence, as the question of labor has come to dominate conflicts in Palghat as well, both areas have nonetheless developed institutions and modalities of class compromise that are unique and that can be causally tied to the timing and pattern of class mobilization and state intervention in each area.

The institutionalization of class struggle marks a dramatic transformation in Kerala's agrarian relations.[2] The economic implications have been much debated and are explored in the next chapter. The objective in this chapter, however, is to examine the institutional underpinnings and political dynamics of class compromise. I do this by focusing on the formalization of the wage issue in the 1980s, a development that has seen the containment of the wage militancy of the past in favor of a negotiated process that explicitly recognizes the interdependency of class interests.

Agricultural Wages in Kerala

The issue of agricultural wages in Kerala has been the subject of countless studies and controversies. Two important facts stand out. The first is that real agricultural wages in Kerala have grown steadily and at a faster rate than in other states. Table 2 shows that both male and female wages have doubled when deflated by the standard agricultural consumer price index and tripled when deflated by the wholesale cost of rice. In comparing growth rates across states, Jose found that a 96-percent increase in real wages for male agricultural workers between 1956–57 and 1985–86 in Kerala was surpassed only by Uttar Pradesh and Andhra Pradesh (1988:tab. 12A). The contrast with Kerala's two neighboring states is even more instructive: Tamil Nadu registered an increase of real wage rates of only 29 percent while agricultural workers in Karnataka saw their wages fall by 8 percent (ibid.). In the most recent comparative study, real wages in Kerala lagged behind only Punjab and West Bengal in 1987 for men and behind only Punjab for women. Male agricultural laborers in Kerala in 1987 received twice the amount of their Tamil Nadu counterparts, and the gap for women was even more pronounced at Rs. 15.9 per day in Kerala and Rs. 6.2 in Tamil Nadu (Krishnan 1991:tab. 1).

Second, numerous studies have tied wage gains to institutional factors,

[2] Of the many studies on agrarian mobilization in Kerala, T. Oommen 1985 is the only one to have explicitly addressed the question of institutionalization.

TABLE 2. Paddy wages and prices in Kerala.

| | In constant 1960 rupees | | | Purchasing power in kgs. of paddy per daily male wage |
| | Average daily wage, paddy work | | Farm price of paddy (100 kgs) | |
	Male	Female		
1965–66	2.22		61.1	3.64
1966–67	2.39		69.0	3.47
1967–68	2.76		81.4	3.19
1968–69	2.43		57.4	4.22
1969–70	2.43		49.5	4.90
1970–71	2.37		42.0	5.65
1971–72	2.57		46.9	5.48
1972–73	2.61		53.8	4.86
1973–74	2.42	1.61	67.7	3.57
1974–75	2.10	1.40	72.8	3.27
1975–76	2.34	1.58	50.0	4.68
1976–77	2.59	1.80	43.9	5.90
1977–78	2.73	1.91	41.3	6.62
1978–79	2.77	1.93	39.8	6.97
1979–80	2.78	1.94	38.0	7.31
1980–81	2.94	2.08	40.1	7.33
1981–82	3.04	2.11	42.7	7.12
1982–83	2.78	1.99	43.5	6.39
1983–84	2.71	1.88	43.1	6.29
1984–85	3.97	2.00	33.8	11.74
1985–86	4.33	2.51	40.1	10.81
1986–87	4.26	2.46	36.7	11.62
1987–88	4.30	2.50	37.1	11.59
1988–89	4.05	2.36	37.4	10.83
1989–90	3.94	2.32	34.3	11.49
1990–91	3.81	2.25	31.8	11.96
1991–92	4.07	2.59	36.9	11.03
1992–93	4.30	2.87	37.4	11.50
1993–94	4.26	2.79	32.6	13.07

Source: Statistics for Planning, Economic Review (annual).
Note: Wages and prices deflated using Agricultural Consumer Price Index.

namely state intervention and unionization (Bardhan 1970; Kannan 1988; Pushpangadan 1992; Krishnan 1991; Baby 1996). Wages began to climb steadily in the mid-1970s, a period of rapid union growth and the implementation of the Kerala Agricultural Workers Act (KAWA), which gave legal sanction to collective bargaining. That no serious reversals of real wage levels have occurred since, despite a continuous decline in the price of rice, suggests that institutional factors have insulated wages from downward pressures. This socialization of wages is all the more noteworthy given that it has taken place against a backdrop of declining demand for labor (the area under paddy cultivation has shrunk continuously) and increasing supply (population growth and persistent unemployment).

Agricultural laborers are, by definition, the most economically vulnerable of all social classes, especially in times of agrarian transformation. That this class has been able to maintain and even improve its economic position in the face of the commodification of labor in a surplus-labor economy points to the working of countervailing forces that Polanyi famously argued are necessary corollaries of markets. One must, however, avoid the functionalist trap of defining all institutions as necessary. Be they defined in the transaction cost logic of institutional economics or in the social externalities sense of Polanyi, institutions do not simply emerge to compensate for market failures. They are the products of concrete historical struggles, in which a particular configuration of social forces has congealed, however imperfectly and unevenly. The institutions that currently shape labor-farmer relations in Kerala are the direct product of the interplay of mobilization and intervention.

The process of negotiating, setting, and enforcing agricultural wages in Kerala is necessarily complicated since it involves slightly over two million agricultural laborers and one million cultivators dispersed over hundreds of thousands of work sites. By definition, small-scale agriculture has none of the formal and permanent characteristics conducive to the regulation of employment conditions and wages. Employment is seasonal, and in the case of paddy, labor demand fluctuates dramatically between periods such as harvesting (for which a medium-sized farmer might require as many as a hundred laborers for two days) and periods when no labor is required. Moreover, the demise of attached labor systems in Kerala has created a mostly casual work force with few permanent ties to any farmer. A seasonal and casual labor force working for a large number of small farmers does not lend itself to organized and regulated wage bargaining. Yet over the past three decades, Kerala has developed a complex and relatively smooth system of wage determination characterized by a high degree of integration between formal state bodies (and procedures) and organized social forces.

Committees on minimum wages represent the top level of the wage-determination process and are appointed on a strict tripartite formula (producer groups, labor, and state) at more or less regular intervals. The committee's role is legitimated in classic interventionist terms of providing both social protection and social order. The 1991 committee asserted, "In a democracy, wages must be fixed through collective bargaining. Because agricultural laborers are vulnerable to exploitation and lack collectivism and conscientization, the government must come forward to provide them protection. If wages are too low, this will lead to tension in the agricultural sector" (GOK, Labour Department 1991a:1).

At the district level, both Palghat and Kuttanad, because of their long histories of acute conflict, have standing industrial relations committees (IRCs) that serve as tripartite consultative bodies with broad mandates to mediate labor relations in agriculture. In contrast to the highly politicized character of most government appointments, all the major unions and associations from both the governing and opposition party coalitions are given representation.[3] The IRCs are not corporatist bodies, however. IRC decisions do not carry the weight of law, and none of the represented bodies has the legal power to enforce decisions on their membership. Nonetheless, as we shall see, the IRCs have created an arena of social concertation by giving explicit recognition to the class power of farmers and laborers and providing the state a channel for scaling up and routinizing the terms of conflict mediation in a competitive democratic polity.

For all the authoritative legitimacy that minimum wage committees, IRCs, and the Labour Department enjoy, their enforcement capabilities remain vitally dependent on the mobilizational power of the KSKTU. As a cohesive voting block with over a million members, the union has the electoral clout to shape political agendas and exert pressure on public officials.[4] But its power to shape agrarian relations rests on its village-level activism and the competitive character of local politics in Kerala. With half of Kerala's agricultural laborers belonging to the KSKTU and with the Left Democratic Front (LDF) usually in control of over half of the panchayat governments, the organizational clout of agricultural workers is felt in most villages. The basic organizing unit of the union, paralleling the structure of the CPM, is the ward (a subunit of the panchayat that encompasses a few hundred households). Ward committees are generally informal and serve primarily as vehicles for grassroots organizing and dues collection. The panchayat committee is the primary formal body, with elected representatives and officeholders, and plays the most active role in negotiations and work actions. At the higher levels of the area and district committees,

---

[3] In interviews, two different labor commissioners confirmed the relative freedom of IRCs from political interference and specifically contrasted them to political fiefdoms such as public-sector enterprises.

[4] Following the lead of the CPM, every major political party in Kerala has sponsored nominally independent unions for agricultural laborers. By all accounts, the bulk of agricultural laborers belong to the KSKTU. Membership in the KSKTU increased from 368,329 in 1980 to 1,106,791 in 1990 (figures provided by KSKTU state office in Alleppey).

the union's activities become almost indistinguishable from those of the Communist Party. Statewide policies and strategy, including wage demands, are formulated by the state committee, whose members are generally high-ranking party officials, including members of the legislative assembly.[5] At this level, the union operates primarily as a wing of the party, in an organizational integration that has favored political unionism over trade unionism.

The presence and power of the KSKTU are both cause and effect of class formation. The erosion of caste-based forms of social control, the increased literacy among dalits (the contemporary term for untouchables), and the bureaucratization of local authority all contributed to eroding the vertical ties of dependency that characterized traditional agrarian relations. Thus in contrast to the paternalistic and deferential ties of the past, agricultural laborers today negotiate their relationship to property owners in contractual terms that are enforced through formal organizations and state laws. The demise of vertical ties of dependency and the crystallization of horizontal identities among agricultural laborers in Kerala have received extensive commentary.[6] The ideological and normative boundaries of exchange relations have dramatically shifted in the space of a single generation. When asked why laborers would demand the "posted" wage, the Chennithala panchayat secretary of the KSKTU explained "in the past laborers were slaves. They depended on the charity of landlords. But the party has taught them the right to demand fair wages. They are now convinced that this is their right." The comments of an untouchable laborer are even more revealing: "In the past, we would have to go the landlords' house to get our pay. We would stand with our head bowed and our hands open. Now he must come to the field to pay us. If he doesn't have exact change, we send him off to get it."[7]

[5] In the 1987 legislative elections, five of the elected members of the legislative assembly (MLAs) were KSKTU officials. The union's state secretary, V. S. Achuthanandan, has long been one of the two most powerful brokers in the CPM.
[6] See, for example, Kannan 1988, Tharamangalam 1981 and K. Alexander 1989. In his comparative survey of four taluks in Kerala (Kuttanad), Karnataka, and Tamil Nadu in 1973, Alexander found that patron-client norms, while still prevalent in Tamil Nadu and Karnataka, had largely dissolved in Kuttanad. An overwhelming majority of farmers he surveyed in Kuttanad acknowledged the right of laborers to bargain for wages and to work fixed hours. And whereas farmers in Tamil Nadu and Karnataka generally endorsed traditional caste practices of deferential speech and behavior and upheld the social segregation of caste groups, these were almost unanimously rejected in Kuttanad (1989:398–99).
[7] Compare this account reported from Tamil Nadu: "When a Harijan (lowest-caste) agricultural laborer is to receive his wage at the end of the working day, a ritual is enacted at the gate of his employer's house. In receiving the money, the Harijan bows, forms his hands into

The actual organizational clout of the KSKTU is probably best measured in the attitudes of farmers. In both panchayats where I conducted fieldwork—Chennithala (Kuttanad) and Pudunagaram (Palghat)—farmers associate laborers with the "party" or the "union." Farmers were frank in saying that they pay the union-declared wage because of the enforcement capacity of the KSKTU. To quote one farmer: "Laborers have all the power. You can't say a word to them because they will break you. If you talk back to them they just go and raise the [Communist] flag. They will drop the bundles [during harvest] and not return for as long as it takes."

How institutions actually function and the degree to which bureaucratic authority actually regulates social behavior cannot be gauged from formal attributes. Laws, agencies, and organizations are power relations that constitute social fields. The intensity of these fields is uneven and invariably weakens as they radiate out from their centers (capital cities, offices, constitutions) and encounter other sources of social control (local strongmen, patriarchal institutions). The high degree of state-society integration in Kerala notwithstanding, it is possible to discern regional variations in the process of wage determination which can be tied to local histories of class mobilization. To fully explore these relationships, I examine three distinct cases. The first briefly considers a region of Kerala that has experienced little if any labor militancy and is, in essence, a proxy for most of India. The second explores Palghat, where labor militancy has historically been high but an uneven pattern of mobilization has limited the role of the state in institutionalizing class conflict. In the face of a rapid agrarian transition, militancy in Palghat has been directed at defending traditional employment security and has slowed, if not altogether stopped, the process of proletarianization. The existence of a significant labor force of "permanent workers" tied to specific farmers has favored local agreements over peak-level mediation. Finally, the case of Kuttanad represents the prototype of fully institutionalized class compromise. The early and thorough proletarianization of the labor force has accentuated the articulation of broad, horizontal class interests, which has favored formal state intervention and forms of collective bargaining that closely approximate the industrial-relations model of conflict resolution.

---

a cup, or beggar-bowl, which he holds in from of him; his employer then drops the money into his cupped hands, and is careful not to touch them" (Djurfeldt and Lindberg 1975, cited in Bardhan 1984a:174).

Unfree Labor

The lowest wages for paddy workers in Kerala are found in the areas of the Chittur taluk in Palghat that border Tamil Nadu.[8] Landlords in this area have successfully recruited nonunion Tamil workers and maintained a labor-repressive system. The *kuddikadapu* (homestead) provisions of the land reforms have never been implemented and organizing efforts by the KSKTU have been met with threats of eviction and the recruitment of *goondas* (thugs). The writ of the state has not penetrated this area, a fact readily acknowledged by district Labour Department officials. Local institutions are directly controlled by landlords. A KSKTU leader who visited the Kozhinjampara panchayat as part of an organizing campaign observed: "In the panchayat, the president—a landlord—sits on a chair while the elected members sit on the floor, simply because he is the landlord. People refused to talk to us when we went there to investigate. They are afraid the landlord will put them on a lorry and send them back to Tamil Nadu. This is the only place where there is still untouchability in Kerala."[9]

The case of unorganized Tamil workers in Chittur illustrates that there are very sharply drawn boundaries—in the literal sense—to the power of unions and the state to effectively regulate agrarian relations. In contrast to the militancy, politicization, and organized power of Kerala laborers, Tamil laborers are still locked into local structures of domination. In the well-irrigated and productive farm area of the Cumbun valley in the neighboring Tamil Nadu district of Madurai, Ramachandran found that green revolution technologies had undermined traditional forms of labor-tying and led to the increasing casualization of the workforce. Yet, "Despite the generalized occurrence of the wage labor form in actual production, extreme poverty, the extension of the land monopoly into the present, staggering levels of inequality in the village, and a *general absence of democratization of village life* are fetters on the creation of a completely free rural work-force (1990:2; emphasis mine).

In his comparative study of Kerala and Tamil Nadu, K. C. Alexander comes to similar conclusions. Noting the exception of East Thanjavur district, one of the few areas in Tamil Nadu where Communists have success-

[8] District Labour Department officials and union leaders unanimously identified Chittur as Palghat's "low-wage" taluk. The district labor officer estimated that the maximum daily male wage was Rs 20, compared to Rs 50 in Alathur taluk.

[9] Interview with C. T. Krishnan, MLA and vice president of the KSKTU, October 21, 1992, Chittur.

fully organized agricultural laborers, he concludes that even where rapid agricultural growth has taken place, in the absence of labor mobilization the traditional labor regime in Tamil Nadu remains largely intact:

> [B]onded labor is widespread; working conditions are mostly unregu-
> lated; laborers in most parts of the state address farmers with honorific
> titles and exhibit various signs of respect towards them; untouchability
> is strictly observed and Harijans are discriminated against in village tea
> shops; beating and other forms of corporal punishment are sometimes
> practiced. Disputes between laborers and cultivators, if they occur, are
> generally settled through village leaders and panchayats dominated by the
> higher castes. (1989:403)

Though the extension of democracy to village India has produced new patterns of mobilization, and in particular has witnessed the rise of rich farmer movements, it has for the most part left local structures of power intact. And though production for the market and the modernization of production have created a demand for wage labor, they have not dissolved the bonds of unfreedom (Ramachandran 1990). The terms of exchange between laborers and farmers thus continue to be governed by local polit-ical and social configurations. Labor markets are tightly bounded by im-perfect information and regulated by personalized and interdependent transactions (Bardhan 1984b). In Kerala, outside of the border areas, this nexus of local economic and political power has been disrupted. As a re-sult, wages have become an object of organized contention and are closely bound up with state-level politics and policies.

Palghat: Uneven Proletarianization and Localized Wage Negotiation

The system of wage determination in Palghat falls in the middle of a range that runs from the elite-dominated exchanges of most of village India to the fully institutionalized labor relations of Kuttanad. Though garnished with all the legal and institutional trappings of an industrial-relations model, the institutionalization of class conflict in Palghat is located in large part outside the formal machinery of the state. Peak institutions such as the IRCs and minimum wage committees have played only a supporting role. Wage agreements have instead been hammered out at the local level. In this form of what Herring (1991a) has called "local corporatism," ne-gotiations have been carried out primarily through intraparty consulta-tions between the CPM's farmer and labor wings. The limited character of direct state intervention can be directly tied to Palghat's history of agrarian mobilization and class formation.

The transition to capitalist agriculture in Palghat has produced a class of agricultural laborers structurally suspended between the reformed vestiges of the traditional labor regime and the proletarianizing impulses of a rapidly modernizing agricultural economy. In general, labor-tying arrangements embedded in the caste system were more common in Palghat than in other parts of the state (Nossiter 1982). Moreover, because the social base of Communist agrarian mobilization in Malabar was the class of tenant-cultivators, labor attachment went unchallenged much longer in Palghat than in Kuttanad. As a result, organized challenges to the economic and social ties binding laborers to landlords did not come until the post-land-reform split of the party's agrarian coalition. Ecological conditions of paddy cultivation have also favored the use of attached labor. In contrast to the flood-prone conditions of Kuttanad, farming operations in Palghat can be easily staggered and, because of the practice of double cropping, are more continuous. Cultivation requires steady rather than concentrated inputs of labor (Kannan 1988:250). Thus both the ecological and social relations of production in Palghat inhibited the growth of a casual labor force solely dependent on wage labor.

All of this began to change rapidly in the late 1960s when green-revolution technologies and the abolition of feudal rents led to the rapid commercialization of paddy cultivation, and the embourgeoisement of the peasantry and the formation of the KSKTU in 1968 polarized the political situation. Because the shorter growth cycles of high-yielding varieties (HYVs) required less but more timely labor input, farmers increasingly favored the use of casual workers (including migrant Tamil workers). Workers, on the other hand, struggled to retain the security of employment associated with attachment while rejecting its social dependencies. This legislated security is precisely what the 1974 passage of KAWA achieved with its "permanent worker" clauses that guaranteed traditional workers quasiproprietary rights of employment. By 1992 the district labor office estimated that the number of permanent and casual workers in Palghat were roughly equal. Thus the work force in Palghat is split between fully proletarianized workers and those who enjoy legalized rights of employment.

The uneven development of labor relations in Palghat is reflected in the variation of wage rates across the district. We have already seen that the border areas have particularly low wages. Labour Department officials note that even within a single taluk, wage rates vary widely. Despite repeated efforts, the Palghat IRC has never successfully prescribed a wage at the district level. Yet real wage rates in Palghat, as in the rest of the state, have risen steadily over the past two decades, far outpacing paddy prices (Baby 1996; Herring 1991a). Significantly, the daily wage in Palghat is more than twice that in Tamil Nadu. Thus, despite the uneven development of agricultural laborers as a class, the variation in labor relations across sizes of holdings and regions, and the limited regulatory impact of the state, wages in Palghat have clearly responded to the bargaining power of laborers. That power, moreover, is exercised with only local and tactical resort to militancy (despite the fact that, with a district-wide membership of 135,000 in 1991, the KSKTU has more support than ever). Over the past decade, IRC records indicate that the KSKTU has threatened to strike over a wage dispute on only one occasion. Labour Department officials, KSKTU leaders, and farmer representatives were all unanimous in observing that conflicts over wages have been few and far between since the large-scale struggles of the early 1970s. The district labor officer in Palghat told me that the situation has become so "normalized" that he fears for his job.

Gaps in the state or district organizations' capacity to regulate labor relations in Palghat have been compensated for by local-level mechanisms. In Pudunagaram, the Chittur panchayat where I conducted fieldwork, the CPM's unions are the key players on both sides of the wage question. The KKS claims to represent one-third (three hundred) of all farmers, and farmers from opposition parties acknowledge the influence of the "Marxists," estimating that 45 percent of farmers vote for the (the CPM-led Left Democratic Front (LDF). The KSKTU represents fourteen hundred out of two thousand laborers in the panchayat and is the only active laborer's union.[10] A few weeks before the cultivation season, informal discussions are held by leaders of the KKS and the KSKTU. The extent to which these negotiations are organizationally bounded is reflected in the fact that the union leadership is more representative of the structure of the party than of class interests. The secretary of the KSKTU in Pudunagaram is a farmer, and the local KSKTU committee meeting I attended was presided over by the secretary of the CPM local committee, also a farmer. Taking the wage increase recommended by the district committee of the KSKTU as a starting point, negotiations center on making the adjustments necessary to gain

[10] This and the following panchayat-level account are based on a total of fifty-four interviews conducted with local officials, laborers, and farmers. Laborers were selected randomly, usually by picking out a house from ward-level clusters. For farmers, I relied mostly on elected "conveners." Because the conveners act as ward-level representatives for farmers, they were the ideal source for exploring the process of wage negotiation.

the cooperation of the KKS. The support of KKS farmers, most of whom are marginal landholders, is seen as enough to declare and effectively implement a wage increase.

The local interorganizational cooperation of the CPM's agrarian wings reflects a district-wide phenomenon. When I interviewed the KKS district president in Chittur I found that he shared office space with the CPM and the KSKTU. At the presidents' insistence, his KSKTU counterpart also participated in the interview. Both bristled at the notion that laborers and farmers are somehow at odds. They insisted that they are both part of the same class, the *karshika vargam* or agrarian class. The increased cooperation between the KKS and the KSKTU in Palghat reflects what appears to be an increase in the strength of the KKS, its district membership having grown to 68,000 by 1991. The CPM's calculated concessions on wage issues and KAWA in recent years have won back some of the farmers it lost to the Congress Party in the aftermath of the land reforms and the conflicts over KAWA. Many farmers have also joined the party out of sheer opportunism. The secretary of the anti-Communist DKS (the KKS's main rival for farmer support) suggested that farmers have joined the CPM in order to get "protection" and to have more "cordial" relations with laborers.

Once a rate has been agreed upon, local KSKTU organizers call ward meetings (there are generally ten to twelve wards in a panchayat) at which the rank and file are informed of the new wage rate and justifications for the increase. The increase in 1991, for example, was justified on the grounds of inflation (blamed on the center), and the recent recommendation of the minimum wage committee. Members are then carefully instructed not to accept a lower wage and to report all "recalcitrant" farmers. Farmers who resist are targeted for strike actions. Over the previous two years the KSKTU had organized strikes against the same farmer "to make an example." The farmer in question, who confirmed the story, was a former large landlord and a well-known activist in the BJP, the Hindu revivalist party. Singling out prominent upper-caste farmers who resist demands has long been a KSKTU tactic.

The union's capacity to effectively wage such strikes or, more important, effectively wield the threat of work stoppage derives directly from the strategic control laborers have over the production process. Given the highly time-bound nature of HYV cultivation, farmers can ill afford strikes. A delayed harvest can subject the crop to flooding, and can also result in the late planting of the second crop. Underscoring this leverage is the high degree of solidarity among workers. Many farmers in Pudunagaram simply refer to the prevailing wage rate as the "union" wage, and one offered a particularly succinct view of the dynamics of the local labor market: "If I paid a lower wage, nobody would come."

The process of wage determination in Palghat is deeply enmeshed in local political configurations. The strength of the KSKTU is the critical factor in determining the extent to which wage rates are the subject of collective bargaining. In the case of Pudunagaram, the predominance of small and marginal farmers, many of whom belong to the KKS, has given the CPM further clout in setting wage rates. But also it is important not to lose sight of the significance of supra-village institutions. The contractual framework and procedural logic of wage negotiations derive from a larger bargaining culture, and the authority of local bargaining agents rests in large part on their organizational ties with the broader political system. And it is only because public legality has permeated local arenas that labor can confront property as a collective category, rather than as a social tie. Minimum wage notifications, labor legislation, and peak-level mediation have provided the reference points, the governing norms, and the public legitimations within which farmer-laborer negotiations can take place at the local level. The diffusion of legality is manifest, for example, in the terms that laborers and farmers use in discussing wages. References to the Consumer Price Index, minimum wages (the "government wage"), and KAWA are common. In sum, while the "union" wage is very much rooted in the idiosyncrasies of local politics, as a contractual relationship governed by supra-local points of legitimation it is indeed a far cry from the personalized ties, bounded information, discretionary gifts, and caste subordination that governed traditional exchange relations.

The comparatively late development of capitalist agriculture, the predominance of small holdings, and the structural unevenness of the wage-labor class have all contributed to limiting the capacity of the state to directly and uniformly regulate labor relations in Palghat. The border areas of Palghat, in fact, remain very much at the margins of the authoritative reach of the state. Even so, while the degree of formal institutionalization of wages in Palghat falls far short of the Kerala norm, it is clear that legislative enactments, public policy, and union politics have provided a broad public-legal (as opposed to the private-discretionary) framework that has to a significant degree percolated down to the village level.

Kuttanad: Proletarianization and Institutionalized Wage Negotiations

Kuttanad represents the prototype of institutionalized agrarian class conflict in Kerala. As in the case of Palghat, wages are the subject of formal negotiations carried out by organized interest groups. But what sets Kuttanad apart from Palghat is the extent to which organized intermediation is governed by its IRC. In this respect, Kuttanad conforms closely to the type of peak-level, industry-wide model of intermediation associated with democratic corporatism.

The displacement of class conflict from the bounded conditions of the village to a state institution is a direct outgrowth of Kuttanad's history of class struggle, agrarian transformation, and state intervention. As we have seen, the early commercialization of agriculture and the ecological particularities of rice cultivation in Kuttanad gave birth to a highly proletarianized agrarian structure in the pre-Independence period. In contrast to the experience in Malabar, Communist-led agrarian mobilization never commanded substantial support from the peasantry (which had secured its property rights in the nineteenth century) and was, for the most part, a movement of agricultural laborers allied with the factory workers of Alleppey. Agrarian conflict in Kuttanad crystallized horizontally and uniformly, pitting wage earners against property owners. Movement demands focused on securing political and administrative regulation of the wage form, which in a context of highly mobilized democratic competition invited early and determined state intervention.

The Kuttanad IRC was constituted in 1957 by the Communist ministry to stabilize and formalize increasingly volatile wage relations. Unionized workers, challenging the traditional prerogatives of landowners in fixing wages and setting work conditions, had created a general crisis in labor relations. In 1958, the IRC recommended fixed wages and successfully negotiated a demand by labor representatives that discretionary gifts of paddy at harvest time be established as a right. Throughout the 1960s the IRC was often a forum for disputes, many of which were effectively resolved, including a negotiated wage settlement in 1967. But on the whole its authority remained limited. This period marked the height of agrarian mobilization in Kuttanad. The Communist Party was launching extraparliamentary agitations for land reform and actively strengthening its mass base among agricultural workers, while landlords were raising private armies and forming their own political party (the Kerala Congress). In this climate of heightened class struggle, there was little scope for institutional mediation. Farmers would often ignore decisions and labor unions—most significantly the KSKTU—readily resorted to strike actions to back up their demands.

In the post-land-reform period the IRC began to play a much more substantial role in wage determination. In 1971 the IRC stipulated that unions submit their demands on a yearly basis before the planting season. Between 1971 and 1984, the Kuttanad IRC negotiated and notified wage increases ten times. In seven cases the decision was unanimous.[11] (No decisions were taken between 1977 and 1979 because of the national authoritarian interlude of the Emergency, during which union activity was curtailed by law). Throughout this period wages were set on a yearly basis, with increases being more or less tied to the Consumer Price Index. This practice mirrored that in the organized industrial sector and government services throughout India of supplementing basic pay with a yearly "dearness allowance" (an inflation adjustment). Providing agricultural laborers with the same benefits as these sectors was a long-standing demand of the unions. In contrast to the 1960s when wage demands were ritually backed up with strikes, IRC records show that with the exception of 1984 there have been no large-scale agitations by laborers or organized resistance by farmers over the wage issue since 1971.

After this first phase, with the institutionalization of labor's bargaining capacity and the decline of militancy, a second stage followed with the forging of explicit corporatist trade-offs. The fragmentation of holdings has increased the number of marginal farmers, the swing class in Kerala's agrarian electoral alignments. As the profitability of rice farming has declined, wage concessions have become an increasingly attractive means of broadening the Communist Party's agrarian base. In the words of one of the party's most prominent union leaders, K. N. Ravindranath:

> The single most important obstacle to left unity is the conflict between the agricultural laborers' unions and farmers. This is because the trade unions are interested only in problems related to the livelihood of their members. At the same time they don't consider the position of farmers. We need to back up the farmers. Supporting their interests is in the interest of laborers. The hue and cry about higher wages of the laborers results from the poor economic condition of the majority of farmers who live in villages. (Conference of Indian Trade Unions 1979)

Beginning in the mid-1970s, real wages grew inexorably, reaching a plateau in 1984–85 (see table 2). But between 1984–85 and 1992–93 the

[11] Interviews, with Varghese Thundiyil, IRC member, October 14–16, 1992, Alleppey.

terms of exchange between laborers and farmers (as measured by the ratio of wages to the farm price of paddy) remained practically constant. The slowdown of wage growth reflected the party's policy of wage restraint and also overlapped with its 1987–91 tenure in power, which saw a dramatic turnaround from the party's traditional strategy of using state power to "further mass struggles." The political risks of restraining wage demands in a competitive electoral polity in which all parties actively court the vote of agricultural workers is obvious. In interviews most KSKTU officials were reluctant to acknowledge that the party was exercising wage restraint, but IRC records clearly show that throughout this period the KSKTU repeatedly rejected and effectively vetoed higher wage demands submitted by non-Communist unions.[12]

The task of enforcing wage agreements at the field level, especially when the fields in question are often tiny, is beyond the logistical capacity of most states. IRC-notified wages (which are not legally binding) have to be transmitted and enforced through local mechanisms. In contrast to Palghat, however, local bargaining in Kuttanad has more of an informational and legitimation function than an actual role in fixing the wage rate. In the panchayat of Chennithala in lower Kuttanad where I did much of my fieldwork, the local rate is little more than a minor adjustment of the IRC notified wage. The leveling impact of district-wide wage determination is, in fact, reflected in the uniformity of wage rates throughout the region.[13]

In order to facilitate implementation and make necessary adjustments for exceptional local circumstances such as flooding, the KSKTU does organize local negotiations. In Chennithala, the union has a commanding presence, claiming 3,800 out of four thousand laborers, and it sets wages through a two-stage process. First, it consults with KKS leaders to fix a mutually agreeable wage "demand" using the IRC-notified rate as a base.[14] This demand is then published in local papers and posted throughout the panchayat. In 1992 the posted demand justified the wage increase on the grounds of inflation (for which the International Monetary Fund (IMF), via the center's program of liberalization, was emphatically blamed) and

---

[12] The representative of the Travancore-Kochi Karshaka Thozhilali Sangham (TKKTS) labor union (one of two Congress Party unions), commenting on the KSKTU's position, acidly remarked that "the communists have declared solidarity with farmers." Interview, October 15, 1992, Alleppey.

[13] Both V. Mukherjee 1989 and Francis 1990 report uniform wage rates across ecological zones and taluks in Kuttanad, with only some variation for men performing more specialized tasks (bund repair, carrying work, and supervision of irrigation).

[14] In 1992 the new wage rate was actually notified by the Minimum Wages Committee and the union organized over three hundred ward meetings in Kuttanad to discuss the notification with the rank and file (KSKTU 1992).

appealed to "patriotic" farmers to "pay the declared wage and thereby help to maintain a peaceful atmosphere in the agricultural field."[15] The demand was then subjected to a round of negotiations with farmers. In contrast to Pudunagaram, the KKS in Chennithala has limited support (reflecting the comparatively weak farmer base of agrarian mobilization in Kuttanad), and conciliation talks must consequently be held outside the party and through the local panchayat government instead. In Chennithala the later has a de facto corporatist character as both the president of the KSKTU and its secretary, as well as two prominent farmers, are members of the panchayat. This process of local mediation has proven quite successful. There have been no major agitations on the wage issue in Chennithala since 1977. On the one occasion when local mediation failed—a dispute over the introduction of tractors in 1988—the CPM member of the legislative assembly (MLA) successfully brokered an agreement.

In contrast to the importance of local bargaining in Palghat (manifest in the significant variation in wage rates across taluks), the Kuttanad IRC has conferred a high degree of predictability and uniformity on the wage process. There is a clear recognition in Chennithala that wages are the product of supra-local political and administrative processes. Farmers complain that paddy prices have not kept pace with wages, but also note that yearly wage increases are necessary because of inflation. A farmer representative on the IRC noted, "The [wage] demand made by laborers is very legitimate. They demand wage hikes only according to price increases, just like the D.A. [the "dearness allowances" paid to government workers and most organized industrial workers]."[16]

In objective terms, the class contradictions of smallholder farming and a high-wage labor force are as sharp as ever (although the recent efforts to restrain wage increases does represent a significant concession to farmers). Wage increases have consistently outpaced farm gate prices and are indeed the highest in south India. Yet labor's normative claim to high wages is no longer contested. Survey results of a study conducted in Kuttanad in 1988–89 showed that when asked about "labor problems," only 7 percent of cultivators cited wage demands.[17] The conflict over wages has indeed been institutionalized, in large part because class demands are managed

---

[15] Notice posted by the KSKTU Mavelikkara Area Committee, Chennithala, August 17, 1992.

[16] Interview with Jacob Mappilassery, November 19, 1992, Champakulam.

[17] Across six different regions, a survey of 391 cultivator households found that over 73 percent of cultivators reported no labor problems. Labor "indiscipline"—slow work, opposition to mechanization—was cited as a problem by 10 percent of respondents (Mukherjee 1989).

through a process of formal concertation that enjoys widespread legitimacy.

The institutionalization of class conflict and the CPM's turn to corporatism in Kerala is marked by significant regional variations. Kuttanad represents the prototype, where the early proletarianization and unionization of the labor force and a long history of state intervention have produced a highly organized and formalized system of labor relations. In Palghat, an incomplete agrarian transition has produced a hybrid system of labor relations in which organized intermediation is rooted primarily in local conditions, though governed by powerful extralocal factors. In both regions, the articulation of formal state institutions and local power configurations has thus produced a complex set of linkages among public policies, organized interest groups, and village-level structures. But understanding how these linkages play themselves out and how actors and institutions actually manage conflict is best illustrated by examining an instance in which the system comes under stress. Somewhat fortuitously (at least as far as making the argument of this chapter is concerned), a crisis presented itself as I was conducting my fieldwork in the summer of 1992.

The 1991–92 Minimum Wage Crisis: Politics vs. Institutions

Though institutionalized, the wage-determination process in Kerala is not immune to politics. In 1989, the CPM-led Left Democratic Front government appointed a minimum wage committee. The committee made its recommendation in June 1991, shortly after the Congress-led United Democratic Front government came to power. Following a series of agitations organized by the KSKTU, in April 1992 the government, under pressure from most political quarters to take action, notified a daily minimum wage of Rs. 30 for women and Rs. 40 for men. The notification was a political bombshell. The 30/40 rate corresponded to what the committee had determined would be in conformity with International Labor Organization (ILO) standards,[18] but in keeping with a carefully calibrated logic of class compromise, the committee had recommended a lower rate of 25/35 "in consideration of the price hike of seeds, fertilizers and pesticides."

---

[18] The committee calculated that the average daily expense of an agricultural laborer's family (three consumer units) was Rs. 36.12. The consumption basket included the cost of food (3,000 calories for a laborer, 2,800 for dependents), clothing, rent, and 20 percent of the minimum for "fuel, lighting, recreation, education and medicine" (GOK, Labour Department 1991a).

(Under pressure from the IMF, the center had recently committed itself to liberalization, including massive cuts in fertilizer subsidies, which media reports suggested would produce a 300-percent cost increase.) The prevailing wage in the Palghat district at the time was Rs. 15–20 for women and Rs. 25–30 for men. In Kuttanad, it was Rs. 19 for women and 30–35 for men. The new minimum wage thus represented a 20 to 50 percent increase over prevailing wages in the main paddy-growing areas of Kerala.

The government's action met with immediate criticism from farmer groups (including its own union), whose protests were given full play in the press. In the weeks following the notification and shortly after the government had announced that it would constitute a high-level committee to review the issue, I made inquiries in four different sites in Kuttanad and two in Palghat. In all the sites, which included a remote block in the Kuttanad backwaters, laborers and farmers all cited the new minimum wage as a major point of contention. Across the board, farmers expressed outrage not only at the sheer magnitude of an increase in wages they could not afford but also at the manner in which the government has short-circuited the established process. A farmer in Chennithala said, "We are mad because the government declared the new minimum wage unilaterally. It was a despotic decision. The minister [of labor] must have been unconscious when he made the decision. It was not discussed with the cabinet, the relevant committees, or the Kuttanad IRC."

The general consensus was that the Congress government was making a rather transparent and cynical attempt to raid the CPM's most dependable vote-bank. Some suggested that the minister in question was simply a drunkard and had acted on his own. An Indian Administrative (IAS) officer who advised the minister claimed that he acted rashly because he was young and inexperienced. Whatever the explanation, the decision was widely perceived, even in Congress ranks, as a mistake. But the government, wary of the appearance of caving in to pressure from farmers, decided to stonewall the issue through the appointment of a high-level committee. Given the general consensus that the wage increase was far beyond what farmers could absorb, the government's refusal to rescind its decision set up a potentially explosive situation.

The minimum-wage increase became an immediate source of tension because it forced the hand of all concerned parties. The district branch of the Congress Party in Alleppey openly challenged their own minister, as did a number of Congress MLAs. The Kerala Congress (KC), the Kuttanad-based Christian party and government coalition partner with two cabinet ministers, demanded restoration of the original committee recommendation. For the first time in years, farmer groups in Kuttanad organized rallies to protest the government's agricultural policies. In Palghat and Kuttanad, farmers filed petitions in court, challenging the legality of the recommendation. And in Kuttanad they threatened to leave their fields fallow for the second crop.[19] On the other side, the KSKTU, unwilling to concede any initiative to the Congress Party on the wage issue, had no choice but to embrace the recommendation. At its March state committee meeting, the union took credit for the government's decision—a disingenuous claim since the KSKTU had officially endorsed the original 25/35 recommendation—and announced the beginning of a massive "propaganda" campaign. Local committees were instructed not to conclude any agreements fixing wages at less than the minimum (KSKTU 1992).

Yet, despite the fact that the lines of conflict were so quickly and sharply drawn, and that the crisis originated in a thinly veiled electoral maneuver by the Congress-led government, the sudden politicization of the wage question did not produce any substantial conflict. In Palghat, the district labor officer and district-level KSKTU officials all reported that the situation was calm. In Kuttanad, there were organized agitations and protests by farmers who were particularly incensed that the notified daily minimum did not make allowance for the fact that the average working day in Kuttanad is fixed at six hours compared to the eight-hour day in the rest of the state. But the conflicts and threatened actions were notable for their relative mildness. Only one protracted strike was reported to the IRC.[20] At public meetings, the Akila Kuttanad Karshaka Vedi (All-Kuttanad Farmers' Association) denounced the government's unilateral action and demanded that the IRC be entrusted with negotiating a compromise.[21] A threat by farmers to leave paddy land fallow never materialized, as a visit to Kuttanad at the time of the harvesting of the second crop made clear.[22] And at a Kuttanad IRC meeting held in Trivandrum in September, the

[19] *Indian Express*, Cochin, May 15, 1992.
[20] The strike was by KSKTU workers on R block, a 40-acre garden-crop area reclaimed from Vembanad Lake. R-block farmers hold relatively large plots and, specializing as they do in cash crops, earn handsome profits. KSKTU activists I interviewed explained that these particular farmers could afford to pay the minimum. The strike was settled in September.
[21] Rally held in Chennithala, October 3, 1992. Most speakers actually railed more against the price increase of fertilizers than against the minimum wage increase.
[22] The *Malayalam Manorama*, the newspaper of the Syrian Christian community and having well-known pro-farmer tendencies, did report that 20,000 hectares were left fallow in Kerala during the second crop. The source for this estimate was not given. Even if this number were correct, it would represent only 8 percent of the 243,611 hectares registered in 1989–90 for the autumn (virippu) crop.

KSKTU representative officially reported that there was no wage dispute, that the harvest was "progressing peacefully," and that all the land had been cultivated. The subcollector from Alleppey town confirmed this, testifying that there had been no "untoward" incidents and that he expected the agricultural season to continue with no major disruptions.

How was such a potentially explosive situation, pitting agricultural laborers with a history of militant mobilization (and official support from both major political forces) against farmers faced with an impossible demand (and little open political support) effectively diffused? Two things happened. First, the state bureaucracy, acting quite independently of the government's politics, took no actions to actually implement the minimum wage and in fact tacitly endorsed local "adjustments." Moreover, all parties to the dispute agreed to allow for a thawing period during which the dispute was referred to various state bodies. Second, recognizing the impracticality of the minimum and in keeping with its determined efforts to build a corporatist alliance, the KSKTU never seriously pushed for the new wage, public pronouncements notwithstanding.

Developments in the Kuttanad IRC capture this set of dynamics at the peak level.[23] During the first part of the September meeting, presided over by the labor commissioner and attended by all the major farmer and labor representatives, both sides made their cases in what were often very emotional terms. Farmer representatives loudly protested the double whammy of increased fertilizer prices and increased wages. They complained that farmers were being "sacrificed" for political purposes and repeatedly evoked the trump card of capital—they would defeat higher wages in a zero-sum game by reducing labor inputs. Predictably, labor representatives invoked the "scientific methodology" of the Minimum Wages Committee, arguing that the new wage simply reflected the subsistence needs of laborers and that farmers could afford to pay. Willing or not, they asserted, farmers were already being made to pay the minimum. A veteran KSKTU leader reasserted labor's proprietary claim and implicitly threatened a withdrawal of consent to private-property capitalism when he reminded the farmers that "you only hold the land in trust for the people. If we have to, we will reclaim it."

The labor commissioner then held separate discussions with both parties. What emerged from those discussions was an understanding that the labor unions could not officially agree to a lower wage for political reasons. But the KSKTU representative later confided to the labor commis-

---

[23] This account is based on my attendance at the meeting and discussions with the labor commissioner on September 23, 1992 in Trivandrum.

sioner that in practice they would demand less. In consultation with the Alleppey district subcollector and the Kuttanad special district labor officer, the labor commissioner decided that government intervention would not be necessary. He later explained that the demand from the farmers that the government reconsider its decision was officially unacceptable. Instead he felt that a tacit understanding at the IRC level that the unions would not actually enforce the minimum was enough to diffuse the situation: "Things will work out for themselves. Some local deals will be made at the padashekaram [contiguous paddy area] level. But because the workers recognize that the increase is too high, they won't make unreasonable demands. Local-level mechanisms should be enough to guarantee smooth negotiations."

Behind its public stance of supporting the new minimum, the KSKTU and the CPM were clearly committed to working out a compromise solution. When it became clear that the government in Trivandrum was not interested in reversing itself, a process of district-level negotiation was undertaken. As early as June, the CPM-controlled Alleppey District Council constituted a coordination body to discuss the wage issue. At a June 20 conciliation conference, V. S. Achuthanandan, KSKTU state secretary and a member of the CPM state secretariat, reportedly agreed that laborers should make local adjustments with farmers. The KSKTU's not-so-secret position was also reported in the press.[24] Yet even as these compromises were being discussed, at both the district and the panchayat level, KSKTU officials steadfastly insisted that they were demanding and receiving the new minimum wage.[25]

This process of public grandstanding and backstage pragmatism was reproduced at the local level. In early October, the KSKTU president in Chennithala (Kuttanad) explained that "we must demand the new wage because it is the minimum." But he went on to add that in the normal course of wage demands "the union would not have demanded as much. We had already decided on demanding an increase of only two rupees. To raise it more would violate the local standard—it wouldn't be harmonious to increase it by so much."

---

[24] The *Indian Express* reported that farmer representatives "said that the trade union leaders, as well as the workers themselves, were privately telling them that the existing wage structure was fair enough, given the economics of paddy cultivation" (May 15, 1992). At the end of the harvesting season five months later, another daily, the *Mangalam*, concluded that "the second crop was done with a secret agreement on wages between farmers and laborers" (October 10, 1992).

[25] Interviews with KSKTU state committee members in Alleppey and Chennithala KSKTU leaders, June and July 1992.

The Chennithala secretary of the KSKTU insisted that the union had little choice in the matter. The rank and file, he explained, would demand the new wage because "they know it is their right." He then suggested a more calculated political reason for the new wage: "Karunakaran [the Congress chief minister] is trying to divide farmers and laborers. He can't lose the support of Congress farmers, but stands to gain the support of laborers. So the government declared 30/40. If the union doesn't demand the minimum, it won't be seen as upholding the interests of workers." He went on to explain that the KSKTU and KKS would make an agreement, and that KKS farmers would then start paying the new wage in December when planting for the *punja* (Summer) crop was to begin. But by late November the local KSKTU officials were clearly embracing the accommodative line of the state-level leadership. Discussions between the KKS and KSKTU at the district level had not produced a compromise; it was agreed instead that local-level adjustments would be made. And this appears to be precisely what happened. Although there is no official data on panchayat-level wages, field investigations and interviews with district officials did point to a high degree of locally adjusted wages. For example, in Onathakarra, a block with a large number of marginal farmers, it was decided not to implement the minimum, whereas in Kuttanad taluk, where yields are among the highest in the state and double-cropping is common, the minimum was enforced.

In Palghat the minimum wage question was essentially brokered within the Communist Party. The KKS took the position that the minimum was too high. In discussions with the KSKTU at the district level they agreed on an Rs. 5 increase over the existing range of Rs. 13–20 for women and Rs. 25–30 for men. In the following year there would be another Rs. 5 increase.[26] Given that yearly demands for wage increases were generally only for one or two rupees, this still represented a substantial increase, although it fell far short of the government's wage of Rs. 30/40. The compromise was possible because, as the KKS district president put it, "the farmers realize that because of inflation wages are too low, and laborers know that paddy cultivation is no longer profitable." In Pudunagaram, interviews with farmers and KSKTU officials confirmed that wages had been increased from Rs. 15/20 to 20/30.[27] The local secretary of the KSKTU in-

[26] Discussions with C. T. Krishnan, the KSKTU district president, and R. Krishnan, the KKS district president (both are also vice presidents of their respective state organizations), October 20 and 21, 1992, Chittur.

[27] These wage adjustments in Palghat district received the full support of the Labour Department. The district labor office, theoretically charged with enforcing minimum wages, reported receiving only a handful of complaints. In such cases the district labor officer actually

sisted that the union had the capacity to press for the minimum, but that it was also its "duty" to look after the interests of marginal farmers. Notably, farmers and the KSKTU organized a joint picketing of the block office to protest the price hike of fertilizers.

What then does this "crisis" and its denouement tell us? In Kerala's climate of intense political competition and multiparty ruling fronts, many observers have argued that coalition politics and jockeying between interest groups have adversely affected the administrative functioning of the state and undermined its capacity to pursue developmental objectives (Nossiter 1982; G. Kumar 1986; John 1991). This view of Kerala politics dovetails neatly with neo-Huntingtonian theories of developing states in general. Political participation in a developing society, it is argued, opens the floodgates to a seemingly endless and unrestrained parade of Olsonian distributional groups that, in their frenzy to capture scarce resources, undermine good governance. Political parties are factionalized, and governments paralyzed.

That democracy in a developing society produces a proliferation of interest groups is not disputed here. What is disputed are the two assumptions that inform the politics-as-patronage and "demand-overload" theses. The first is the disaggregated nature of the interests assumed to be at work. In keeping with the rigid dichotomies of modernization theory, developing societies are cast as societies in flux, overwhelmed by a proliferation of diffuse and fractured interests readily exploited by savvy political entrepreneurs. The second assumption is that high rates of mobilization are a sign of weak integrative institutions.

The Congress government's decision to dramatically increase the minimum wage was a transparent attempt to capture Kerala's largest single voting block, agricultural laborers. Motivated as it was by political considerations, the policy decision had no economic rationale. The labor unions, also motivated by political considerations (in this case those of a fiercely competitive multiunion environment), embraced the government's decision. The situation had all the ingredients for a crisis of demand overload as politicians and unionists happily played to their constituents. As we have seen, however, the outcome was not dictated by these particular political dynamics. A relatively independent state bureaucracy helped absorb and manage the crisis by providing a forum for peak-level negotiations and by prodding concerned interest groups to make their own accommodations. Within this flexible institutional environment, laborers

---

recommended that parties to a dispute agree on a 30/35 wage. This, he added, was acceptable because the unions knew that the minimum was too high.

and farmers were able to reach workable compromises through established negotiating practices. The type of public-private linkages that produced this outcome conforms to Evans's typology of embedded autonomy—"the apparently contradictory combination of corporate coherence and connectedness" (1995:12). The state was immersed in society, both through the standard channels of political influence of an electoral polity and through the labour department's mediating functions which provided informational and collaborative links to key societal actors. Counterbalancing this immersion in society was the general robustness of public institutions, most palpably the professionalism of the labor department, but more abstractly, and more important, the density and autonomy, from the peak-level down to the village, of public legality.

The denouement to this crisis demonstrates that partisan electoral politics and the politicization of the developmental state represent only the most visible manifestation of what can and should be properly called "politics." Underlying the highly visible, fissiparous dynamics of party and interest-group competition are, on the one hand, an institutional context that does not simply bend to the political whims of the day and, on the other, a balance of class forces that produces its own political logic—in this case, democratic corporatism.

The institutionalization of conflict in Kerala and the CPM's turn to corporatism are statewide phenomena that reflect both structural and political developments. Against this backdrop, there are significant regional variations. The paddy field in Kuttanad today looks much like a factory governed by work rules and industry-wide regulations. Crops are harvested by armies of casual workers who often travel great distances; the workday begins and ends with the punctual blasting of a siren or the raising of a flag;[28] and wages are decided upon by career unionists and farmer lobbyists meeting in the state capital. In Palghat, traditional and customary arrangements governing the organization of paddy production have proven more resilient. An uneven and incomplete transition in the social relations of production has created a terrain of class exchange still very much bounded by local conditions.

These variations notwithstanding, throughout Kerala the dense, person-

---

[28] Sirens were first installed by the government in the mid-1970s following an IRC decision. Farmers had found the established practice of raising the party flag—the hammer and sickle—inflammatory and objectionable. In one Kuttanad padashekaram I visited, the nearest siren was out of earshot, so the practice of raising a flag to signal the end of the workday was still used, but with a concession: though the flag was red, the hammer and sickle were gone.

alized, interlocking relations of traditional agrarian systems have been replaced by formal intermediation among organized interest groups. The state has penetrated agrarian relations directly, either as arbitrator or judge, through tripartite committees and the rule of law, or, less directly but nonetheless significantly, through a long history of effective and democratic intervention (benefiting both farmers and laborers) that has underscored the legitimacy of rational-legal authority. Irrespective of the party in power, organized interests in Kerala have, by and large, accepted the mediation role and the particular modus operandi of the bureaucracy. Hence the willingness of all parties to refer differences to the IRCs, and the referential and ideological weight that minimum wage decisions and tripartite negotiations carry.

As I have described it here, the decline of conflict and the consolidation of public authority cannot be understood simply as the result of "ideal-typical" institutions. If these institutions work, the reason lies less in their formal characteristics than in their dynamic relationship to society, a relationship born of particular histories of state-society engagement. Most broadly stated, the effectiveness of public institutions in Kerala has been underwritten by the general democratization of rural life. The formation of the agrarian lower classes as a unified force swept away the social and cultural edifice of the traditional caste-based social order. The demise of landlordism, and more generally of the fragmented forms of social control that have so often frustrated state-building projects (see Migdal 1988), opened the door to expansion of the forms of authority associated with the modern bureaucratic state, specifically public legality. It is important here to analytically highlight the affinity between bureaucratic state capacity and class-based interests. Class-based movements make encompassing demands, especially for social leveling and protection from the injustice of purely market-based resource distributions (Cohen and Rogers 1992). Because such demands define beneficiaries in broad socioeconomic categories, they lend themselves to the instrumentalities of the modern states. Such demands are if effect public goods. This last point is important because it helps explain why a pattern of state-society engagement driven by conflict produced effective governance and not institutional collapse.

The contrast here with the general situation in India needs to be emphasized. In discussing state capacity it is useful to make a distinction between infrastructural power and authoritative power. On the first count, India and Kerala are isomorphic, enjoying many of the Weberian attributes of a modern bureaucratic state. But on the dimension of authoritative power they part company. As democratically accountable states, both have of necessity become enmeshed in society, but the historical pattern of engagement has been different. Under Congress Party hegemony, the Indian state extended its reach to the countryside by nurturing clientalistic bases of support through the mediation of local notables or through various forms of agrarian populism. This pattern of engagement has meant marshaling support on the strength of loosely defined coalitions that produce flabby, rather than programmatic, policy regimes. Typically, populist mobilization depends on plebiscitary or personalistic appeals that tend to be unstable and make building and sustaining organizations difficult. In either scenario, the state compromises its capacity to engage in transformative projects. Most states in India have passed land reform legislation, instituted minimum wages, declared bonded labor illegal, and earmarked resources for marginal farmers and the landless. But in the absence of linkages to organized subordinate groups, legal interventions have been successfully resisted and distributional interventions have been diverted by entrenched social and economic elites. And while these accommodations with powerful social forces have sustained democratic *rule*, which is no mean achievement in a country as poor and as heterogeneous as India, they have come at the expense of democratic *legality*. Because the state's authoritative reach stops where landed power or caste domination begins, public legality and effective citizenship have been compromised. In the past two decades political observers have thus pointed to the "deinstitutionalization" of the Indian polity and some observers have gone so far as to argue that the Indian state increasingly fails the most elemental test of "stateness"—the capacity to provide the master public good, the rule of law: "The combination of increased group violence, decline of legitimate political authority in the countryside, politicization and criminalization of the police, and their involvement in incidents of violence has contributed to an increasingly pervasive Hobbesian state of disorder, unpredictability and fear of violence among ordinary people in the rural areas of India" (Brass 1994:60).

What distinguishes Kerala is thus not so much the character of the state—its specific interests and formal characteristics—but the fact that its institutions and its authority have permeated societal relations. The politics of society, which in Kerala have been instrumentally focused along the sharply delineated lines of class conflict, are in other words closely integrated with the procedural logic of a modern bureaucratic state and a democratic polity. Hence, the process of wage determination, once deeply embedded in asymmetrical and vertical social ties, is now subject to collective bargaining and contractual enforcement.

The significance of these changes is not simply that laborers have rights and that conflict has been curtailed. The formalization of exchange relations has also set the stage for a coordination of class interests. The CPM's efforts to build bridges between farmers and laborers has of course been prompted by electoral considerations. Walking the line between class interests is of course an inherently delicate process, subject to periodic crises, renegotiation and regional variations. Such a balancing act is possible only because the institutionalization of conflict has reduced the strategic necessity of militancy and has secured labor's claim to a share of the social surplus. As two officials noted in the party's theoretical quarterly, "wage increases are customary and no longer require agitation" (Thomas Isaac and Shridharan 1992). Even more telling was the political logic underlying the 1987 CPM ministry's promotion of a scheme to provide cooperatively managed farm inputs (Group Farming Scheme). Designed and specifically directed at small and marginal farmers, the scheme was the centerpiece of the CPM government's agricultural policy, and marked a clear transition from the politics of redistribution to the politics of growth. When asked how the anticipated productivity increases would benefit labor, the agricultural minister remarked simply that "the wage system is such that labor will get a share."[29]

Accordingly, the KSKTU no longer presses for wage increases out of political compulsion. Through iterated cycles of conflict and state intervention, the union has secured its bargaining leverage and has developed a strategic understanding of the structural interdependence of marginal farmers and laborers. At the 1988 state conference, union officials noted: "The unity of farmers and agricultural laborers is increasing. The situation that prevailed in the beginning is no more. A consciousness has arisen amongst farmers that the working class should be paid well. And among the laborers there is a consciousness that they should work for the wages they get. This is the result of the joint efforts of our two unions, the KSKTU and Karshaka Sangam" (KSKTU 1988:4).

In this chapter we have seen how labor secured its capacity to command a share of the agrarian surplus. This success in turn set the stage for class compromise, an explicit recognition that in a capitalist economy the long-term interests of labor depend on private investment decisions. But how has the history of militancy actually affected the agrarian economy, and what, if any, effect has class compromise had on labor's welfare and on private accumulation?

[29] Interview with V. V. Raghavan, June 19, 1992, Trichur.

4

Class Compromise and the Development of Capitalist Agriculture

By most conventional definitions, Kerala's agricultural economy is capitalist. Control over labor and property is no longer rooted in the social and political power of landed elites. The wage-labor form has replaced the attached-labor systems and dyadic patron-client relations of the past, and the rent-generating property structures that once provided the material basis for the leisurely existence of a class of mostly upper-caste Hindu landlords have been legislated out of existence.

But Kerala's agrarian economy is not one of large or even medium-sized capitalist farms. With the exception of small rubber planters, the sturdy middle class of "bullock capitalists" that Lloyd and Susan Rudolph (1987) have identified as the carriers of agrarian capitalism in India today are largely absent from rural Kerala. The rural landscape is instead dominated by marginal and small holdings. Of Kerala's 5.4 million operational holdings, 92 percent were less than one hectare in size in 1991 (GOK, Department of Ecomomics and Statistics, *Statistics for Planning* 1993). For many, farming has become a secondary occupation; most farmers also work as teachers, shopkeepers, civil servants, traders, and agricultural laborers. The 1991 census revealed that only 12.4 percent of all full-time workers in Kerala reported "cultivation" as their primary source of work, the lowest percentage in any state and one-third the national average of 38.7 percent.

Conversely, agricultural laborers represented 27 percent of the work force in 1991, the third highest percentage in India. The rapid spread of education and the expansion of service sector employment, including well-paid and secure government jobs, has increased the opportunity costs of using family labor. Moreover, caste-status injunctions continue to keep

118

many farmers and their families from being directly involved in agricultural work. Thus agricultural production in Kerala depends heavily on wage labor. For both coconut and rice, Kerala's two most important food crops, 90 percent of the labor is hired (GOK, Department of Economics and Statistics, *Cost of Cultivation* 1988). The rural social structure of Kerala thus rests on a precarious material base: on the one hand it is highly proletarianized, on the other hand its property-owning class is economically marginal.

Under capitalism, there is by definition always a trade-off between the welfare of wage earners and the profits of property owners. In Kerala, that trade-off is acute. The smallest shift in the terms of interclass exchange can have dramatic consequences, especially for those who must sell their labor to subsist. As we have seen, agricultural wages in Kerala have been "socialized"—sheltered from the market by administrative and political interventions. And despite the wage restraint exercised since the late 1980s, wages remain comparatively high (twice the prevailing nominal rates in neighboring Tamil Nadu). How, then, have farmers coped with a wage regime that fixes wages well above market-clearing levels? More generally, what impact has labor militancy and the subsequent political institutionalization of distributional conflicts had on farm-level economic decision making? How has lower-class mobilization and redistribution in the form of high wages affected capitalist development?

There are three possible answers to these questions. (1) Labor militancy has produced a "class stalemate" and a negative-sum game: high wages and restricted managerial prerogative have forced farmers to reduce investment and even withdraw from cultivation, and laborers have suffered from the subsequent loss of employment. (2) The outcome has been a zero-sum game in which there has indeed been growth, but at the expense of laborers; "compromises" have in effect been "concessions," marking the ascendancy of the economic logic of capital. (3) Class compromises negotiated around explicitly recognized class interdependencies have not only resolved conflicts politically, but have also resulted in a positive-sum coordination of growth and redistribution.

The first section of this chapter examines the development of agriculture in the post-land-reform period. I argue that the sluggish agricultural growth rates cited in the widely held "stagnation thesis" are misleading because they fail to take into account important structural and institutional changes. Specifically, there is evidence that points to: (1) an increase in farmer investment; (2) a market-conforming rationalization of the cropping structure (primarily in the form of a shift from food crops to cash crops); and (3) increases in labor-household incomes that, coupled with state-sponsored welfare programs, have significantly diminished rural poverty. In the second section, which is divided between Palghat and Kuttanad, I examine how these transformations have been mediated. The central focus is on the capitalist, but negotiated, rationalization of the labor process.

Labor Militancy and Agricultural Stagnation

The stagnation of Kerala's agricultural economy in the period following land and labor reform is well documented. Although the growth rate of output was a modest but respectable 3.6 percent between 1962–63 and 1974–75, in the following decade the agricultural sector experienced a negative growth rate of 0.7 percent (Kannan and Pushpangadan 1988: A121). The poor performance of agriculture has been directly tied to stagnation in the yield of the state's principal crops (Kannan and Pushpangadan 1990). As we shall see later, however, these growth figures paint an exaggerated picture of stagnation and conceal important structural changes in agriculture. The more immediate concern here is to evaluate the extent to which post-land-reform class relations, and more specifically what Herring (1991a) calls the class "stalemate," have acted as a fetter on agricultural growth.

A number of observers, most notably the famous Indian economist K. N. Raj, have tied the stagnation of the agricultural sector to wage militancy. Raj has specifically argued that the "negative rate of growth of agriculture output, which set in towards the middle of the 1970s, appears to have been sparked off primarily by the sharp rise in the wage rates of agricultural labor from then on" (1991:40). A more nuanced and thorough exposition of this argument is found in Herring's work, which first examines struggles over the labor process and only then draws cautious inferences about macro effects. Citing the aggregate data and drawing on extensive field work, Herring concludes:

KAWA [Kerala Agricultural Workers Act, the legislation that formalized labor relations and institutionalized downward sticky wages] and the accompanying militancy produced a stalemated class conflict, with neither antagonist possessing sufficient power to resolve the situation on their own terms. Farmers responded to labor legislation with reluctance to invest because of lower profit margins, taking marginal land out of production because of wage increases, and sometimes leaving land fallow to 'teach the workers a lesson.' (1991a:8.15)[1]

The net outcome of labor militancy, Herring concludes, has not only thwarted accumulation but threatens to undermine redistributional gains. In particular, the increase in real wages has been negated through a dramatic decline in the number of days of employment. "[T]he market defeats the laborers' strategy of raising wages to compensate for inadequate days of employment, as farmers retain strategic power to reduce the total wage bill" (Herring 1991a:185).

Field studies leave little doubt that class conflict had a disruptive effect on the agrarian economy in the mid-1970s.[2] In response to the upsurge of labor militancy, farmers withheld or redirected capital, and the sudden transformation in the labor regime certainly disrupted the organization of production. But to what extent did these conflicts harden into irreconcilable class interests that blocked economic development? Has labor militancy been self-defeating?

The Crisis of Paddy Cultivation

Central to the stagnation thesis is the claim about disinvestment, specifically the large-scale decline in the area of land under paddy cultivation since the mid-1970s. Herring and others have interpreted this as capital flight (in the form of redeployment), arguing that in the face of rising wage costs and the loss of managerial prerogative resulting from the demise of the traditional labor regime, farmers have opted out of labor-intensive paddy cultivation in favor of less labor-intensive tree crops, particularly coconut and to a lesser extent rubber.

The relationship between conversion and labor militancy rests on a historical trend that at first glance is striking. The area coverage of paddy reached a peak in 1974–75 (881,470 hectares)—just a few years after the height of farmer-labor conflict and implementation of KAWA—and then began an uneven but constant decline that has yet to abate (table 3). But this trend is deceptive. If conversion is a response to actual conflict (strikes and other actions), and one assumes a lag effect of two or three years, one would expect the rate of conversion to be highest in the late 1970s. Yet it

---

[1] See also Mencher 1978.
[2] See Herring 1991a, Mencher 1978, and Kannan 1988.

TABLE 3. Area of major crops in Kerala, in 1,000 hectares.

	Rice	Coconut	Rubber
1960–61	778.91	500.76	120.00
1965–66	802.33	586.31	150.00
1970–71	874.06	707.84	179.00
1974–75	881.47	748.17	
1975–76	876.02	692.95	205.00
1976–77	854.37	694.99	
1977–78	840.37	673.48	
1978–79	799.24	660.63	
1979–80	793.27	662.66	
1980–81	801.70	651.37	237.80
1981–82	806.92	652.88	248.00
1982–83	797.89	674.38	259.70
1983–84	740.09	682.28	294.30
1984–85	730.38	687.48	310.20
1985–86	678.28	704.68	330.31
1986–87	663.13	706.11	347.14
1987–88	604.08	775.37	358.96
1988–89	577.56	816.88	366.50
1989–90	583.39	832.17	376.80
1990–91	559.45	864.06	384.00
1991–92	541.32	840.28	
1992–93	537.60	877.01	428.86
1993–94	507.83	882.29	437.14
1994–95	503.29	990.96	443.30
1995–96	471.15	982.10	449.00

Sources: 1980–96 figures from *Economic Review* (various years). Pre-1980 figures from *Report of the Steering Committee on Agriculture and Allied Sectors* (State Planning Board 1989b). Pre-1980 rubber figures from Narayana 1990.

actually stabilizes somewhat during this period (1978–82). It accelerates dramatically thereafter, during a period of labor quiescence. If the issue is wage levels rather than just conflict, the relationship is equally difficult to establish. Thus during nine years (1984–1993) when wages did not move against the farm gate price of paddy (indicating constant terms of exchange between capital and labor), the rate of conversion continued at a record pace (see tables 2 and 3). Moreover, when examined at the district level, militancy is definitely not associated with conversion rates. Two separate studies (Kannan and Pushpangadan 1990; P. George and Mukherjee 1986) have shown that decline of paddy coverage has been much slower in Palghat and Kuttanad, the two areas in which the labor militancy of the 1970s was most pronounced (and where the KSKTU had 40 percent of its total membership in 1980). Despite being the scene of the most violent large-scale confrontations in the early 1970s, between 1975 and 1984 Palghat was the only district to record simultaneous positive growth rates in yield, production, and acreage of paddy (P. George and Mukherjee 1986:26).

When the pattern of conversion is examined in a broader context, a different explanation emerges. With its tropical soils and abundant rains, Kerala has a comparative advantage in perennial crops. It produces over 80 percent of the country's rubber and 58 percent of its coconut and has a virtual monopoly on a number of spice crops (cardamom, ginger, pepper). Its undulating terrain and mostly rain-fed irrigation, on the other hand, puts it at a comparative disadvantage in rice cultivation. Despite the early commercialization of rice cultivation, Kerala has been a rice-deficit state since the 1880s: most of its food requirements are met through private-channel imports from other states or central government allocations. Kerala's food dependency has had important political and economic consequences. In the mid-1960s, a precarious national food-grain situation caused widespread hunger. Political parties unanimously called for greater food self-sufficiency, and subsidies to the rice-farming sector were increased. The center's restrictions on the interstate movement of grains effectively protected the local market and inflated local prices (Radhakrishnan, Thomas, and Thomas 1994:165). Farmers responded by bringing marginal lands under cultivation and increasing the area under paddy.

Since the early 1970s, however, increases in national food-grain production that came with the green revolution and deregulation of interstate sales have depressed harvest prices in Kerala. A number of studies have shown that relative prices, which favored rice before the mid-1970s, shifted in favor of tree crops thereafter (Narayana 1990; P. George and Mukherjee 1986). Taking 1975 as a base year, the 1992 wholesale money price index of rice had climbed to only 201, compared to 399 for coconut and 294 for rubber (GOK, *Statistics for Planning* 1993:284). By 1995 a farmer producing at average levels could generate, on one hectare, Rs. 9,588 of revenue growing paddy, Rs. 19,390 with coconut, and Rs. 53,050 with rubber.[3]

The pattern of conversion, moreover, is clearly correlated with regional levels of productivity. In their analysis of all fifty-six rice-growing taluks, Kannan and Pushpangadan (1990) found that the loss of paddy area was concentrated in areas with low yields. Most of the decline has, in fact,

[3] Calculated from GOK, *Economic Review* 1996.

been concentrated in regions that have not traditionally specialized in rice cultivation but where coverage increased in the 1960s because of shortages and inflated prices. The three districts that experienced the greatest absolute and percentage losses of paddy between 1975–76 and 1995–96— Kozhikode, Cannanore, and Malappuram—also had the lowest average yields.[4]

In a smallholder agricultural economy such as Kerala's, farmers are extremely sensitive to fluctuations in input and output prices. Aggregate trends provide at best an imperfect picture of the factors shaping farm-level decisions. The weight of the evidence does suggest, however, that dramatic shifts in the relative prices of crops played a much more decisive role than wage escalation. What is even clearer is that the overall outcome does not reflect an agricultural economy frozen in class stalemate. On the contrary, the evidence across time and across regions suggests that the shift to a cash-crop economy represents a rationalization of cropping patterns dictated by an increasing responsiveness to market forces. As economic maximizers, Kerala's farmers have responded to shifting price signals by reallocating their resources from paddy to more lucrative crops.

The extent of transformation is difficult to exaggerate and certainly belies any suggestion of a stagnant rural sector. Though Kerala's agriculture has long been subject to commercial forces, the post-land-reform period has seen more land redeployed in answer to market forces than at any other time in history. In 1975, paddy was Kerala's most important crop, covering 884,020 hectares. By 1995, 404,870 hectares had been taken out of paddy cultivation, a 46-percent decline. In area it now ranks behind both coconut (982,100) and rubber (449,000), which have increased respectively by 42 and 119 percent since 1975.[5] When viewed against the national picture, the magnitude of the transformation is even more telling: between 1980–81 and 1990–91 the area under nonfood crops in India increased 8.4 percent, compared to 20.8 percent in Kerala (CMIE 1994a: tab. 6.3–2).

---

[4] Calculated from GOK, *Statistics for Planning* 1988 and GOK, *Economic Review* 1995.
[5] Crop substitution varies with agro-climatic endowments, and not all of the tree crop gains have come at the expense of paddy. Thus more of the paddy conversion has been in favor of coconut, while the extension of rubber has come at the expense of Kerala's other major food crop, tapioca. A significant share of paddy lands has also been lost to urban expansion and private construction.

The Consolidation of Capitalist Farming

In the decade of negative growth (1975–85) that immediately followed the peak in Kerala's agrarian conflict, conventional indicators clearly point to a pattern of stagnating investment. Although the total area under cultivation remained stable, there was little movement in the productivity of major crops, suggesting that farmers lacked either the incentive or the means to make improvements in the land. Yet if one closely examines actual investment behavior rather than inferring it from overall agricultural performance, some interesting patterns emerge.

The large-scale conversion of paddy land to tree crops represents a sizable shift from moderate seasonal investments in inputs (seeds, fertilizer, pesticides) to significant capital investments. Planting tree crops is costly both in terms of initial investment and the opportunity costs of land. Converted land often has to be raised, trees have to be purchased and planted, and the prebearing period can be as long as eight years for rubber and ten for coconut, with optimal yields coming only later. Given the lengthened time horizons that such investments represent, large-scale conversion points to increasing confidence in the stability of the agricultural economy.

The extent of agricultural investment is reflected in—and indeed has been facilitated by—the buoyancy of the credit market. Poorly developed credit markets have often been identified as a key obstacle to agrarian accumulation in India. In Kerala, despite the predominance of marginal landholdings and the absence, outside the plantation sector, of large capitalist farmers, institutional credit has become widely available. Desai has calculated that Kerala is the only state in India where the credit needs of farmers are fully met at 102 percent of demand, compared to a 12-percent all-India figure (1988:347). Because of the relatively early commercialization of agriculture in Travancore, the banking sector in Kerala has always been strong, and its expansion has been especially pronounced over the past two decades. In 1970, Kerala ranked a distant second to Tamil Nadu in commercial lending to the agricultural sector, and ranked eighth among fifteen major states in loans advanced by the cooperative land development banks (CMIE 1991:tab. 13.17). By 1987, the combined total of outstanding loans advanced to agriculture from both commercial banks and cooperative land development banks in Kerala was Rs. 3,759 per hectare of gross cropped area, the highest figure for all states. Tamil Nadu ranked second at Rs. 3,062, with the all-India average at Rs. 1,084 (ibid.).

The cooperative sector, which accounts for 60 percent of the total credit advanced to agriculture in Kerala (Sunanda 1991:85) and has a far more extensive network of branches than the commercial sector, has been especially instrumental in providing loans to smallholders. Despite the declining size of holdings, total credit advanced by the agricultural cooperative sector (primary development banks and primary agricultural credit societies—PACS) increased in constant 1960 rupees from 67 million in 1960–61, to 304 million in 1972–73, to 2,175 million in 1993–94.[6] There has also been a notable shift in lending patterns from short-term to long-term loans. Overall, Sunanda estimates that as a share of total cooperative credit disbursed by PACS and the development banks, short-term loans fell from a peak of over 70 percent in 1969–70 to 37 percent in 1985–86 (1991:tab. 3.13). This points to a shift in investment patterns from current agricultural operations (crop loans) to long-term improvements in land and productive assets, a phenomenon clearly associated with the conversion from paddy to tree crops.[7]

From the above it is clear that the productive transformation of capitalist agriculture in Kerala has been institutionally facilitated. First, the agricultural sector has generated high levels of savings, reflected in the extraordinary success of PACS in mobilizing deposits. Between 1980 and 1993, total deposits increased from Rs. 1.4 billion to Rs. 18.9 billion. In 1996, Kerala accounted for just over half of the total national deposits in PACS.[8] Second, farmers have made effective use of credit. Kerala's rate of overdue loans, which over the period 1983–86 was 21.9 percent, is the lowest of any state and well below the national average of 42 percent (GOI, Reserve Bank of India 1989:543).[9]

In the absence of well-developed institutional credit markets, access to credit continues to be an obstacle to capitalist development in much of rural India. The dependency on noninstitutional sources of credit not

---

[6] All figures on the cooperative sector are calculated from GOK, *Statistics for Planning* 1977, 1980 and GOK, Registrar of Co-operative Societies (various years).

[7] A case study of the Irinjalakuda Primary Co-operative Agricultural Development Bank (Paranjothi and Ushadevi 1989) found that over a fifteen-year period loans were equally disbursed among minor irrigation, land improvement (leveling, bunding, terracing), and material additions (tillers, sheds, fencing, pump-houses).

[8] See *Economic and Political Weekly*, October 25, 1997, p. 2779. The Report of the Agricultural Credit Review Committee (GOI, Reserve Bank of India 1989) noted that the success of Kerala's PACS contradicted the conventional view that the rural poor don't save.

[9] Misuse of loans in India is chronic. Stories of wedding ceremonies or motorcycles paid for with agricultural loans abound. The available evidence suggests, however, that the problem is less pronounced in Kerala. A planning board survey conducted in 1987 found that of 497 sample loanees, only 17 percent misused loans (cited in Sunanda 1991:105). A survey conducted on a primary agricultural credit society in Palghat found no evidence of misuse (Radhakrishnan and Mukundan 1987).

only perpetuates the clientalistic nexus of interlocked credit, labor, and land markets, but also privileges the accumulation of merchant over productive capital (Bandyopadhyay and Von Eschen 1993:128). Kerala's highly developed network of agricultural credit institutions thus represents, by the standards of the subcontinent, a critical institutional breakthrough toward more dynamic forms of capitalist agriculture. Underlying this institutional transformation has been the synergistic quality of state-society relations.

High deposit levels and low-level leakage reflects the institutional legitimacy of PACS, which results from a combination of bureaucratic robustness and democratic accountability.[10] Despite their small size (compared to commercial banks) and their local character, PACS are staffed by career professionals from the cooperative department. Within the lending and financing guidelines set by the department (requirements for collateral, debt/deposit ratios, and so on), general policy and loan disbursements are made by the elected board. Political control of cooperatives in India often translates into capture by local factions or the dominant class,[11] but in Kerala's climate of vibrant local democracy, both political fronts actively contest cooperative elections.[12] Because board directors are elected on a single-member ward basis, most cooperatives have multiparty representation. The resulting mutual suspicion and scrutiny provides a powerful check against transforming PACS into sources of patronage. And because a cooperative society directorship is often the first step in both the Congress Party's and CPM's career ladders, directors have an incentive to perform well.[13]

The performance of Kerala's cooperative societies can also be tied to local stocks of social capital (Putnam 1993). High levels of literacy and direct community involvement have contributed directly to good governance. In interviews, cooperative officials and elected representatives re-

---

[10] This account is based on interviews with officials of the cooperative department and field visits to three PACS.

[11] The thin coverage, low membership, and financial weakness of the Indian cooperative sector represents an endemic institutional failure. Notable exceptions include the dairy cooperatives of Gujarat that received exceptional levels of state and foreign assistance and enjoyed favorable marketing conditions, and the sugar cooperatives of Maharashtra which benefited from the cohesive domination of one of India's most powerful rural lobbies (see the essays in Attwood and Baviskar 1993).

[12] Battles over control of cooperative societies in Kerala are widely reported in the press. The registrar of co-operatives estimated that membership turnout for elections was 70 to 80 percent. Interview with V. S. Senthil, April 14, 1992, Trivandrum.

[13] One cooperative secretary attributed the low rate of loan default to the role of directors in personally pursuing defaulters, noting that their political reputations were at stake.

peatedly noted that mismanagement and political favoritism were curbed by a culture of whistle-blowing and willingness to take legal action. The synergy of bureaucratic intervention and politicized boards is most evident in the extraordinary success of the PACS' annual deposit mobilization schemes that date back to 1975. The cooperative department sets the targets, provides financial incentives, and helps identify potential depositors, but it is the local credit societies that actively solicit deposits, organizing information campaigns complete with village festivals and the participation of prominent community members. The deep immersion of these state-sponsored institutions in local political and social life is complemented by the relative insulation of the cooperative sector from state politics. Though parties in Kerala are eager to control cooperative societies, the critical developmental and legitimating role of the cooperative sector enjoys broad political support. Thus the practice in many Indian states of declaring "loan holidays" (forgiving debts) shortly before elections is unknown in Kerala, despite the narrow and shifting electoral margins that separate the Congress Party from the CPM-led fronts.

There is one final measure of capitalist transformation that can be inferred from the shifting profile of cooperative-sector lending patterns. Between 1978–79 and 1989–90, the volume of nonagricultural loans disbursed by PACS jumped from 37.7 percent of total loans to 57.7 percent.[14] This increase has not come at the expense of agricultural loans but rather on the strength of an absolute increase in the volume of credit available from agricultural credit cooperatives. If the buoyancy of agricultural credit institutions has provided the supply for the expansion of nonagricultural loans, the demand has come in large part from the linkage effects of the conversion to tree crops. Thus, the decade corresponding to the "stagnation" period was marked by an explosion of agro-processing industries, particularly in rubber (Sunanda 1991:90). Between 1975 and 1986, the number of registered rubber and rubber-product factories increased from 217 to 926 (GOK, *Statistics for Planning* 1977, 1988). There was also a notable expansion of small-scale industrial units (most of which are located in rural areas) during this period, and their numbers have since exploded.[15] In the absence of more detailed data, causal inferences must be qualified, but the sheer magnitude of growth in small-scale

[14] Calculated from GOK, Registrar of Cooperative Societies 1991:tab. 7.
[15] Between 1980 and 1996 the number of registered small-scale units increased from 19,931 to 143,123 (GOK, State Planning Board 1996a).

industries over the past fifteen years (a five-and-a-half-fold increase) does suggest that financial buoyancy and the linkage effects of agricultural transformation have had a multiplier effect.

If the growth of agricultural credit and the conversion to more capital-intensive tree crops during the 1980s indicates increased capitalist activity, how then does one explain that total agricultural output in 1986–87 was no higher than in 1970–71? Given the amount of attention that the negative growth performance of this period has received, the answer is astoundingly simple, and serves as a reminder that growth figures, especially for agriculture, do not necessarily paint an accurate picture of economic performance. The growth performance of tree crops has two important particularities: long gestation periods and high variability of yields over a tree's life span. Unless trees are planted in even and staggered cycles, total output will thus vary dramatically. In a study using 1986–87 as an endpoint, Narayana examined planting patterns beginning in the mid-1970s and argued that the observed decrease in output of rubber and coconut in the 1970s reflected the high percentage of new or young and hence low-yielding trees that were a result of conversion. Rejecting the stagnancy thesis, he concluded: "In fact, the period could as well be one of intense investment activity in replanting, under-planting and intermixed cropping" (1990:29).

The most recent figures confirm Narayana's hypothesis. Table 4 presents figures for three-year averages in total production and yield per hectare of coconut, rice, and rubber. The production of rubber and coconut has increased by 155.4 percent and 74.2 percent, respectively, in a decade. This growth has been fueled by area expansion (at the expense of paddy) but also by significant yield increases. Over the same period, the yield of rubber per hectare has increased by nearly 80 percent, and even coconut, which is only beginning to recover from the devastating root-will disease, has increased by 30.5 percent. As marginal land has been converted to other crops, paddy has also experienced a yield increase of 17 percent. These figures, coupled with the investment trends documented above, suggest that in fact there may never have been a severe economic crisis in the post-land-reform period of Kerala's agriculture. The negative growth rates registered during that period had more to do with a reconfiguration of productive assets than with a crisis of accumulation. Taking into account the appropriate time lag, one sees that institutional and social transformation in Kerala agriculture have underscored a new and fairly dynamic pattern of growth. And, much as the above analysis highlights the need to treat aggregate growth figures with caution, it is worth noting that be-

TABLE 4. Production and yield of major crops in Kerala.

	Coconut		Rice		Rubber	
	P*	Y*	P	Y	P	Y
1982/83–84/85	3,144	4,535	1,212	1,694	173	555
1993/94–95/96	5,478	5,919	977	1,979	442	996
% change	+74.2	+30.5	−19.4	+16.8	+155.4	+79.4

Note: P = 1,000 tonnes, P* = million nuts
   Y = kg. per hectare, Y* = nuts per hectare
Sources: GOK, *Economic Review* 1992:tables 4.5 and 4.6. GOK, *Economic Review* 1996:tables 4.8, 4.12, and 4.18.

tween 1986–87 and 1993–94 total agricultural income in constant prices grew at an annual compounded rate of 5.5 percent.[16]

The Distributive Effects of Capitalist Consolidation

The modernization of Kerala's agricultural economy has clearly benefited its broad smallholder base. The overall impact on wage-labor households is less clear. The shift to tree crops, which are less labor-intensive than paddy, represents a dramatic decrease in the overall labor-absorbing capacity of agriculture. Thus one must ask whether the aggregate increase in investment and the rationalization of resource deployment in agriculture has come at the expense of labor. Has the political capacity of labor to secure high wages been economically defeated by the reconfiguration of capital? For all their organizational power and state protection, Kerala's agricultural workers are not immune from the classic dilemma of labor: the trade-off between wages (current consumption) and investment (future wages). A number of authors have concluded that despite wage militancy and labor-market controls the capitalist development of agriculture has resulted in the immiseration of the landless.

This argument rests on a central trend, namely the decline in days of employment per year for agricultural laborers. A survey conducted by the Kerala Department of Economics and Statistics on the socioeconomic conditions of rural labor (hereafter SSEC)[17] reported that in 1964–65 male

[16] Calculated from GOK, *Economic Review* 1996.
[17] GOK, *Report of the Survey on Socio-Economic Conditions of Agricultural and Other Rural Laborers in Kerala—1983–1984* (1985).

agricultural laborers worked an average of 198 days a year, and female laborers—the bulk of paddy workers—164 days. In 1974–75 the figure had fallen to 169 days for men and 126 for women, and in 1983–84 to 147 and 112. On the strength of these findings and their own field investigations, Herring (1991a) and Kannan (1988:303) both draw a direct connection between labor militancy and a capital strike. Herring concludes: "The strategy of raising wage rates, particularly in excess of productivity gains, induces capital to lower the aggregate wage bill, primarily by reducing the days of work offered, the parameter over which it has most ready control" (7.2).

Two possible arguments can be made here. The first is that paddy farmers cut back on certain operations (such as the number of weedings) and introduced labor-saving technologies, as a number of field studies have reported (Kannan 1988; Herring 1991a; Mencher 1978). It is doubtful, however, that these actions significantly reduced aggregate employment over the long run. The marginal returns to labor for rice cultivation are high compared to other crops and tend to increase with the adoption of high-yielding varieties (HYVs), which require increased applications of fertilizer and more weeding. Mechanization, as we shall see in detail later, has not displaced labor. The farmers I interviewed insisted that there is little scope in paddy cultivation for cutting back on operations without incurring substantial yield losses. Survey data for the 1970s show that average labor input per hectare declined only marginally, from 1,458 person-hours in 1970–71 to 1,423 in 1979–80 (Natarajan 1982). My own calculations based on the Cost of Cultivation reports (GOK, Department of Economics and Statistics 1986, 1990) indicate that there was, in fact, a slight increase in labor inputs in the subsequent period (1980 to 1988).

The second argument is that the loss of employment days per year is the direct result of the conversion of labor-intensive paddy land to cash crops. In assessing the actual trade-off that this represents in the capital-labor equation, the critical question becomes what impact shifting employment patterns have had on aggregate income. Though loss of paddy has clearly resulted in a net loss of employment, the higher wages paid for cash-crop cultivation has actually resulted in an increase of total income.[18] Estimates by the Task Force on Agricultural Employment found that conversion to

[18] Coconut tree climbers and toddy tappers (toddy is the local "poor man's wine" tapped from the coconut tree) are highly unionized and have some of the most formidable entry barriers of any occupation in Kerala. Their wages are subject to minimum-wage laws and periodic government wage prescriptions. Rubber workers fall under the plantation sector in which wages are regulated by an IRC. Wages for rubber workers tend to be slightly higher than those of the paddy sector, and have risen steadily since the early 1970s. From 1970 to

cash crops has produced a higher aggregate wage bill (GOK, State Planning Board 1989a:13). Even within paddy cultivation, loss of employment has been compensated for by rising real wages. The overall effect has been dramatic. Using the SSEC data, Kannan has compared average agricultural household income with the income required to pass the poverty line. He finds that whereas in 1964–65 average income represented 55 percent of the required income, and fell to 49 percent in 1974–75, by 1983–84 it had climbed to 89 percent of required income (1990b:72).

The findings from the 1985 SSEC survey highlight two other factors that point to an improvement in the relative economic position of the rural wage force. First, usurious moneylending, a key factor in the rural cycle of poverty in India, has become the exception in Kerala. Traditional moneylenders accounted for only 10 percent of the loans extended to agricultural workers' households, with the bulk of loans coming from institutional sources (government, cooperatives, banks) (GOK, SSEC 1985:32). Second, the incidence of absolute landlessness has declined dramatically. In 1964–65, 66.8 percent of rural workers' households owned land. In 1983–84 the figure was 93.3 percent. Though average holdings remain minuscule (.15 hectares), ownership of dwellings and small garden crops represent significant economic assets for the rural poor.[19]

At least one study (Datt and Ravallion 1996) has tied the decline in rural poverty in part to the income windfall from wages remitted by Kerala workers in the Gulf countries, which in the late 1980s was estimated to be 13 percent of the state domestic production (Nair and Pillai 1994:18). The effects, however, have been secondary at best. Because the bulk of remittances have gone to consumption activities concentrated in consumer durables and construction materials which are imported from other states, and to residential land purchases, there have been few direct employment-generating effects (Nair and Pillai 1994). Of course the construction boom has increased the demand for labor, but much of the low-skill demand has been filled by low-wage workers from Tamil Nadu. In a surplus-labor economy such as Kerala's, where unemployment rates have remained consistently high, trickle-down mechanisms alone cannot explain the increase in rural income. When examined against the national situation, the role of institutional factors comes into sharper profile.

1984, the real daily wage rate of rubber workers increased from Rs. 3.75 to Rs. 5.83 (Raman 1986:300).

[19] Most of the increase comes from the "hutment dwellers" provision of the 1970 land reforms, but there is evidence that agricultural workers' households have been purchasing more land. The 1985 survey found that 25 percent of borrowed money has gone to land acquisition.

Reviewing the literature on rural employment in India, Harriss (1992) argues that although the declining rate of landlessness, the increased agricultural ouput, and the rise in nonagricultural rural employment have all contributed to a general tightening of rural labor markets, these have not, by and large, translated into higher wages (see Jose 1988). Though local wage solidarity has made wages "downwards sticky," persistent intervillage wage disparities suggest that "mutuality may be confined to, and is in a sense defined by, the boundaries of a small neighborhood and caste or kin group so that laborers within even a small area may enter into competition with each other" (Harriss 1992:206). If labor-market segmentation reflects social embeddedness (differentiations of gender, caste, and locality), it also reflects explicit strategies of labor control such as exclusion of local labor, dividing casual laborers into high-wage young workers and low-wage fringe workers (the elderly and children), and the reforging of attached-labor relationships (1992:207). Under these social and political conditions, wage-raising market forces are effectively canceled out.

In Kerala, despite levels of rural unemployment that are still the highest in India, these segmentations and their wage desolidarizing effects have been significantly dissolved. We have already seen that within paddy cultivation, the institutionalization of wage determination has leveled the effects of locality and social differentiations in setting wages. Just as significantly, however, high rates of unionization, union entry barriers, widespread literacy, and strong social norms governing wage mutuality *across villages and occupations* have created what Krishnan has dubbed "interrelated" labor markets. Analyzing wage rates in eight categories of rural labor in agriculture and construction, Krishnan found that the "wage rates [across markets] are mutually related and operate through feedback mechanisms when wage parities are disturbed until they are reestablished" (1991:A86). In addition to finding causal wage linkages across rural and urban, skilled and unskilled markets, Krishnan found that wages moved in tandem even across the most persistent social barrier, namely gender. Thus, despite the fact that decreased demand for labor in paddy cultivation has disproportionately affected women, who constitute an estimated 63 percent of paddy labor (and almost 100 percent of the "unskilled" categories), the wage ratios between males and females have remained constant.[20] Krishnan's findings underscore the general observation that wage gains in one sector (be they the result of market or bargaining dynamics) are quickly passed on to other sectors.

[20] Female wages over three-year averages in 1973–76 and 1993–96 were constant at 66 percent of male wages (see table 2).

Interrelated labor markets have had the effect of producing an informal social wage.

Finally, strong welfare institutions have helped mitigate the social costs of agrarian transformation and especially the effects of declining employment in paddy cultivation. The material and qualitative benefits of Kerala's high social expenditures cannot be overestimated. In comparative terms, the rural poor in Kerala receive more education and better health care than in any other state (Dreze and Sen 1995).[21] But the direct impact of the welfare state on disposable income is also substantial. Laborers over the age of sixty receive a pension of Rs. 60 per month,[22] a not inconsiderable sum when compared to the Rs. 113 per capita monthly expenditure defined as the poverty line by the central planning commission.[23] Kerala's public distribution system (PDS), a network of 13,028 ration shops that provides subsidized staples to virtually all households and is by far the most extensive and comprehensive in all of India, accounted for more than 50 percent of poor rural households' consumption of rice and over 90 percent of wheat (Ramachandran 1996:249). In a context where poverty is as much a function of income as of exchange entitlements and where the effects of inflation are potentially devastating, the role of PDS in stabilizing market prices and subsidizing basic consumption has been critical, especially in light of Kerala's increased dependency on the national market for food grains. And reversing his 1988 assessment that workers were less well off in the 1980s, Kannan found in a 1990 study that transfer payments considerably supplemented household incomes. The combined income from the Integrated Rural Development Programme (IRDP), rural employment schemes, the income subsidy from PDS, the noon meal scheme for primary school children, pensions, and other welfare payments amounted to Rs. 1,162 per rural labor household, 24 percent of the average income of agricultural workers' households in 1983 (1990b:13). State subsidization of incomes, Kannan notes, has also contributed to the higher reserve price of labor (ibid).[24]

[21] See table 1. Kerala's school retention rate is the highest in India. Besides the obvious benefits of education, high retention rates have made education a "catchment" area that relieves pressure on a saturated labor market.

[22] Started in 1980, Kerala's agricultural workers' pension scheme is the only one of its kind in India. In 1993, 344,946 laborers received pensions (GOK, State Planning Board 1996b). Gulati calculates that the pension is sufficient to pay for basic food requirements through the public distribution system (1990:341).

[23] Report of the expert group appointed by the planning commission, submitted in 1993 and reviewed in EPW Foundation 1993. The figure is for the year 1987–88 and represents the "minimum standard of living."

[24] For a detailed and comprehensive village-level study that comes to similar conclusions, see Franke 1993.

The decline in rural poverty is captured in studies based on data from the National Sample Survey. Although these studies use different measurements and come to different conclusions concerning the absolute levels of poverty, they all indicate that the incidence of rural poverty in Kerala has been rapidly declining over the past two decades, and at a pace that is matched by only a few other states.[25] Three studies show that as late as the mid-1960s Kerala was the poorest state in India, both in terms of the percentage of the rural population below the poverty line (more than 70 percent) and in terms of Amartya Sen's more comprehensive poverty index (1973). All five studies cited by the EPW Research Foundation review found that by 1987–88 Kerala ranked in the top half of the least poor states, ranging from the seventh (Minhas et al. 1991) to the third (GOI, Expert Group 1993) lowest percentage of rural poor of fifteen major states. A recent World Bank study (Datt and Ravallion 1996) found that between 1957–58 and 1990–91 Kerala experienced the most rapid decline in poverty of any major state, including the Punjab and Haryana, India's success stories of capitalist growth.[26] The decline in poverty in the post-land-reform period has been especially rapid. The planning commission's expert group on poverty found that the percentage of rural poor in Kerala declined from 54.2 percent in 1973–74 to 24.4 percent in 1987–88. The estimated number of rural poor decreased from 10.2 million to 5.5 million.[27]

The Capitalist Labor Process and Negotiated Proletarianization

Since land reform in Kerala, farmers and laborers have both been winners. In the 1990s growth has been strong, and redistributive mechanisms have spread the new wealth. At the sectoral level, the terms of the class compromise are clear: labor has consented to private property in exchange for

[25] For a compilation of results see EPW Foundation 1993. The most important studies for which findings are presented here are: GOI, Planning Commission Expert Group on Poverty 1993; Ahluwalia 1978; Dev, Suryanarayana, and Parikh 1991; Minhas et al. 1991; and A. Sen 1973.

[26] The annual decline was 2.26 percent on the head-count index and 3.93 percent on the poverty-gap index (Datt and Ravallion 1996:30).

[27] Figures from the study that diverge most from the planning commission's findings present different absolute numbers but comparable trends. Thus Minhas et al. (1991) found that between 1970–71 and 1987–88 the percentage of the rural poor declined from 69 to 44 percent. While most states registered an increase in the absolute number of rural poor, Kerala's decrease (19 percent) was surpassed only by Haryana and Andhra Pradesh.

high wages. Thus the KSKTU no longer raises the issue of land reform, and has refrained from invoking the Land Utilization Act of 1975 which prohibits the conversion of paddy land.[28] And farmers no longer contest labor's right to bargain collectively. But what has become of the labor process itself, especially in the rice-farming sector where the material basis of class compromise is so precarious? Have labor control and state regulation inhibited the market discipline and managerial discretion of a capitalist organization of production?

The dramatic changes in agrarian relations over the past few decades profoundly transformed the organization of rice farming. The demise of the traditional labor regime, which was embedded in a complex, caste-based social order of patron-client ties and customary reciprocities, was rapid and unequivocal. What emerged in its place was from the outset an object of class struggle. Lacking the extraeconomic levers of landlordism, farmers were eager to rationalize the labor process by relying on market discipline. An organized labor force, determined to secure its bargaining leverage, sought control over the labor process. Tractors were burned and labor-market controls were imposed. The capitalist rationalization of production was fettered. Labor, as we shall see, did in the end relinquish control over the labor process. It did so not because it was politically defeated or trumped by market forces, but rather through a negotiated process that secured material concessions (the high wage regime) and, just as critically, minimized the dislocations that rapid commodification of labor in a labor-surplus economy entails.

In telling the last part of this story of a socially mediated capitalist transformation, I want to situate Kerala between two dominant narratives of agrarian transformation. The first is the familiar story of the inexorable logic of the technical modernization of agriculture and the casualization of the labor force under the imperatives of an emerging capitalist economy. In the reductionist vision of formal development models, existing social arrangements are swept away and agencyless peasants and workers are

---

[28] That the KSKTU has retained the capacity to withdraw consent to conversion is clear from the events of 1997. Professing publicly to be alarmed by the continuing pace of conversion, the KSKTU launched an agitation in which CPM legislators led workers into "illegally" converted fields and forcibly reconverted them by uprooting coconut trees and destroying banana crops. Centered in Kuttanad, the agitation monopolized headlines through the summer and became a major political embarrassment to the CPM-led government. The agitation was diffused, and subsequently it became clear that it was triggered more than anything else by internal party feuding. Nonetheless, though the union's tactics of crop destruction were roundly condemned, even within the CPM, as an unfortunate return to the "politics of confrontation," the cause behind the union's protest evoked widespread sympathy in the media and across the political spectrum.

absorbed into new, dynamic sectors of the economy. But even when political and social factors are brought back in, the outcome is all too often the
same, especially when the process is overseen by an authoritarian state. In
Scott's vivid account of the dismantling of the traditional moral economy
in a Malaysian village (1985), the conscious, active, and at times violent
resistance of small tenants and field laborers is tragically futile. Combined
with political controls, market forces proved irresistible as tenants were
dispossessed of their land and field laborers were subordinated to unmediated wage relations or simply displaced by mechanization. The story of
agrarian transformation in Latin America has been much the same (de
Janvry 1981; Grindle 1986). The second narrative is Polanyi's. Beginning
with the recognition that market forces, when left to their own devices, are
self-destructive, Polanyi (1944) identifies the existence of "countervailing"
forces that provide the necessary forms of social protection that ultimately
sustain the "great transformation."

The pace of transformation in Kerala has certainly been rapid, with dramatic changes in property relations and the form of labor. But the logic of
commodification has been contested. The countervailing forces at hand,
moreover, have not been, as in Polanyi's account, the outcome of what
was functionally necessary for the market to prosper without destroying
its own social foundations.[29] These forces emerged instead from political
realignments that tied the state to the most vulnerable segments of rural
society. We have already seen that the socialization of wages and the expansion of the welfare state, which have sheltered labor from the full effects of commodification, were the result of concrete struggles. But what
has transpired at the point of production has been just as significant.
Labor, with the help of the state, has sought to regulate proletarianization.
The specific points of conflict and forms of intervention have varied with
local production conditions, established labor practices, and mobilizational histories. In Palghat, struggles over the labor process in the early
1970s focused on the loss of customary employment security that came
with the demise of the traditional attached labor regime. The passage of

---

[29] "The natural aim of all social protection was to destroy such an institution [free labor
market] and make its existence impossible. Actually, the labor market was allowed to retain
its main function only on condition that wages and conditions of work, standards and regulations should be such as to safeguard the human character of the alleged commodity, labor.
To argue that social legislation, factory laws, unemployment insurance, and, above all, trade
unions have not interfered with the mobility of labor and the flexibility of wages, as is sometimes done, is to imply that those institutions have entirely failed in their purpose, which was
exactly that of interfering with the laws of supply and demand in respect to human labor, and
removing it from the orbit of the market" (Polanyi 1944:177).

KAWA was designed to give legal sanction to customary rights. In Kuttanad, early proletarianization and the development of a relatively free labor market mooted the question of employment security. Instead, contested proletarianization took the form of resisting mechanization. But the paddy field, as Herring notes, is not a factory, and bureaucratic efforts to regulate the minutia of the labor process failed in Kerala. As Scott has argued in *Seeing Like a State* (1998), state attempts to inject uniformity and standardization into productive practices are often defeated by the sheer complexity and diversity of local conditions. By intervening to regulate contestation, however, the state in Kerala did provide opportunities for local actors to arrive at their own accommodations. And those accommodations, when taken as a whole, have produced a socially mediated transformation to a capitalist labor process.

Palghat: Late Proletarianization and the Struggle over Employment Security

In response to labor mobilizations of the post-land-reform period (see Chapter 2), the government sought to interpose itself directly between laborers and farmers by enacting comprehensive labor legislation in 1974. Hailed by the CPI-led and Congress-supported government as the "Magna Carta of the toiling masses" and as a "model bill" by the central government, the Kerala Agricultural Workers Act (KAWA) was intended to contain the CPM-led mobilization of agricultural laborers (Kannan 1988: 281). But the Act was supported by the CPM, which through picketing and mass demonstrations pushed for speedy implementation. The costs of militancy by then had become increasingly apparent, and the CPM welcomed the Act "as providing security for workers and an institutional framework for localized corporatism as an alternative to class struggle" (Herring 1991b:182).

Patterned in many respects after the formalized system of labor relations in Kuttanad, KAWA was statewide in its coverage, but its effects were most pronounced in Palghat. Two of its major provisions—fixing the maximum number of working hours at eight for adults and six for children and statutorily enforcing prescribed wages—were already well-established practices in Kuttanad. Measures that established conciliation machinery and gave more power to the Labour Department to mediate conflicts met with no significant opposition. It was the conferment of employment that became a flashpoint.

The Act granted the legal status of "permanent worker," with a guaranteed right to employment, to any laborer "bound by custom or contract or otherwise to work in the agricultural land of that landowner" (GOK, KAWA 1976:5). In codifying the customary rights of the worker and granting quasiproprietary rights to work, the state substituted itself for the traditional patron, replacing the diffuse sanctions and material dependency of labor-tying arrangements with contractual obligations backed by new administrative machinery.[30] Actual implementation fell far short of what legislators and government officials had envisioned, for the certification and registration of hundreds of thousands of laborers was beyond the logistical capacity of the Labour Department. Politically, rather than defusing class struggle, in its initial impact KAWA had the effect of hardening conflicts in what was a particularly acute instance of a state's awkward efforts to bureaucratize social relations.

Derisively referred to by farmers as the "factory acts" (Herring 1991a: 6.10), KAWA deprived farmers of their traditional control over the quantity and quality of labor inputs. In granting legal protection against dismissal, the permanency clause provided labor with new leverage. The KSKTU rapidly translated the employment guarantee into an entry barrier, demanding that all agricultural operations in a given field be undertaken exclusively by permanent laborers.[31] Farmers thus not only lost the power to discipline labor through a credible threat of dismissal but were also in practice denied the flexibility of hiring additional workers for peak-season activities. The stringently time-bound rhythms of HYV cultivation requires large and concentrated inputs of labor, and thus lends itself to the use of casual labor. Permanent workers with fixed hours and exclusive rights to work could not satisfy peak labor demand. Control over harvesting operations was especially contentious. Because it is paid in kind—one-seventh of what the laborer harvests—harvesting work protects wages against inflation and guarantees labor a share of any productivity increases. Erecting entry barriers was thus critical to maintaining labor's bargaining leverage. For farmers, a quick harvest limits the exposure of

[30] KAWA provided for the direct intercession of the state between landowner and laborer by defining all disputes and differences over denial or termination of employment as "agricultural disputes" subject to the law's provisions. It specifically mandated the maintenance of registers of permanent workers, granted enforcement powers to labor officers in wage matters, and created new conciliation machinery including conciliation officers and agricultural tribunals.

[31] This practice was, in fact, contrary to the provisions of the act. KAWA specifically entitled the farmer to hire additional laborers if the number of permanent workers "is less than the number required by the landowner for the agricultural operation in his land" (GOK, KAWA 1976:6).

the crop and allows for the more timely planting of a second crop. Thus in
its formal application KAWA instituted a labor regime that was incompatible with the new technical requirements of paddy cultivation and literally
fettered farmers in their efforts to reorganize cultivation as a capitalist enterprise.

Paradoxically, KAWA aggravated conflicts over the labor process. Not
only did it impose production rigidities which were unacceptable to farmers, but by severing traditional ties of dependency and neutralizing the
whip of the market, it also increased the capacity of workers to agitate.[32]
Between 1974–75 and 1976–77 the number of agricultural disputes referred to the department increased from 444 to 4,279.[33] In contrast to the
organized mobilization and large-scale protests that had given birth to the
Act, however, conflict in its aftermath was more localized and generally
took the form of referral to the government's grievance machinery.[34]

Social legislation aimed at regulating exchange relations, particularly in
an agrarian context with an uneven social terrain, has rarely proven successful.[35] But to simply evaluate the impact of KAWA by measuring it
against its formal objectives is to uncritically take the "bureaucratizing"
impact of the state on society as a given. Efforts to extend rational-legal
authority into social domains are always contested. Typically, the end result represents a delicate accommodation between state power and social
forces which at best only approximates the original bureaucratic vision.
KAWA was enacted in a context of heightened class conflict in which the
traditional labor regime was not only being socially and politically challenged by labor mobilization, but was also becoming increasingly obsolete
from a technical point of view. In providing legal restrictions on the prerogatives of farmers and curtailing the whip of the market, KAWA in effect

---

[32] As T. K. Oommen has specifically observed in the Kerala context, the conventional wisdom that the bureaucratization of class conflict demobilizes workers fails to take into account the new forms of struggle that the difficult process of implementation itself engenders
(1985:238).

[33] These figures are taken from the annual GOK Labour Department administrative reports.
Although the figures are for the state as a whole, it is clear that most of the increase can be attributed to the implementation of KAWA in Palghat.

[34] For all the difficulties of administering KAWA and conciliating conflicts between individual parties at the local level, the increased role of the Labour Department was significant. In
1977–78, for example, of the 2,367 disputes that could not be settled through voluntary negotiations, 873 were successfully conciliated by labor officers. By comparison, in the year before implementation of KAWA the department conciliated only ninety-three disputes.

[35] Even in states that enjoy considerably more infrastructural power, the regulation of agrarian relations has proven to be an elusive goal. The case of migrant workers in California is
only one of many telling examples.

instituted organized labor's capacity to resist full commodification. In its initial phase of implementation—at a time when farmer-labor relations were still acrimonious—it undoubtedly had the effect of rigidifying the labor process, to which farmers responded by scaling back operations. Yet precisely because it made the costs of excessive labor militancy transparent and provided the administrative and legal framework for an institutionalized bargaining environment—one in which the unilateral power of property ownership was balanced by social rights—it provided organized labor with both the economic overview and the strategic leverage to underwrite calculated concessions in the actual implementation of KAWA.

In 1981, the DKS, the most powerful farm lobby in Palghat, presented a "Charter of Demands" to the Palghat IRC, demanding that "the farmer should have the absolute authority to employ workers as per the needs of the crop."[36] The most pointed complaint was that restrictions on labor hiring—specifically the exclusive rights of permanent workers to harvesting work—were making it difficult to finish operations in time. The DKS threatened to back up its demands by leaving land fallow. The strike was averted when the IRC agreed to appoint a deputy director of agriculture, K. Ramankutty, to study the problem and propose a more adequate land/labor ratio of permanent workers.

Ramankutty's report and recommendations are revealing because they explicitly acknowledge the tension between labor's claim of a proprietary right to work as a welfare entitlement and the serious production constraints presented by limited managerial discretion in a modernizing agricultural economy. The report begins by noting that the ratio recommended by labor representatives—one and a half permanent workers per acre—"was quite sufficient for carrying out the work a few years back when local varieties of paddy were cultivated. But at present the major area is under High Yielding Varieties, cultivated by applying modern technology, which requires time-bound operations and more labour" (GOK, Ramankutty 1982:30). After consulting with unions, farmer organizations, and agricultural experts, Ramankutty made a base recommendation of two permanent laborers per acre. Noting that labor requirements varied with the size of the holding,[37] he proposed a sliding-scale labor ratio, with smaller holdings benefiting from a higher labor ratio. The ratio for every acre of land over seven acres was fixed at one and a half, the same as rec-

---

[36] DKS "Charter of Demands" submitted to the Palghat IRC on January 1, 1981.
[37] Smaller holdings provide less scope for effective utilization of labor, and small cultivators are often engaged in other employments, requiring that agricultural operations be finished "as quickly as possible" (GOK, Ramankutty 1982:31).

ommended by the KSKTU. In compromising between labor and capital, the government, in other words, made important concessions to small farmers, but largely sided with labor against large farmers.

Farmer organizations quickly accepted the recommendation, but the KSKTU, citing low wages and arguing that the recommended ratio would result in a loss of employment, balked. Subsequent discussions conducted in a series of IRC meetings stalled, with farmers continuing to complain of a shortage of labor at harvest time and the KSKTU refusing to concede. An agreement was finally hammered out in 1986. The KSKTU gave its consent to the recommendation when farmers agreed to recognize the exclusive rights of permanent workers to harvest operations on the condition that the work be finished within fifteen days. With this workable accommodation, the question of permanency, the focal point of contested proletarianization in Palghat, was in effect depoliticized.

Peak-level accords notwithstanding, the mediation of KAWA has been mainly a local affair. This is reflected in its uneven impact. A government report found that permanency was widespread in Palghat taluk but virtually nonexistent in Ottapalam taluk (GOK, Nair Ramankutty 1982:25). Drawing on a village-level survey, Kannan concludes that farmers were largely successful in retrenching permanent workers and accelerating the casualization of the labor force that KAWA was intended to arrest, though he goes on to note that "as a compromise, the farmers agreed to give priority to permanent workers for harvesting work" (1988:284). Herring, in contrast, finds that "the power of the laborers, as represented by strength on the ground and extensive union membership, is such that a *proprietary* claim of the permanent laborers in the land is now widely recognized in practice" (1991a:6.25). In surveys conducted in four villages in two Palghat blocks, Sankar found that 62 percent of agricultural laborers were permanent (1985:52); surveying five Palghat villages, Lukose puts the figure at 69 percent (1991:43).

My own fieldwork in the Pudunagaram panchayat of Chittur taluk revealed that most farmers with holdings of one hectare or more rely exclusively on permanent workers for harvesting and generally have limited hiring discretion for other operations. In all, permanent workers accounted for roughly half of the local labor force. At a KSKTU meeting in Pudunagaram, when asked if the defense of permanency was due to the law (KAWA) or the union, the chorus response was "the union's law." This was no boastful claim. In a typical characterization, one farmer noted that permanent workers "make their own laws," preventing the hiring of outside workers and coming to work "as they please." The most common complaint was that labor shortages would lead to a slow or delayed harvest, resulting in crop losses. The attached labor system that predominated in Palghat well into the 1960s was well suited to the organization of traditional paddy cultivation. With pre–green revolution long-duration seeds it was possible to stagger operations among fields, and the labor of even a few workers could easily be spread across time. The close personal ties to the landlord guaranteed timely and flexible inputs.[38] The consequences of politicizing what had once been highly personalized forms of farmer-laborer interdependency are captured in the nostalgic musings of one farmer: "To be successful in agriculture, there must be a father-son relationship between the farmer and his laborer. The relationship has to be cordial. In the past, if a farmer overslept, the laborer would come wake him. If the laborer overslept, the farmer would come wake him. But now the politicians have come in between and divided them into two strata. And the politicians are intent upon keeping farmers and laborers apart."

Yet for other farmers the use of permanent workers was little more than an extension of the old patron-client system. One of the panchayat's most successful cultivators spoke of his permanent workers as "family members" and claimed that he still gave the customary gifts and was allowed to hire outside when "there was a need."

Whether as a carryover of the attached-labor system or as a protected right to employment enforced by closed-shop unionism, permanency in Pudunagaram has by all accounts declined appreciably over the last decade. The decline is due to attrition rather than retrenchment. In sharp contrast to the attached-labor system, in which generations of laborers were tied to the land, the intergenerational transfer of permanency is neither recognized by the law nor enforced by the KSKTU. This change reflects the profound social transformation that Kerala's agrarian structure has undergone since Independence. The politics of class, mass education, and declining fertility have eroded the rigid stratification of the caste system and accelerated status mobility.[39] Despite high rates of unemployment, young educated dalits are increasingly reluctant to take on the low-status

[38] Herring notes that "workers were on call 24 hours a day, and would frequently work through the night with torches to save a harvest or redirect excess water which threatened crops. Now, as farmers say (and many laborers agree), 'they are only interested in the clock' " (1991a:816–17).

[39] The dramatic intergenerational social transformations that have taken place in rural Kerala are particularly well captured in Sankar's survey results on age groups and literacy in two Palghat blocks. Whereas male agricultural laborers in the 36–45 age group had a literacy rate of only 29.6 percent, the 26–35 age group was 79 percent literate (1985:tab. 5.5).

work of paddy labor. As one farmer put it, "a man with an SSLC [high school diploma] does not want to get his dhoti [loincloth] muddy." A second factor contributing to the attrition of permanency is the sale of paddy land. Historically, attached laborers were included in land transfers. Although KAWA itself is silent on the question, the KSKTU, in defining permanency as a proprietary right, enforced the transferability of permanency with all land transactions. In fact, the union specifically violated KAWA's exemption of holdings of less than one hectare from the permanency provision by demanding that when land was parceled, permanent workers be retained. Rigid enforcement of transfer rights has been moderated, however, by a buyout clause. In a practice that has become established policy since 1987, the KSKTU routinely negotiates the severance of permanency in exchange for monetary compensation from new landowners. Respondents reported compensation rates ranging from Rs. 2,000 to 7,000. Invoking the "golden handshake" practice common in the factory sector, the KSKTU has demanded that the compensation package for retrenchment be fixed by law at 10 percent of the price of the land (KSKTU 1991).

The union's relaxation of the permanency question is somewhat surprising, as the permanent labor force in Palghat, with its security, has been the backbone of the organization. The militant defense of permanency was as much dictated by the strategic advantages of closed-shop unionism as by welfare considerations. Not surprisingly, concessions on permanency have met with resistance by the rank and file. Some permanent workers in Pudunagaram bitterly complained that compensation packages were being negotiated against their will and that the increase in casual workers was having a downward impact on wages.

The change in the union's position is tied to two important developments. The first is an explicit recognition, which follows from the CPM's embrace of corporatist class alliances, that the institution of permanency has become increasingly incompatible with the technical requirements of modern small-scale paddy cultivation. In explaining the KSKTU's concessions, the Pudunagaram area secretary pointed out that the increased use of HYVs, chemical fertilizers, and tractors had made cultivation more time-bound, increasing the demand for seasonal labor. The fragmentation of landholdings in Palghat has also increased the number of marginal farmers, the key partners in the CPM's corporatist alliance.[40] These farmers, as the KSKTU leaders are well aware, are particularly inclined to rely

---

[40] In 1971–72, 65.6 percent of all holdings were two acres or less in Palghat. By 1980–81 the figure had increased to 81.5 percent. From the Civil Supplies Department as quoted in GOK, Ramaukutty 1982.

on casual workers. The second development relates to the KSKTU's overall organizational position. Concessions on permanency have been made from a position of strength. Originally, the union took a militant stand on the rights of permanent workers in response to farmers' resistance to wage demands in the early 1970s. But as wage increases have become institutionalized, permanency, as a means of exercising bargaining leverage on wages, has outlived its strategic usefulness. The KSKTU has, in other words, explicitly traded rights of control over the labor process for wage increases.

The development of a fully free labor market in Palghat is still constrained by the strength of unions and social legislation, yet two conclusions can be drawn. The first is that KAWA is no longer a contested issue.[41] Even KAWA's most vociferous detractors have come to accept the rules and modalities of the legislation. The secretary of the DKS acknowledged that in defending farmers' interests the organization now regularly invokes provisions of KAWA in making its demands. The fact that DKS agitations have been largely restricted to petitioning courts or the IRC in the past decade speaks volumes. The second conclusion is that KAWA has not had a sclerotic impact on the development of market forces. As a "factory act" —a formal, bureaucratized labor regime—the legislation did threaten to cripple farm-level management decisions. But through its imperfections and compromises, its actual effect has been as an important countervailing force to market forces that would have torn the agrarian social structure apart. It has slowed the pace of proletarianization and provided labor with protections against the virulence of the market (reducing recourse to militancy) without obstructing the overall process of casualizing the workforce and rationalizing the production process.

Rice farmers in Palghat today are the most productive in Kerala. Yield rates in the district have consistently been the highest in the state and have grown steadily, if not spectacularly, since the mid-1970s. In 1972 the district had only 482 tractors; twenty years later it had 2,042, half of the state total.[42] Though it is difficult to prove a correlation, high wages and artificial labor shortages created by permanency probably provided a powerful incentive for the increased use of tractors. And in contrast to Kuttanad, where tractors were resisted, the employment protections for workers in Palghat minimized labor opposition to mechanization.

---

[41] The labor office in Palghat no longer has records for the 1970s, but the labor officer confirmed that the disputes over permanency in the 1970s numbered in the thousands. In 1981 the district office handled 569 cases. By 1992 the number was below two hundred.

[42] See GOK, *Statistics for Planning* 1977 and *Economic Review* 1992.

The typical farm in Palghat is increasingly run as a small business. Most farmers in Pudunagaram keep detailed accounts of their expenditures, experiment periodically with new seed varieties, and are quick to adopt new practices recommended by the local agricultural extension office. There is also a surprisingly high degree of cooperation among farmers. Tractors are contracted by each padashekaram on the basis of sealed bids and fertilizers are purchased in bulk from a farmers' cooperative that was organized in 1977. When the Group Farming Scheme was introduced in 1990–91, farmers readily adopted the recommendations of the local agricultural office. Pesticide application was coordinated, a new transplanting method was used, and fertilizers were applied in more carefully calculated ratios. The subsequent yields were 30 percent higher than before the scheme and 60 percent higher than the state average.[43]

Farmers in Palghat are small even by Indian standards, and do not, as a rule, dispose of large surpluses. High wages, increasing costs of inputs, and stagnant paddy prices have kept profit margins relatively low. But within these constraints, Palghat farmers have transformed the production process, using modern cultivation techniques, mechanizing ploughing operations, relying increasingly on hired labor, and in general managing their assets as capitalist farmers. They bear little resemblance to the poor rack-rented tenants who once made up the cultivating class in Malabar.

Kuttanad: Early Proletarianization and the Struggle over Mechanization

While contested proletarianization in Palghat in the postreform period centered on regulating the labor market, in Kuttanad it took the form of regulating mechanization. The work force in Kuttanad has been largely casual since Independence. The early unionization of agricultural laborers invited efforts by the state to regulate work conditions and the rural labor market as early as the 1950s. Thus, while KAWA was a focal point of farmer-labor conflicts in Palghat, it had a negligible impact in Kuttanad. The question of permanency had little bearing on Kuttanad's casual work force, and the rest of KAWA's provisions—prescribed wages, dispute machinery, regulated work hours—had become established practices in Kuttanad well before the 1970s.

---

[43] Based on records from the Pudunagaram agricultural office.

Post-land-reform challenges to the development of capitalist agriculture in Kuttanad assumed a very different character. Given the early predominance of wage labor and the relatively open character of the labor market, the bargaining power of laborers in Kuttanad has rested more on controlling the overall terms of trade between labor and land than on regulating the labor market. Labor's exposure to the market was aggravated in the 1960s when the size of the agricultural labor force was bloated by declining employment in the nearby coir and fishing industries. Mencher's field observations capture the severity of labor's dilemma: "Nowadays, during the harvest season, the workers measure the amount of time employed in minutes, not in hours or days. . . . Thus, in 1976, it was not only the landowners who feared the loss of crops at harvest time (when literally thousands crowd into some of the larger fields at 8 am in order to begin the harvesting, which might be completed two hours later) but also the local labourers, who have seen their earnings diminish as the number of hours of harvesting dwindle due to the pressure of numbers of people" (358–59).

In contrast to the post-KAWA legal rights of their Palghat counterparts, paddy workers in Kuttanad have no formal rights to employment. And whereas lucrative harvesting work in Palghat is exclusively reserved for permanent workers, it is open to all in Kuttanad. In part the difference lies simply in the fact that Kuttanad's unique water-control conditions require that harvesting operations be conducted simultaneously in contiguous fields, requiring concentrated inputs of labor. There is a second reason for which harvesting has traditionally been open to all, in contrast to other operations which in practice are generally reserved for locals. Because the harvesting wage is paid in kind, it functions as a subsistence guarantee. One might speculate that, as a social institution, this practice evolved as a means of sharing the burden of scarcity and mitigating the danger of famine in a labor market where proletarianization long ago dissolved the reciprocities of the traditional labor regime. This at least is what one elderly laborer suggested: "Anybody can come and harvest. We [the locals] can't say no. It's for food they come. Food is given by God."

Because of this structural dependency on the aggregate supply of employment, labor's strategy has focused on pushing up wages. This, as we have seen, has been largely successful. Wages in Kuttanad have been consistently higher than in other Kerala districts, and in the early seventies were twice as high as in Palghat (GOK, Report of the Kuttanad Inquiry Commission 1971). In response, farmers turned to mechanization to reduce their wage costs. The central point of conflict in the capitalist development of agriculture in Kuttanad in the post-land-reform period has thus been resistance to labor-displacing machinery, specifically tractors.[44]

In 1969, a study sponsored by the Kerala State Planning Board ("A Study of Tractor Use and its Impact on the Farm Economy of Kerala") concluded that the widespread introduction of tractors would significantly enhance productivity. The study's authors pointed out that tractor ploughing was cheaper than traditional bullock ploughing, provided higher-quality soil preparation, and, by shortening preparation time, allowed for the introduction of an additional crop in many areas. The authors also warned, however, against labor displacement. Full use of tractors, they estimated, would displace 270,000 ploughmen (GOK, State Planning Board 1969:22). Allowing for the facts that ploughmen also engaged in non-ploughing agricultural labor and that the operation of tractors would create new employment, they calculated that net unemployment would amount to 121,000 workers. In 1966, Kerala had a total of 652 tractors and 250 power tillers. The planning board estimated that to bring all tractor-plowable paddy land in the state (1.5 million acres) under tractor ploughing would require 7,000 tractors. It was hoped that this could be achieved within twenty years.

Planning estimates are notoriously optimistic. Yet in this case the planners were nothing short of prophetic. In 1991, Kerala counted 6,665 tractors and 2,069 tillers (GOK, *Economic Review* 1991, app. 7.11) which, given the 36-percent decrease in the coverage of paddy land since the late 1960s, was well above the planners' target. Though it is difficult to assess the actual utilization rate of tractors, interviews with agricultural officers and farmer representatives suggest that tractor ploughing in Kerala is widespread. In Kuttanad and Palghat it is the norm in all but a few pockets. Indeed, my calculations show that of the four southern states, Kerala has by far the highest density of tractors per food-crop hectare.[45]

The mechanization of agriculture is generally treated as a teleological phenomenon. Given the obvious advantages in productivity, it is only a matter of time before tractors are adopted in a commercialized agricultural sector. The determining factors are strictly economic: the costs of tractors, supply of adequate credit, and economies of scale. In Kuttanad's particular circumstances, however, this implacable economic logic could not be disentangled from its social implications. Introduction of tractors was from the outset an object of class struggle. State officials,

---

[44] Resistance in Kuttanad to the mechanization of agricultural operations is discussed in Jose 1977, 1984, T. Oommen 1985, and Tharamangalam 1981.
[45] Calculated from CMIE 1994a:tabs. 6.3–1 and 6.11.

moreover, were acutely aware of this and were determined to manage the problem.[46]

The first tractors were introduced in Kuttanad in 1954 by a handful of large landlords. Coming at the height of the KSKTU efforts to organize the agricultural work force, the action was viewed as a direct challenge to labor. Under pressure from the unions (including the Congress unions), the IRC in 1959 decided to ban the renting of tractors. Unsatisfied, the CPM's ploughman union, the Kuttanad Taluka Uzhavv Thozhilali Union (KTUTU), continued to agitate for a complete ban. The union threatened to forcibly plough fields manually and demanded monetary compensation for tractor ploughing (Tharamangalam 1981:78). Bowing to the pressure, the IRC decided in 1962 that "hired tractors should not be used if as a result a worker is denied labour," thus effectively banning the use of tractors.[47]

As the use of high-yielding varieties of rice spread, there were renewed pressures to introduce mechanized ploughing. The new seeds, which were of shorter duration and required more timely and meticulous field preparation, made the use of tractors particularly attractive. The wages of ploughmen, pushed upward by monopoly control, provided a further incentive for farmers to use tractors. By the mid-1960s, farmers' organizations were regularly petitioning the IRC to reconsider the restrictions on tractor use. Locally, some farmers did introduce tractors, only to be confronted with union-organized *satyagrahas*. The police were repeatedly forced to intervene. With the CPM's return to power in 1967, the situation came to a head: declaring that laborers should not be made the "scapegoats of the Green Revolution," the party made the decision to "mobilise its energies for starting direct action against mechanization of agriculture" (Varughese 1978:142–43).[48]

---

[46] In its 1971 report, the Kuttanad Inquiry Commission explicitly endorsed the need for a planned and integrated introduction of tractors. "We feel that is high time for adopting tractor ploughing in the Kuttanad areas. We are, however, conscious of the fact that the sudden switch over to mechanization will affect a considerable number of ploughmen and because of this important factor, we recommend that tractor ploughing should be introduced only as a phased programme." The commission endorsed the efforts of the IRC to work out a compromise formula and added: "In the meanwhile, ways and means have to be evolved for providing alternate employment to the displaced ploughman. They can be given proper training in the use of tractors and they should be given preference in employment while implementing the schemes contained in our recommendations" (GOK, *Report of the Kuttanad Inquiry Commission* 1971:29).

[47] IRC minutes, April 4, 1962.

[48] The party's opposition to mechanization became one of the more divisive issues that eventually led to the Left-coalition ministry's fall. Protesting the party's decision to mobilize, the

The CPM's opposition was short-lived. After lengthy negotiations and an IRC subcommittee study, a compromise solution was reached in 1969. Farmers were granted the right to use tractors on the condition that a portion of ploughing work be set aside for manual ploughing. Specifically, the accord stipulated that tractors could be used for the first round of ploughing—generally conducted when the land was dry—with additional rounds of wet-land ploughing set aside for ploughmen (one round in regular *karapadom* fields, two in the *kayal* lakefields). The agreement was a complex formal compromise that weighed the efficiency gains of tractors against the social costs of labor displacement. From a technical point of view the compromise was anything but optimal. Though manual ploughing is in some cases more suitable to wet-land ploughing, costs are higher, productivity is lower, and quality control is poor. One IRC member complained that "when they plough under water there is no way of telling if they have done a good job. It is like singing in a crowd." Of course, had efficiency been the only criteria, full introduction of tractors would have proceeded unimpeded. But by reserving some work for traditional ploughmen, the agreement codified the material terms of a class compromise: ploughmen would receive financial compensation through what was, in effect, a social tax, borne by farmers, on mechanization. Even with the costs of compensation, however, the returns on tractor use from increased productivity and lower overall costs produced a net benefit for farmers.

In 1977 the IRC worked out another compromise that was specifically designed to increase overall production. Improved pumping facilities, increased government subsidies, and higher paddy prices had made growing a second crop more attractive (traditionally Kuttanad has specialized in the single *punja* crop). Because a second crop would increase employment opportunities, the unions agreed to allow full use of tractors without compensation for the second crop. The agreement was made possible when the KSKTU openly defied the opposition of its own ploughmen's union. The increases in productivity and days of employment for agricultural laborers were held to far outweigh the need to protect the interests of ploughman.[49]

The IRC, in conjunction with the Labour Department, has played the central role in implementing this compromise, often acting to settle disputes and make local adjustments. In 1983 it granted the Labour Depart-

---

CPI minister of agriculture, M. N. Govindan Nair, argued that opposing tractors would adversely effect production: "Adding fuel to the fire you are harassing the small peasants instead of befriending them and you are unleashing terror both against the peasants and agricultural workers who are not politically loyal to you in areas where you are strong" (quoted in Varughese 1978:142).

[49] Interviews with Varghese Thundiyil, IRC member, October 14–16, 1992, Alleppey.

ment the authority to enforce compensatory payments to ploughmen denied work after three consecutive years of employment. The IRC has also periodically fixed wages for ploughmen. By all accounts implementation has not posed any significant difficulties. All of the IRC members I interviewed reported that the IRC agreements had been widely respected.[50] Labour Department officials in Alleppey described the arrangement as "smooth" and had no records or recollection of serious disputes in recent years. As in the case of wage determination, many local accommodations have been reached. In a fairly prosperous panchayat in Kuttanad taluk, dominated by large holdings, I found that farmers are now offering one-time, lump-sum severance packages, equivalent to two or three years of work, to their traditional ploughmen. A prominent farmer speculated that within five years ploughmen would completely disappear from the area. This appears to be the trend throughout lower Kuttanad. One official at the Department of Agriculture in Alleppey described the situation as one of "tractor saturation."

Traditional manual ploughing has been more resilient in upper Kuttanad. My primary field site, Chennithala panchayat, was in fact the last area in Kuttanad to work out a compromise in 1989. With its extremely small average holding,[51] few farmers could actually afford to own tractors, and many were ploughmen themselves. Furthermore, with only one crop a year to provide employment, the unions were reluctant to allow mechanization. Two factors turned the tide. First, the rental market for tractors has developed rapidly over the past decade, reducing the economies of scale problem. Second, the 1987–91 CPM-led LDF ministry, as part of its concerted effort to increase productivity in paddy agriculture, introduced the Group Farming Scheme, through which farmer committees can now contract tractor use for an entire *padashekaram* or purchase a tractor with government subsidies. In making the political pitch for this project, the minister of Agriculture, V. V. Rhagavan, launched a high-profile campaign to convince workers that tractors would enhance productivity.[52] The intimate degree to which the state in Kerala is involved in forging class compromises is reflected in the fact that a panchayat-level accord (based on the IRC formula) was reached in 1989 when a CPM MLA and then the minister himself finalized negotiations with the local committee of the KSKTU. By 1992, the conveners of the Group Farming committees in all

---

[50] Three farmer representatives and three laborer representatives sitting on the 1991 committee were interviewed.
[51] In the Mavelikara block of Chennithala, 20,070 out of 23,372 holdings are below .5 hectares in size (GOK, Department of Economic and Statistics 1989).
[52] Interview with V. V. Rhagavan, June 19, 1992, Trichur.

eleven of the Chennithala's *padashekarams* reported that tractors were being contracted for use by the committees, although where "necessary" ploughmen were still being hired for the first crop.

The introduction of tractors in Kuttanad can be interpreted as a victory of landowners against laborers (Mencher 1978; Kannan 1988). In lifting state regulations and ending union opposition that prevented mechanization, farmers were indeed given greater flexibility over farm management and investment decisions and thus greater control over labor. But in the case of Kuttanad, introduction of tractors was based on both implicit and explicit class compromises. The explicit compromise was the compensation formula for ploughmen, which not only institutionalized a redistribution of the gains from use of tractors, but also slowed the pace of labor displacement. The implicit compromise was rooted in the institutionalized capacity of labor to maintain high wage rates. With downward sticky wages, labor could relax control over the labor process, without adversely affecting the aggregate terms of exchange.

Class compromises are necessarily complex. They require first that the concerned actors act *as* classes (recognizing the interdependency of interests inherent in a class society), and second that the institutional environment provide the formal rules and normative boundaries that must underwrite any process of negotiation. With conflicts and compromises over tractors came important political lessons and institutional learning. In 1988 the IRC opened discussions on the question of introducing threshing machines (used to separate rice grains from the harvested plant), which would significantly reduce harvesting time. What was remarkable about these discussions was that threshers had yet to be introduced by farmers. Indeed, existing models had not yet been technologically adapted to Kuttanad's waterlogged conditions. Farmers nonetheless expressed an interest in accelerating development (a public enterprise was developing a new prototype) and, in anticipation of resistance from labor unions, began by submitting a memorandum to the IRC in which they committed themselves to social regulation, pledging that labor displacement would be minimized. They specifically cited the model of negotiated use of tractors in which "labourers were not made to suffer." After repeated rounds of IRC discussions, in 1991 the KSKTU endorsed the introduction of threshers in areas of Kuttanad where labor supply for harvesting operations is tight. And in 1992–93 alone, the Department of Agriculture supplied 965 threshers to group farming associations (GOK, Department of Agriculture 1996:13).

In the classic case of the English enclosures and in much of Latin America, South Asia, and parts of East Asia, the commercialization of farming has often been accompanied by the commodification of labor. The demise of traditional subsistence guarantees, the displacement of subsistence crops by nonfood crops, and the introduction of capital-intensive production techniques have all had wrenching effects on the small peasantry and the landless. Because we associate modern capitalism with industrialization, we often forget that the unregulated proletarianization of the tillers of the land is the root cause of both the urban and rural poverty that so often accompanies the transition to capitalism.

If the peasantry in Kerala has escaped this fate, the difference lies specifically in the patterns of social and political mobilization that underwrote the agrarian transformation. If the transformation has been mediated and its social costs minimized, the outcome was the result of neither fortuitous economic circumstances nor enlightened social policies. What shaped the outcome were iterated cycles of social conflict, state intervention, institutional learning, and political compromise. That the cycle has been mostly virtuous and has been marked by little of the organized or silent violence that grips much of the Indian countryside is because it was enabled by a democratically accountable and embedded state and even more critically by the democratization of local arenas.

The formation of a grand agrarian coalition precipitated the demise of landlordism and of a traditional labor regime rooted in social domination. With land reforms came secure proprietorship and the abolition of rents, two institutional developments that promised to promote capitalist farming. But these changes also threatened the traditional moral economy and endangered the livelihood of the most vulnerable of social classes, rural wage earners. Thus, while class mobilization set capitalist relations of production into motion, it also defined the limits. This limiting effect, as Przeworski argues, is intrinsic to the nature of capitalist democracy: "Just as it freed accumulation from the restraint of the feudal order, the bourgeoisie was forced to subject it to the constraint of popular control exercised through universal suffrage. The combination of private property of the means of production with universal suffrage is a compromise, and this compromise implies that the logic of accumulation is not exclusively the logic of private actors" (1985:219).

In Kerala the constraints took the form of the institutionalizing of high wages, through which labor laid claim to its share of the rent fund, and the increased farm income that has resulted from the modernization of agriculture. And to preserve aggregate employment and leverage its overall bargaining position, labor, with the help of the state, exerted some control over the pace and modalities of proletarianization. But as economists are always quick to remind us, there is no such thing as a free lunch.

Under capitalism, social welfare, labor market control, and wage increases come at the expense of private investment. But such limits to the *absolute* scale on which capital accumulation can take place do not rule out the specific type of dynamism associated with capitalism and do not preclude the creation of institutional forms that can, over the long run, nurture accumulation.

First, the organization of wage workers as a class has spawned new relations of production. In the past, propertied classes secured surpluses through the social and political subjugation of labor. Today, farmers must play the market by developing comparative advantages or by deploying the factors of production more efficiently in the pursuit of profit. Second, insofar as labor militancy crystallized class demands (classes-for-themselves are, following Przeworski's dictum, the *effects* of class struggle), it laid the basis for class compromise. The institutionalization of class conflict, which saw labor consent to private property, has created a more stable investment environment judging by the extended time horizon that the massive conversion to tree crops represents. Because wages have of late behaved somewhat more predictably than the erratic fluctuations of prices and the spiraling costs of inputs, the institutionalization of distributional demands has arguably improved the decision-making climate for farmers. It also underwrote a negotiated trade-off between high wages and increased managerial flexibility, as in the Kuttanad case of tractor use and the Palghat case of relaxation of labor market controls.

Finally, effective state interventions in mediating class relations have strengthened the authority and legitimacy of public institutions, many of which now play a critical role in promoting economic development. The role of the cooperative credit sector is a case in point. Income redistribution has limited the size of capital in private hands, but by the same token it has increased the availability of institutional capital. The economies of scale faced by small farmers are presently being addressed through improved agricultural extension services, state-assisted mechanization, and efforts to create farmer purchasing cooperatives (Group Farming). The comprehensive decentralization of financial resources, administrative structures, and development planning that began in 1997 with the implementation of Kerala's ninth five-year plan is specifically geared to increasing the accountability and efficacy of overcentralized state bureaucracies and has already triggered significant increases in local-level initiatives for minor irrigation, resource management, and mixed-cropping strategies (Thomas Isaac 1998).

It is, of course, too early to assert that capital accumulation in agriculture has become self-sustaining. If nothing else, the double dependency of

Kerala's cash-crop economy on the central government's pricing policies and world commodity prices suggests that the growth fortunes of agriculture will in large part be exogenously determined.[53] What is clear is that the barriers to accumulation that resulted from labor militancy have been removed, not as a result of some ineluctable triumph of the logic of capital or the political defeat of labor but through a process of negotiated democratic class compromise.

[53] The prospects for rubber are extremely good, however. Total production of rubber in India in 1993–94 was 435,000 tons, of which 93 percent was produced in Kerala. Per capita consumption of rubber in India is 580 grams compared to twelve kilograms in developed counties. It is estimated that domestic demand will be about 680,000 tons by the year 2000 and 1.2 million tons in 2010. Xinhua News Agency, July 8, 1994.

II

Industry

Rather than supposing that class accommodations followed from economic growth, it is at least as plausible to suppose that the long run of economic growth that the West experienced after 1950 was a consequence of the industrial, agricultural, welfare, and other policies that the earlier social pacts had set in train. Waiting for affluence to cause social peace and political stability may be like waiting for Godot.

Gregory Luebbert, *Liberalism, Fascism, or Social Democracy*, 1991

There are many factors particular to agriculture that have been favorable to learning the limits of class struggle and the need to compromise. First, the organization of the labor process and the terms of trade-off between the profits of the farmer and the wages of class-conscious laborers are acutely and directly experienced in agriculture. In Kerala, crop-shifting and declining days of employment palpably exposed the relationship between wages and investment. Second, the character of capital in agriculture makes compromise more likely. Most farmers in Kerala are smallholders and enjoy neither the economic nor the political power to act unilaterally. The phenomenon of embourgeoisement notwithstanding, many farmers still support the CPM, and this support has clearly facilitated the political rapprochement between farmers and laborers. And small farmer capital, locked up as it is mostly in the form of land, enjoys only the limited exit option of conversion. The most important private asset in agriculture is not subject to flight.

The constraints on and opportunities for class compromise in industry are quite different. When confronted with militant labor, capital has a wide range of options. Flight is the most obvious, but even where capital is not footloose (as in agro-processing industries) it has the option of reorganizing the scale and process of production. Workshop and home-based production have often supplanted factories as a means of circumventing unions and labor laws. The economic effects of class struggle in industry are thus potentially more severe than in agriculture. As I argue in Chapter

6, labor militancy in Kerala's unorganized sector (traditional and informal industries) is largely accountable for the state's poor performance on the industrial front. Traditional industries have low levels of capital investment, and profit margins depend on keeping labor costs at a minimum. Wage militancy has thus resulted in capital flight in footloose industries and in capital reconfiguration in locally embedded industries. In sectors such as construction and headload work (loading and unloading of goods), capital flight or reconfiguration is not an option. Militancy here has been particularly rewarding for workers, but it has exacted a high price in the rest of the economy as the burden of wage increases has simply been passed on to consumers or other industries. Moreover, the high costs of transportation and construction are often cited as the most serious obstacle to increased investment in Kerala.

The modern industrial sector (organized factories), examined in Chapter 7, is by definition highly capital-dependent. Here, class mobilization raises an acute collective action problem. As a subnational economy with a poorly developed industrial base, Kerala relies heavily on attracting national capital. At the factory level, labor has every incentive to be militant. The trade-off between wages and investment is opaque because all industrial units in India, be they public or private, are sheltered by state regulations and subsidies from market forces and hence from hard budget constraints. Wage increases can thus be passed on to the government (which routinely takes over "sick" private units) or to downstream workers in the unorganized sector. The negative externalities of labor militancy are high, however, because militancy discourages future investments. Though militancy at the factory level carries few costs, its cumulative effect in Kerala has been to create a poor business environment.

But there is more to class interests than the trade-offs between wages and investments. Their structural characteristics aside, agriculture and industry in Kerala share important political and institutional features. Politically and historically, the militancy of agricultural laborers and industrial workers has been closely related. From the outset, the CPI's project of class formation provided a strong organizational and programmatic link between these two sections of the wage-earning class. The politics of class are not given. They are experienced, sometimes assimilated as strategy, sometimes subordinated to other interests, but they are always learned. Thus, across sectors and despite very different conditions of conflict and compromise, the role of the party in shaping the experience of class has been fundamental. The character and role of the state have also provided a degree of continuity to the evolution of class dynamics in both sectors. By virtue of its embeddedness in society, the state has had more of a role in mediating labor-capital conflicts in Kerala than in the rest of the country, and because of the incidence and intensity of conflict, institutional learning and diffusion of knowledge have been high. Forms of state intervention developed in one sector—such as the tripartite committees—have often been extended to the other.

The historical sequences and linkages I explore in the following chapters will be familiar. A first period of mobilization and militancy saw the working class solidify its organizational clout and its political influence. High levels of unionization coupled with state interventions in the labor market and on the social front increased labor's leverage. Large expanses of the informal sector were formalized. Labor's redistributive and regulatory gains in turn precipitated a crisis of accumulation marked by stagnant levels of private investment and increasing levels of unemployment. Against this backdrop of a deepening economic crisis, the CPM and its unions abandoned the politics of class struggle in favor of the politics of class compromise. As I have already noted, the timing and modalities of these sequences have varied rather dramatically across industrial sectors. The variations are tied to levels of organizing, the structural characteristics of the capital-labor relationship, and the capacity of the state to effectively penetrate and regulate given industries. But from headload workers to factory workers, there has been a strategic withdrawal of militancy, and there has been a fundamental shift in the role of the state from regulating capital to nurturing capital.

5

Mobilization and Transformation in Industry

In many respects, Kerala's industrial economy mirrors the national picture. Industry accounts for 25.5 percent of Kerala's total economy, only marginally less than the 27.9-percent share of industry at the national level. Its 1.17 million manufacturing workers represent 4.1 percent of the national total, a figure slightly higher than its share of population (3.4 percent). As is true of the Indian economy overall, the bulk of manufacturing workers are located in traditional, labor-intensive industries, and most of the capital-intensive industries are in the public sector.

But behind these broad similarities lie critical differences in class relations and the role of the state. The working class in Kerala has a long history of mobilization and is more organized than in any other Indian state. Although reliable figures are unavailable, it is widely acknowledged that Kerala has the highest rate of unionization in the country.[1] Because of the demonstration effect of the organizing successes of the Communists, every major political formation in Kerala has sponsored and nurtured its own labor federations and mass organizations. Labor's leverage extends from rural and industrial workers to government workers, and has been cemented through networks of leaders and activists that cut across unions, political parties, and state agencies.[2] Because of its social movement char-

---

[1] Official data give at best a very rough picture because figures are based on self-reporting. In 1988 there were 8,662 registered unions in Kerala, which represented 19 percent of all registered unions in India (GOI, *Indian Labour Yearbook* 1988:74).

[2] Having a union base is virtually a prerequisite for making a political career in Kerala. In the 1991–96 Congress-led government, more than half of the ministers were trade union leaders. The chief minister, K. Karunakaran, founded the Kerala chapter of the Indian National Trade Union Congress (INTUC, the Congress Party union federation), and Vayalar Ravi was president of both the organizational wing of the Congress Party and the INTUC.

acter and the dominance of the Congress of Indian Trade Unions (CITU, the CPM's labor federation), labor in Kerala has developed along far more ideological and programmatic lines than its Indian counterparts. As a cohesively organized political force it has profoundly influenced social and economic policy, driving the expansion of the welfare state and securing significant controls over the labor market. It would hardly be a stretch to assert that, much as the developmental character of the East Asian state is a function of its close relationship with business elites, so the (redistributive) developmental character of the Kerala state is a function of its intimate links with the labor movement.

The second theme developed in this chapter is the impact of labor mobilization on the social structure of Kerala's economy. Lloyd and Susan Rudolph have convincingly argued that the weak impulse of class politics and the centrist nature of Indian politics can be explained by the simple fact that "the 90% of the work force in the unorganized economy has remained beyond the ambition or capability of organized labor" (1987:22). But in Kerala, unions, and through them the state, have extended beyond the organized sector (the Indian term for the formal economy) to cover large segments of the unorganized or informal sector. The organization of the unorganized in Kerala, running against the global trend of the informalization of production and signaling a dramatic transformation in the social basis of Kerala's industrial economy, emerges as the leitmotif of this chapter. To the extent that the state and unions have gone beyond the confines of the organized sector to regulate labor relations and provide some degree of social protection in the unorganized sector, they have, in effect, transformed the conditions under which capital can reproduce itself.

The Unorganized Sector in India

No amount of space and detail could do justice to the sheer immensity and diversity of India's unorganized sector. What is offered here is, at best, a very rough picture, which will highlight two critical comparative and theoretical points. Though the unorganized sector (defined by despotic labor relations) has been disintegrating in Kerala, it has proven remarkably resilient elsewhere in India despite the development of market forces and the consolidation of democratic rights. The difference between Kerala and the rest of India must be located in respective histories of labor mobilization and state-society interactions. As we shall see, the socially fragmented and disorganized character of Indian labor is what makes the continued existence of the unorganized sector possible. Second, as profitability in the unorganized sector depends on squeezing labor rather than improving labor productivity, the persistence of the unorganized sector can be identified as the root cause of the underdevelopment of capitalism in India.

The case that has been made for economic liberalization in India (which started in the 1980s and accelerated with the historic reforms of 1991) has centered on the rent-seeking effects of state intervention, the failure of import-substitution industrialization, the legislated rigidity of labor markets, and the market-suffocating effects of bureaucratic regulation (the infamous license-permit raj). Though compelling, these arguments miss the larger picture. As policy prescriptions, liberalization and deregulation bear only on the organized factory sector, where public and monopoly capital and no-exit labor market policies (it is virtually impossible to fire workers in the organized sector) have indeed blunted the competitive forces of the market. The irony here is that most of India's economy is still located in the unorganized sector, which is characterized by small-scale units, low entry barriers, intense competition, and completely unregulated labor markets. And though driven by and oriented toward the market, and comparatively free of state regulation, this sector of the economy has not displayed the systemic attributes—technological innovation and the rationalization of the labor process—of dynamic capitalism. The problem, moreover, lies not in a shortage of capital, as most theories of economic development assume, but rather in its relationship to labor. My argument is simple: because capital's control over labor remains essentially despotic, the logic of accumulation in India has been one of labor-squeezing rather than innovation.

Capital is not an entity in its own right, with a logic all its own. Capital is, as Marx was at pains to demonstrate, a social relation. It becomes dynamic in the capitalist sense when it organizes production by revolutionizing it. In its less dynamic manifestations capital can reproduce itself without developing the forces of production. From the point of view of economic development, the critical distinction that differentiates dynamic from nondynamic forms of capital is not how much surplus is extracted, but how it is generated. Brenner makes this point succinctly:

[C]apitalism differs from all pre-capitalist modes of production in its systematic tendency to unprecedented, though neither continuous nor unlimited, economic development—in particular through the expansion of what might be called (after Marx's terminology) relative as opposed to absolute surplus labor. That is, under capitalism, surplus is systematically achieved for the first time through increases of labor productivity, leading to the cheapening of goods and a greater total output from a given labor force (with a given working day, intensity of labor and real wage). This makes it possible for the capitalist class to increase its surplus, without necessarily having to resort to methods of increasing absolute surplus labor which dominated pre-capitalist modes—i.e. the extension of the working day, the intensification of work, and the decrease in the standard of living of the labor force. (1977:30)

The revolutionary character of capitalism must then be sought in its particular mode of creating surplus value, that is, the specific means by which surplus labor is expropriated. And while the *mode* of surplus extraction is indeed an economic relationship, it is rooted in a historically specific configuration of social and political forces that structures the relationship between labor and property and determines how labor is organized and appropriated. This is the social *regime* of surplus extraction.

In its Indian usage, the term "unorganized" is a residual category used to describe the full range of economic activities, spanning agriculture, industry, and services, that are outside the modern (registered) factory sector and government employment. By most estimates, the unorganized sector encompasses 90 percent of the labor force. Officially, all economic activities that fall outside the purview of factory and labor legislation—that is, beyond the regulatory capacity of the state—are defined as unorganized.[3] There are obvious problems with this definition but I use it here because it is practical (official data on employment follow the stated dichotomy) and more important because the term "unorganized" captures a fundamental difference between sectors: production in the unorganized sector relies basically on a supply of unfree or cheap labor reproduced within a configuration of social relations largely beyond the reach of the bureaucratic state and modern political institutions, whereas the organized sector is characterized by the contractual relations of a class-based social organization of production, closely linked with the development of the modern state.[4] De-

---

[3] The Central Statistical Organization defines the unorganized sector as "All unincorporated enterprises and household industries, other than organized ones which are not regulated by any of the Acts, and which do not maintain annual accounts and balance sheets" (Banerjee 1988:73).

[4] Portes and Castells define the informal sector as "unregulated by the institutions of society, in a legal and social environment in which similar activities are regulated" (1989:12). The implication of this definition is diametrically opposed to De Soto's treatment of the informal sector in Latin America (1989). For De Soto, the informal sector consists of extralegal economic activities organized in resistance to the overregulation of a predatory state—what might be called "popular capitalism." In India, however, the resiliency of the unorganized

fined as such, the concepts of "organized" and "unorganized" become critical to our understanding of economic development because they concretely link the organization of the labor process with the social regime of surplus extraction.

Because workers in the unorganized sectors are not organized as a class, or even as craft associations or other economic interest groups, and are not protected by labor legislation, returns to labor are pushed to the subsistence level.[5] This capacity to squeeze wages, though often associated with the use of extraeconomic coercion, for the most part does not depend on "unfree" labor in the absolute sense. Surpluses in the unorganized sector are extracted through the wage form or through the exchange of a finished commodity. There are, however, to recall Miles's term (1987), "degrees of unfree labor." Thus, while wage labor in India is free in Marx's (and Weber's) double sense of the term, and surplus does appear in the form of unpaid labor, the formal transactional nature of this relationship should not obscure its inherently social character. Portes notes that "Because of the absence of state regulation, informal transactions are commonly portrayed as the play of pure market forces" (1994:429); the paradox of this view, he goes on to comment, "is that the more it [the informal sector] approaches the model of the true market, the more it is dependent on social ties for its effective functioning" (430). And as studies of the informal sector in India invariably emphasize, the networks in which informal-sector activities are embedded are not characterized by the benign forms of trust associated with closely knit groups, but by deeply asymmetrical relations of dependency and domination. Labor is legally free (although there are documented cases of bonded labor) but socially embedded in a tapestry of power relations.

After four decades of planned development with a heavy emphasis on industrialization and a strong political commitment to the social and economic uplift of the poor, the vast majority of India's population still secures its livelihood in the unorganized sector (table 5). Of 286 million main workers (employed 183 days or more per year) enumerated in the

---

sector is symptomatic of Migdal's weak-state/strong-society model. The persistence of cheap labor as a strategy of production reflects the resiliency of precapitalist social institutions that have effectively resisted the penetration of the modern state.

[5] As a basis for solidarity, caste sometimes serves as a form of protection. The closed occupational categories of the caste system (*jatis*) have provided some protection from competition, but the more significant effect has been to enforce a rigid and hierarchical division of labor defined by unequal exchanges. Moreover, unlike craft associations, caste groupings never enjoyed market advantages enforced by the state.

TABLE 5. Composition of work force in Kerala and India, 1991, in thousands.

	Kerala	India
Census		
Main workers	8,299	285,932
Nonagricultural	4,296	94,592
Manufacturing	1,176	28,671
Organized sector (EMI)	1,162	26,657
as % of main	14.0	9.3
% of nonag	27.0	28.2
Registered factory	265	8,319
as % of main	3.2	2.9
% of nonag	6.2	8.8
% of manufacturing	22.5	29.0

Sources: Census and EMI from CMIE, *Basic Statistics Relating to the Indian Economy* 1993:tables 9.5 and 9.6. Registered factory from CMIE, B*asic Statistics Relating to States of India* 1994:table 9.9.

Note: "Main" workers are those who worked for at least 183 days in the year of enumeration.

1991 Census, only 9.3 percent were in enterprises classified as organized (all public-sector enterprises and all nonagricultural private enterprises with ten or more workers).[6] Even as a percentage of the nonagricultural workforce, the organized sector accounted for only 28.2 percent of total employment. In sum, almost three-quarters of the nonagricultural workers in India are either service workers employed on a casual or semipermanent basis, manufacturing workers employed in small workshops or unregistered factories, or self-employed workers.

As our concern here is primarily with industrial workers, table 5 also presents data for workers employed in registered factories.[7] This category, which corresponds to what is generally thought of as an industrial working class, represents at the all-India level only 2.9 percent of the work force. The most striking feature of India's work-force composition is the ratio of registered factory workers to total manufacturing workers. In 1991 there were 28.6 million workers enumerated in the census category "manufacturing," which includes both household and nonhousehold

[6] Official estimates of organized-sector employment come from data collected from employment exchanges as part of the Employment Market Information Programme (EMI).

[7] Registered factories are registered under the Factories Act of 1948, which covers all factories employing twenty or more workers and not using electric power or ten or more workers with power and some factories with less than ten workers specially notified by state governments.

workers. If we subtract workers in registered factories (8.3 million), we find that 20.3 million or 71 percent of India's manufacturing class work in domestic industries or in workshops that employ fewer than twenty workers and do not use electric power or employ fewer than ten workers and use power. Though these data are rough at best, it is nonetheless clear that the bulk of the manufacturing work force is located in the unorganized sector.

The commercialization of the economy in the post-Independence period and a robust industrial growth rate of 6.4 percent from 1953 to 1990 (Jalan 1991:58) have not significantly eroded the size of the unorganized economy. Between 1971 and 1991 organized-sector employment grew only 2 percent annually, well below the rate of population growth (CMIE 1993:tab. 9.6). The organized sector represented 10.2 percent of the work force in 1981, but only 9.3 percent in 1991. The absolute increase in numbers of workers employed in the unorganized sector between 1981 and 1991 was 59.5 million, twice the total number of workers in the organized sector in 1991. Growth of registered factory employment has also stagnated, averaging only 2.6 percent per year between 1971 and 1989.[8] Naidu presents data which show that in manufacturing alone between 1973 and 1987, employment in the unorganized sector grew at three times the rate in the organized sector (1993:26–27). Papola has estimated that between 1973 and 1987 the share of the unorganized sector in industrial employment increased from 67 to 76 percent (1992:37).

In the rough picture of the unorganized sector, four distinct forms of organization of production (two or more of which often coexist in the same industry) can be identified.[9] The most basic form is independent, household-based, petty commodity production. Here the producer owns the instruments of production, draws on traditional craft skills, and organizes the labor process. Though there are celebrated cases of family-based enterprise dynamism (as in Taiwan), caste segmentations, lack of institutional support, limited market access, and low levels of education and technology have condemned most such units to surviving largely on the strength of Chayanovian-like self-exploitation. As in the case of the home-based segment of Agra's footwear industry (see Knorringa 1996), most of the surplus is siphoned off through merchants' control over the cost of raw materials and output prices, and ties of dependency are maintained through intricate relations of obligation and debt.[10]

In the second form, the putting-out system, labor is still household-

[8] Calculated from the *Indian Labour Yearbook*.
[9] The general categories are borrowed from Singh 1991:29–40.
[10] In the case of Tamil Nadu's gem-cutting industry, Kapadia has documented the existence of hereditary debt bondage as a mechanism of worker control. Workers actually

based and subject to patriarchal authority. But through a subdivision of production instruments and raw inputs, merchant capital organizes a more detailed division of labor. The lace industry of West Godavari in Andhra Pradesh is a typical example. Spread over hundreds of villages, women perform the various tasks of lace-making for agents who provide the raw material and market the finished product to exporters. In this instance, the institution of *purdah*—female seclusion—provides the social basis for unfree labor (Mies 1982). The beedi (Indian cigarette) industry, which is estimated to provide work to over three million workers, including a high proportion of children, operates similarly, although workshop production is also common (Prasad and Prasad 1990).

The third form, sweatshop production, represents manufacturing proper. Here workers are assembled in a workshop or factory, and the labor process is directly organized and supervised by capital or intermediaries. Here the logic of surplus extraction is absolute, in that competitive advantage is secured through labor-tying (for example, debt bondage) and labor-squeezing strategies. Production is primarily manual (does not rely on energy sources) and is located in small decentralized units that facilitate capital's strategy of engaging the most exploitable forms of labor power, generally women and children drawn from huge reserves of rural lower-caste labor. The match industry, the workshop beedi industry, and the weaving sector of the coir industry are all examples. Except for the fact that workers are assembled in relatively large factories, the cashew-processing industry, as well as many other food product industries, also fall into this category.

The final form of unorganized industry approximates capitalist factory production itself, but can still be distinguished by its labor regime and the predominance of merchant capital. In these small-scale factories, the use of machinery suggests a movement toward relative (that is, productivity-enhancing) forms of surplus production, and in some cases there have been significant innovations that have drawn qualified parallels to the Third Italy (Cawthorne 1995). Generally, though, the social and institutional conditions associated with the "high road" to flexible specialization are absent. Furthermore, the increasingly widespread use of subcontracting that has driven the growth of this sector in India has been tied to the "defensive" variant of flexible specialization which depends on unregulated wages, neo-Taylorist management (separation of design and production), and minimal social overheads (Holmström 1993).[11]

---

refer to themselves as kottadimai (the traditional word for personal slave) (1995: 447).

[11] Bombay's textile industry has been decentralized and "defactorized" in response to labor militancy during the 1970s and 1980s. Factories were closed in Bombay and Ahmedabad,

The labor-squeezing logic of the unorganized sector is driven by a supply of cheap and abundant labor. Separation from the land in the classic scenario of primitive accumulation has not been a strong factor in proletarianizing Indian labor, but land fragmentation and demographic growth have. Supply-side dynamics alone (what Marx called "the dull compulsion of the market") cannot, however, explain low wage levels. The critical determinants instead are the institutional and social conditions under which labor takes the commodity form. The social embeddedness of labor markets in India is characterized by two structural features. The first is the deep segmentation of work conditions and entry barriers along caste, gender, and regional lines. A study of casual laborers in Bombay found that forms of labor stratification largely replicated those of the village (Deshpande 1983:39). Research conducted in Coimbatore—a fast-growing center in Tamil Nadu—identified eight distinct labor status groups with degrees of security, protection and wages that varied with "inherited characteristics" (Harriss, Kannan, and Rodgers 1990). Numerous other studies have documented the pervasive exclusionary effects of caste on labor markets (Mies 1982; Singh 1991; Breman 1996; Kapadia 1995; Knorringa 1996). The second feature relates to the forms of vertical dependency that condition the terms of labor recruitment. Breman's study of South Gujarat's "footloose proletariat" describes an extraordinary tapestry of networks of dependency through which workers are recruited for jobs as varied as bricklaying, diamond cutting, construction, sugar-cane harvesting, and weaving.[12] Because of the oversupply of unskilled casual labor, workers are locked into asymmetrical contractual relations with jobbers, recruiters, gang bosses, and other intermediaries, often kinsmen or caste mates. Thus, not only is the relationship to capital heavily mediated, but intraclass relations are fragmented along caste, communal, or parochial lines. And as Breman notes, "The immobilizing effect caused by horizontal division is increased by the pressure emanating from the need to invest in vertical dependency relationships" (Breman 1996:245). In the unorganized sectors of the Indian labor market, wage labor confronts capital not as a universal category but as the expression of social particularities.

---

and power looms were transferred to small-scale enterprises in Surat, a fast-growing industrial center in Gujarat. "[T]he considerable reduction in overheads caused by transferring production to new growth poles such as Surat, has been achieved primarily by exploiting labor more intensively" (Breman 1996:58).

[12] Employers, Breman notes, legitimate segmentation on grounds of imputed caste/regional attributes: thus Rajasthanis are the best construction workers, Khandeshis most suited to sugar-cane harvesting, and Halpatis skilled in bricklaying (1996).

In much of the recent literature, analysts focusing on developed countries and Latin America have depicted informalization as a product of the reconfiguration of capital, arguing that increasing globalization and competition have driven "formal sector capital, acting with the complicity of the state, to reduce wage costs and enhance flexibility by making use of unprotected workers in the informal sector" (Meagher 1995:260). Such strategies exploit the institutional unevenness of social rights. Portes and Castells, for instance, note that the vulnerability of informal-sector workers stems from all "social situations that are marked by some kind of social stigma: ethnic minorities, women, and youth are common subjects of discrimination and, hence potential candidates for working at home, part-time, and as temporary replacements" (1989:26). In the Indian case, however, although the informal sector is certainly articulated with the formal sector, it remains deeply rooted in social structures that must be considered autonomous from the logic of capitalism. The vulnerabilities that characterize informal labor markets are not the product of "social marginalities" that have been strategically exploited by a dominant capitalist system, but are an intrinsic part of the prevailing system of social domination in which structured social differences, local dependencies, low levels of human capital formation, and low-density citizenship systematically reproduce vulnerability.

The powerlessness of workers in this sector is matched only by the powerlessness of the state. Parliamentary committees, inquiry commissions, and expert groups have denounced the wages and work conditions that prevail in unorganized industries. The Supreme Court has ruled that minimum wages are an absolute right that must be secured independently of economic performance. Yet the slew of minimum wage notifications issued by the central government and the states have gone unenforced. Of 1,500,674 establishments covered under the rules framed by the states under the Minimum Wages Act of 1948, only 87,103 even submitted returns as required by law (GOI, Labour Bureau 1984:84).

Breman's account of failed efforts to legislate the unorganized sector in Gujarat paints the picture of a supine state. In the absence of trade unions, labor inspectors implement rules indifferently. Violators are threatened with official action only in order to extort bribes. In the brick factories Breman studied, workers refused to report abuses out of fear of dismissal. In a cynical formal application of the rules, wage notifications and rules were posted in English. And when labor agitations broke out, they were met with state repression. Breman concludes that state officials are simply unwilling to confront the power of manufacturers (1996: chap. 7). The inability of the state to curb exploitative labor practices is nowhere more visible than in the area of child labor. Despite legislated prohibitions, estimates put the number of working children in India anywhere between thirteen and forty-four million.[13] For all its bureaucratic capacity, the Indian state has by and large failed to penetrate the unorganized sector, a fact captured quite appropriately in the official usage of the term "unorganized."

The failure of the state to bridge the gap between the organized and unorganized sectors, and the implications for economic development, are now widely recognized.[14] Kannan (1994) notes that the persistence of stratified and discriminatory labor markets has a number of adverse effects on growth. The most serious, as I have already noted, is the disincentive to technological innovation created by the availability of cheap labor. The second is the limited scope for stimulating growth through effective demand. Raising the wage floor would have far more dynamic consumption effects, both in absolute and linkage terms, than the current strategy of promoting middle-class consumption through liberalization. Finally, the persistence of the unorganized sector and its reproduction of traditional economic and social inequalities have stymied the development of human resources, and hence productivity and innovation. The link between the persistence of the dual economy and labor's lack of wage leverage has recently been underlined by the National Commission on Rural Labour: "The conspicuous co-existence of mushrooming high-wage islands in the organized sector on the one hand and miserable conditions of labor in informal urban and rural sector (both farm and non-farm) on the other and the corresponding dualism in capital/labor intensities and associated levels of productivity are the result of our inability or even unwillingness to implement a sound and firm wage policy" (GOI, Ministry of Labour 1991:1:23).

---

[13] Thirteen million is the figure provided by the 1981 Census. A study sponsored by the Ministry of Labour included children paid in kind as well as in cash and put the number at forty-four million (Weiner 1991:21).

[14] Drawing on national accounts statistics, Abhijit Sen has calculated that 1984–85 yearly income per worker (in 1970 prices) in the unorganized sector was Rs. 1,324, compared to Rs. 6,300 in the organized (private) sector. The gap has been steadily increasing, with unorganized wages falling from 26.6 percent of organized wages in 1960–61 to 21.0 percent in 1984–85 (1991:tab. 3). In a detailed survey of sixteen occupations in Bombay, Deshpande found that factory workers earned Rs. 477 per month compared to Rs. 280 for small-sector workers and Rs. 181 for casual (unorganized) workers (1983:26).

The Labor Movement in Kerala

The labor movement in Kerala was born in the crucible of the political and social transformations of the 1930s (see Chapter 2). Incipient forms of craft- or industrial-based unionism were, from the outset, absorbed into a more encompassing and more politicized project of challenging the traditional social order and its despotic labor regime. The early consolidation of the mass-mobilizational character of Kerala's labor movement, marked most critically by the transformative politics of the CPI and its organizational bridging of the rural-urban divide, stands in sharp contrast to the narrow trade unionism of the Indian labor movement.

The state's first labor union, the Travancore Labour Association (TLA), was organized in 1922 by workers in the coir factories of the coastal town of Alleppey, Travancore's industrial center. As social-movement theorists have observed, collective action often first takes place through the mobilization of traditional networks (Tarrow 1994). Coir workers were predominantly of the Ezhava caste. For these workers in large factories owned and managed by British capital, emerging solidarities first took the form of lower-caste self-assertion. The TLA was a direct outgrowth of the caste-reform movement and in its early years functioned as a caste association, providing "social upliftment" and education through reading rooms, night school, welfare schemes, and an ayurvedic hospital. "The workers," noted a union activist of the time, "were active in movements for prohibition, eradication of untouchability and temple entry . . . It was such movements and not struggles against the employers in the factories that agitated the workers" (Govindan 1986:14)

Within two years of its formation, and before it had even engaged in a major strike, the TLA passed a resolution demanding representation in the Travancore legislature. Moreover, the association undertook the organization of workers in other Alleppey industries, and by the mid-1930s was demanding the passage of protective labor legislation to cover all workers. In 1935 the TLA participated in the first All-Kerala Workers Conference organized by the Kerala Congress Socialist Party (KCSP). That caste reform movements were rapidly absorbed into a larger and more radicalized movement is also illustrated by the case of beedi workers in Malabar. The first beedi association was formed in Tellicherry in 1934 and named after the revered Ezhava reformer, Sree Narayana Guru. As the association extended its organizational activities to other towns, it rejected its community identity by dropping the reformer's name, the union vice president declaring that "all workers whatever be their caste or religion are basically workers. All workers have the same work, same wages and same working time" (Thomas Isaac, Franke, and Raghavan 1998:2–14).

The movement's political character solidified with the general strike of 1938. Under the influence of KCSP activists, many of whom were recruited from Malabar, the TLA had voiced support for the "responsible government" movement led by the Travancore State Congress. The socialists were determined to draw the labor movement into a broader political struggle.[15] Protesting the banning of the State Congress and demanding an end to the autocratic reign of the maharajah, forty thousand workers struck for over three weeks and repeatedly clashed with police (Nossiter 1988:51). The general strike "proved to be a school of mass education for the workers" (Thomas Isaac 1985:14). Moderate leaders, influenced by the State Congress and the leadership of the SNDP (the powerful Ezhava caste association), brokered a settlement with the government that was denounced by the socialists. Two years later the break between an increasingly conservative SNDP and the Alleppey working class was consummated. Workers ousted the moderate trade union leadership in favor of the KCSP and its political line of building independent class organizations of peasants and workers. The trade union movement, now firmly under the control of the socialists, emerged as the dominant force in the nationalist and democratic movement in Travancore.

Under the direction of the KCSP, the labor movement in both Malabar and Travancore not only grew rapidly itself but also built organizational bridges to the agrarian movement. Shortly after the general strike of 1938, at the All-Kerala Workers Conference, the trade union movement explicitly committed itself to organizing agricultural workers, and cadres from Alleppey's coir factories were dispatched into the Travancore countryside to organize agricultural laborers (Kannan 1988:112). The class-encompassing political logic of the KCSP was also reflected in its strategy of forming central union councils—local "peak" organizations—and only then organizing factory and ward committees (109). Beedi workers in Malabar were among the first to organize an industry-wide union, and in Quilon, Travancore's second largest industrial center, the Quilon Factory Workers Union covered textile mills, sawmills, and cashew factories (K. Nair 1994:334). In Cochin, toddy tappers successfully organized a union, and in 1946 the Vellanikkara Thattil Estate Union (VTEU) in Trichur

[15] P. Krishna Pillai, founder of the CPI, wrote: "The main purpose of organizing the strike at this time was to strengthen the political struggle of the Travancore State Congress for Responsible Government rather than the economic demands of workers" (quoted in Kannan 1988:111).

struck to have plantations recognized as an industry and brought under the purview of the Trades Disputes Act. The courts eventually ruled in the union's favor, setting an important national precedent (K. Nair 1973:103). From the outset, then, the making of Kerala's working class stretched across the organized factory sector (coir manufacturing), workshop industries (beedi), services (boatmen), traditional agro-processing (cashew, toddy tapping), and agriculture. By 1952 there were 555 registered unions in Travancore-Cochin alone, most of which were affiliated to the CPI (Peter 1957:161).

In the late 1940s, the Communist mobilization of workers and peasants took a revolutionary turn as efforts by the Travancore state and the Congress Party government in Malabar to repress the CPI were met with local uprisings. In Travancore, a severe economic downturn, food shortages, and the maharajah's obstinate refusal to relinquish power prompted elements within the party to call for an all-out insurrection. As the police joined forces with the private armies of landlords to attack Communist organizers, workers organized paramilitary training camps and the CPI called for a general strike. The strike rapidly escalated into a series of large-scale and deadly confrontations. The Punnapra-Vayalar revolt, as it came to be known, was the first urban working-class uprising in Indian history. Though the uprising was quickly crushed, it established the CPI as the leading political force in the struggle against an autocratic Brahmanical government. The uprising also soldered the trade union movement to the politics of mass democracy. Agricultural workers, fishermen, boat workers, and coir workers had openly defied and attacked the absolutist state. Although sixty-one unions and affiliated cultural and social organizations were banned, martial law declared, and Communists leaders forced into hiding, within a year the maharajah had abdicated.

This period of escalating conflict also saw determined efforts by the state to mediate and regulate labor-management relations. Following the 1938 general strike, the maharajah's government passed wage legislation for the coir industry (Das 1983:202) and in 1940 facilitated the formation of an industrial relations committee, the first of its kind its India (Pillai 1972:180). By 1946, unions had successfully negotiated for the payment of bonuses in a number of Cochin factories (K. Nair 1973:85). With Independence came a rise in labor militancy and more active interventions by the state. Bipartite industry-wide consultations were replaced with tripartite bodies. A leader of the coir union, P. N. Krishna Pillai, was appointed labor commissioner. The concept of state-mediated conferences was extended to other industries, and minimum wages were fixed for cashew-processing workers, the largest factory-based industry. The government of Travancore-Cochin also legislated a number of welfare and labor laws including maternity benefits and a bonus law that predated national legislation by two decades.

To Govern or to Struggle?

When the Communists came to power in 1957, the party's strategic line of using the state as an instrument of mass struggle was initially subordinated to the imperative of promoting growth in a subnational capitalist economy. Recognizing that Kerala's weak industrial base precluded state-led autocentric industrialization, the chief minister, E. M. S. Namboodiripad, made efforts to assuage the "apprehensions" of industrialists, declaring that his government would follow the industrialization policy of the center, "reserving only the most important industries for the public sector and leaving a large field of industries for the private sector to operate" (1957:19). Promising to do the utmost "to attract private capital into the field of industries" (18), Namboodiripad emphasized the role that the government would play in actively promoting industrial peace and called upon workers "to realise that it is as much in their interest to help the development of new industries as in the interest of the employers; as a matter of fact, it is far more in their interest because it is only through the most rapid development of industries, that the central problem of the working class—the problem of unemployment—can be successfully tackled. The trade unionists, therefore, have to carry on a systematic campaign among the working class for a policy of industrial peace" (21).

The government extended IRCs to every major industry and sponsored a comprehensive industrial relations bill designed to promote collective bargaining. This conciliatory approach, which would resurface in the 1980s as the centerpiece of the party's conversion to class compromise, proved politically unsustainable. Namboodiripad's firm hold over the ministerial wing notwithstanding, the organizational wing of the party continued to espouse the mass militancy line.[16] Working-class mobilization had, after all, proven particularly effective, and remained critical to building the party's support base. The installation of a Communist ministry had

---

[16] For example, an accord the government reached with G. D. Birla, one of India's largest industrialists, for the opening of a pulp factory was denounced by the CPI labor federation, the All-Indian Trade Union Congress (AITUC), as an "anti-Working Class agreement with Private Capital" (Lieten 1982:60).

severely disrupted the old social order, creating new opportunities for collective action. The government's pro-labor credentials and rhetoric were themselves an invitation to increased militancy. Thus while the government expressed its commitment to industrial peace, it also declared that the police would not be used to suppress "just workers' struggles" and that its overall labor policy would by guided by the resolutions of the All-Indian Trade Union Congress (AITUC), the party's labor federation.[17] Finally, the bandwagon effect of the party's success had attracted new and often opportunistic political entrepreneurs, diluting its cadre base and weakening party discipline. Party leaders blamed a number of excesses on these "anti-social" elements (Nossiter 1988:69). Still the ministerial wing of the party might have been able to deliver the promised working-class discipline had it not been for the determination of the opposition to bring down the government. The Congress-led "liberation struggle" was met by the mobilization of Communist unions and peasant organizations. Industrial unrest spread, as the number of man-days lost increased from 204,730 in 1956–57 to 1,222,378 in 1957–58 (J. Alexander 1972:173).

Through the 1960s and well into the 1970s working-class militancy escalated, and the "politics of confrontation" became the norm. The antidemocratic toppling of the 1957 ministry underscored the party's distrust of the "parliamentary road" and strengthened its class-struggle line. The deployment of Communist unions as front organizations, coupled with fierce interparty competition for the support of labor, created a volatile industrial relations climate. The acrimonious 1965 split in the CPI proved to be particularly destabilizing. The newly formed CPM actively and aggressively raided the membership of the Communist labor federation AITUC, which had remained affiliated to the CPI. Tactics such as unnotified strikes and various forms of intimidation (including *gheraos* in which an official is surrounded and prevented from leaving a site) became increasingly common as the CPM mobilized rank-and-file members to dislodge the "rightist leadership" of the AITUC.

During the 1967 ministry, the CPM adopted the tactical line that, in the words of party secretary E. K Nayanar, the "ministry [be used] as an instrument of struggle against the bourgeois-landlord system" (Nayanar 1982:141). Administrative patronage was liberally dispensed to strengthen the party's mass organizations (Nossiter 1982:244). CPM unions, backed by the Ministry of Labour, launched political strikes, attacking rival unions (Varughese 1978:108). The number of man-days (the government's term) lost to industrial disputes reached an all-time high of

[17] *New Kerala*, January 3, 1958.

2.5 million. When T. V. Thomas, the industries minister from the CPI coalition partner and a development-oriented policymaker, pushed for "responsible trade unionism," he was denounced as an arch-revisionist by the CPM (Nossiter 1982:244).

Shut out of power through the 1970s by the CPI's alliance with the Congress Party, the CPM concentrated its resources on building class organizations and strengthening its mass base. Strike data for this period confirm a picture of labor militancy. Between 1969 and 1978, Kerala accounted for 8.64 percent of the man-days lost to disputes in India, almost double its 4.42-percent share of employment (M. Kumar 1989:tab. 6.1.1). With the factory sector fully organized, the CPM and its labor federation, the CITU, which had rapidly become the most powerful in Kerala, undertook the organization of the unorganized sector. Other political parties, mindful as always of the need in Kerala's political climate to cultivate a mass base, followed suit. In the coir industry, unions pushed out from the factory-based weaving sector to the small-shop and household-based processing sector (extraction and spinning of coir). By the 1980s, Kerala's two largest casual labor markets, construction and headload work, had been extensively organized. Here class struggles assumed a particularly volatile character as rival political unions of construction workers and headload workers (otherwise known as "coolies") resorted to extortionate practices and strong-arm tactics in securing control over labor markets. The inflationary impact of the wage escalation that ensued produced a middle-class backlash that was in part responsible for the toppling of the short-lived third CPM ministry (1980–82).

Much as I argued in the case of agriculture, one has to be cautious about drawing causal connections between labor militancy and economic outcomes. There are important historical legacies (no indigenous bourgeoisie, dominance of merchant capital) and structural conditions (weak linkages to the national market) that can explain Kerala's underdeveloped industrial economy. But the greater mobility of capital in industry than in agriculture does heighten the potential costs of militancy, and one can make a fairly strong case that militancy did precipitate a crisis of accumulation in Kerala, especially in the 1975–85 period during which industrial growth slowed to 1.7 percent a year. The relationship between militancy and investment is directly evident in some sectors and, indirectly but plausibly evident in others. In coir and cashew, as we shall see in the next chapter, capital responded to unionization and regulation by either reorganizing and literally demechanizing production or relocating to Tamil Nadu. In the factory sector there have been few instances of capital flight (which is essentially prohibited by law), but militancy has severely affected Kerala's ability to compete for scarce private investment.

Whatever the immediate effect of militancy on investment levels, the organized character of labor and embryonic character of capital present an interesting juxtaposition. The remainder of this chapter makes the case that although Kerala's productive base has remained largely underdeveloped, its social relations of production have been transformed. As social rights have been extended, traditional modes of labor control and exploitation have been significantly undermined. Patron-client employment relations have been displaced in favor of contractual wage relations. The rigid and caste-stratified occupational structure of the past has made way for state-regulated or union-controlled labor markets. Despotic management practices have been replaced by a sophisticated industrial-relations regime. And a labor force that is almost fully literate enjoys a high degree of mobility and skill.

Organizing the Unorganized

The official figures presented in table 5 indicate that unorganized workers in Kerala account for three-quarters of the total nonagricultural labor force, roughly the same as the national ratio. But the term "unorganized" in Kerala is a misnomer. A large segment of workers outside the public sector and outside the registered factory sector (those officially counted as part of the organized sector) are in fact organized (Kannan 1988; K. Nair 1994; Krishnan 1991). Workers in Kerala's largest traditional industries, cashew and coir, and its two largest casual labor markets, construction and headload work, are unionized.[18] In the beedi industry, unions have not only organized workers, but have also organized the largest and most successful producer-cooperative in the state with a membership of over thirty thousand. Even mahouts (elephant drivers) have a union. Because only unions in the organized sector submit official returns, however, there are no official data by which to assess the extent of unionization in the unorganized sector.[19] Figures obtained from the CITU for the district of Trivan-

[18] Technically speaking, the cashew industry is classified as organized because processing of cashews takes place in factories that employ more than ten workers, and are as such "registered" factories. It is treated here as part of the unorganized sector because it is a traditional industry that bears all the characteristics of absolute surplus extraction.
[19] One labor department official did estimate that 45 percent of workers in the unorganized sector have ties to unions. Whatever the actual figure, there is general agreement that Kerala

drum provide a rough measure. Although the CITU is nominally an industrial trade union federation, over 80 percent of its registered members were in the unorganized sector. Of 63,031 members, almost two-thirds were headload, construction, or coir workers.

The penetration of labor organizations into the unorganized sector can be traced back to the multiplier effect of the early and successful organization of unions in Travancore. As we saw earlier, the first unionized workers in the factory sector of the coir industry embraced a broad political vision of social and economic reform. Unionization was about class formation, which was closely tied to the CPI's political project. The organizing strategies and demands of a small but militant core of coir factory workers were quickly extended to coir workers in the rural household sector, other nonfactory occupations, and agricultural workers. Thus even before Independence agricultural laborers and other rural workers were demanding the same benefits granted to industrial workers, including security of employment, fixed work days, and the right to bargain collectively (K. Nair 1994).

The state in Kerala has actively intervened in the unorganized sector, and the thrust of these interventions has been in direct response to the politics of class struggle. Through a series of regulatory and organizational measures, the state has limited labor's vulnerability to the market and curtailed the prerogatives and flexibility of capital. To minimize the role of merchant capital, for example, the state actively supported unions in organizing and financing labor cooperatives for toddy tappers, beedi workers, coir-processing workers, cashew-processing workers, and handloom weavers (Kannan 1992:12). Responding to fears of labor displacement—which have always been particularly acute in Kerala's high-labor-surplus economy—the state banned mechanization in the coir industry. The state also intervened to control the supply of raw materials in agro-processing industries, establishing monopoly control over the supply of cashew nuts and introducing price controls for coconut husks. When capital fled, as in the case of the cashew industry, the state took over production directly, incorporating thirty-four factories and 34,000 workers into a state cooperative. Minimum wage committees were appointed for the coir and cashew industries and gradually extended to forty-five other industries including the "handling and care of elephants" (GOK, Labour Department 1990). Finally, during the 1980s, social protection in the form of pension and

---

is the only state in India where a sizable section of workers in this sector have been unionized (Singh 1991; Kannan 1992).

welfare funds was extended to twenty-five unorganized sectors including headload and construction workers, artisans, fisherman, coir workers, cashew workers, and handloom and khadi workers (Duvvury 1994).[20]

The most discernible impact of increased state intervention and labor organization has been their leveling effect. As the unorganized sector has become more formalized and workers have developed the capacity to bargain collectively, the gap between work conditions and wage levels in the organized and unorganized sectors has narrowed. Kannan (1990ab:62) presents data on real wages for construction work, toddy tapping, and cashew processing between 1963 and 1985. Across all occupations, including skilled and unskilled categories and male and female workers in construction, real wages increased steadily, with the lowest increase for toddy tappers (42 percent) and the highest for female construction workers (76 percent). Of particular significance is that real wage increases for unskilled construction workers surpassed those for skilled construction workers, indicating a leveling of the earning gap within these industries.

In a later study, Kannan (1992) compares the changes in daily wages in unorganized industries to those in the modern factory sector between two time periods (1960–61 to 1974–75 and 1975–76 to 1985–86). Of sixteen occupations in the unorganized sector for which he presents data, seven experienced gains vis-à-vis factory workers, six maintained parity (an increase or decrease of 1 percent or less), and three experienced a relative decline. Those experiencing a relative decline were male paddy workers (whose wages, as we have seen, have nonetheless climbed significantly), and two categories of skilled construction workers whose wages in the second period still amounted to as much as 95 percent of factory workers wages.[21]

An examination of wages in the manufacturing portion of the unorganized sector confirms the picture of a narrow wage differential with registered-factory workers. Albin found that while workers' share of value added in the registered (organized) factory sector is comparable to the all-

---

[20] The benefits available under the schemes remain modest and coverage is uneven. In the cashew industry 90 percent of workers are reported as registered, compared to only 17 percent for coir workers. Nonetheless, under the ten major new welfare schemes enacted since 1980, over 1.9 million new beneficiaries have been registered (GOK, State Planning Board 1996b). In 1995–96, total social security and welfare expenditures exceeded one billion rupees (GOK, *Economic Review* 1996).

[21] Though unions have clearly been successful in breaking down wage barriers between the modern and traditional sectors, they have done little to challenge the most tenacious traditional source of income discrimination and segmentation. Thus all six of the female occupational categories command lower daily wages than the ten male occupational categories (Kannan 1992:20).

India average, in the unregistered (unorganized) manufacturing sector the share of wages in value added is much higher than the all-India figure and higher than in all southern states. Particularly striking are units with less than six workers and/or a turnover of less than 100,000 rupees. Here, workers in Kerala secure almost twice as high a percentage of the value added as the national average, 21.34 percent versus 12.21 percent (Albin 1992:tab. 2).[22] Albin concludes that the high share of wages in the smaller units in part explains the more even distribution of income in Kerala.

Wage increases in the unorganized sector have not been uniform and are clearly tied to the strategic leverage of specific unions. The occupations that have made the most significant strides in reducing the earnings differential with the organized sector are the most highly unionized—headload, toddy, and cashew (Kannan 1992:20). The key factors here appear to be control over the labor process and the capacity of capital to relocate or reorganize. In occupations with a specialized skill component and low capital mobility, unions have successfully restricted entry to traditional craftworkers, as in toddy tapping, skilled construction work, and coconut-tree climbing.[23] In construction and headload work, local unions operate as clearinghouses, distributing work within and between unions. These practices, while limiting interoccupational mobility, have favored more even employment distribution within labor markets and have increased worker solidarity by displacing patron-client dependencies. Union control of these labor markets has, in effect, limited capital's access to an undifferentiated reserve army of labor.

Even where local-level unionism has been weak, state interventions have extended social rights and created a safety net. Broad-based access to education and long-standing affirmative action have reduced the role of caste in determining employment opportunities (Mukherjee and Thomas Isaac 1994). Minimum wage legislation, the upward pressure on wages exercised by the cooperative sector, and social welfare measures for the "weaker" sections have created, piecemeal, a wage floor. This wage floor has been critical for workers in labor-intensive manufacturing industries; these function as residual employment sectors (Thomas Isaac and Pyarelal 1990) drawing on underemployed rural female laborers, a labor market

---

[22] See also Thampy's study of small-scale units (1990).

[23] A particularity of the history of unionization in Kerala has been the success with which unions drew on traditional occupational categories to consolidate labor solidarity. In the larger context of ideologically powerful social-reform movements, caste-based occupational specializations were used as the basis for organizing closed-shop unions. Drawing on caste solidarity, the unions effectively established control over the labor market by limiting employment to traditional workers (Kannan 1992).

over which unions have had difficulty exercising any bargaining power. Wages in this sector thus remain comparatively low by Kerala standards, but are nonetheless higher than in neighboring states.[24]

Finally, the impact of social development and the emergence of a culture of wage solidarity must also be noted. High literacy has eliminated many of the spatial boundaries and information asymmetries associated with traditional labor markets. Workers in Kerala are very much aware of wage legislation and prevailing wages in other industries. This awareness, Krishnan (1991) notes, explains the rapidity with which wage increases in one occupation are passed on to another. Moreover, the stigma among educated and politicized workers that is associated with accepting wages below the prevailing level explains how wages have remained downward sticky despite increasing unemployment (Krishnan 1991). And mass education, by removing children from the labor reserve has also propped up wages. The percentage of children who complete the fifth grade is 82 percent in Kerala as against 26 percent for India (Weiner 1991:174). The 1981 Census reported a .72 percent work participation rate for children in Kerala in the 0–14 age group, and 17 percent for the 15–19 age group, both figures being the lowest of any state. The all-India figures were respectively 4.2 percent and 34.8 percent.[25]

Crisis in the Unorganized Sector

Capital may indeed be revolutionary, but not, to play on Marx's famous dictum, under circumstances of its own choosing. Advocates of liberalization argue that market forces will inject new sources of dynamism and innovation into the Indian economy. This may certainly be the case for an organized factory sector strangled by monopolies and regulation, but the unorganized sector has always been marked by intense competition, entrepreneurialism, and flexible labor markets. Market forces alone have failed to transform the labor process. As long as the opportunities for squeezing labor abound, capital has little incentive to reorganize production. At a minimum then, any significant transformation in how production is organized will necessarily involve changes in the institutional and social structures of the despotic labor regime. And since the logic through which these

[24] Even in the lowest-paying traditional industry, cashew processing, which draws primarily on lower-caste women, wages in Kerala are significantly higher than in Tamil Nadu (M. Oommen 1979).
[25] GOI, *Analysis of Work Force in India* 1988:tab. 3.4. Figures given are the unweighted average of male and female rates.

structures are reproduced is social and not economic, such a transformation requires a social agent. In the classic English case of capitalist development, that agent was of course the bourgeoisie. In the case of the East Asian Tigers, the state played the catalytic role.

In Kerala, that agent has been the working class. Insofar as working-class mobilization has challenged the social and political institutions of the traditional labor regime, it has transformed the conditions under which capital can extract surplus. Political empowerment and social interventions have curtailed the power of capital in the unorganized sector to draw on traditional modes of labor control and recruitment in organizing production. Unionization and state intervention, including both direct regulatory measures and redistributive interventions, have provided workers in the state's unorganized sector with more bargaining power, more control over the labor process, and higher wages than in any other Indian state. The unorganized sector has been organized. Class mobilization has imposed social and political limits on the despotic labor regime. But if the old is dying, it has not simply given way to the new. The transition *within* capitalism continues to be contested. The next chapter explores the birth pangs of an emerging but uneven hegemonic labor regime.

6

Crisis and Compromise in the Unorganized Sector

Robert Brenner (1986) has argued that when labor-squeezing strategies for extracting surplus are restricted, capital will, when possible, respond by seeking new methods of organizing production. This argument, of course, draws directly on Marx's discussion of the development of English industry. In *Capital*, Marx argues that successful efforts by the working class, with the help of the state, to regulate the length of the workday through the Factory Acts compelled manufacturing capital, under the competitive pressures of the market, to resort to innovation and technological upgrading in restoring profitability. In this sense, social struggles to impose limits on capital can have the effect of stimulating economic transformation. But the trajectory is anything but unilinear. In his richly detailed investigation of the genesis of English capitalism Marx locates the dynamic of economic transformation at multiple points of engagement between labor and capital and identifies a wide range of reconfigurations. Driving these multiple processes, though, was a constant: the contested commodification of labor.

Economic transformation in Kerala has likewise been driven by social struggles over the form of labor, but under very different circumstances that have produced different engagements and different outcomes. First, the time frame has been briefer and the "stages" of development collapsed: between the demise of the precapitalist order and the emergence of organized resistance to the wage labor form there has hardly been time to breathe. Second, in contrast to nineteenth-century England, Kerala is far more dependent on the world economy, and in fact has no economic boundaries of its own. The economic margin of maneuver has been consequently narrower, the trade-offs more acute, the social costs potentially

183

higher. Third, and most important, because labor was politically enfran-
chised and organized *before* it was fully commodified, the politics of transformation have been especially contentious and played out not just at the
point of production but also in formal political arenas.

Thus the crisis of despotic capitalism in Kerala, rather than leading in
linear fashion to a "higher" and more dynamic stage of capitalism (as
Brenner's thesis would predict), has in fact produced a highly contested
and uncertain transition. Between 1970–71 and 1986–87, the unregistered
factory sector grew at an anemic annual rate of .9 percent compared to a
national rate of 4.8 percent.[1] Many factors contributed to this decline, not
least of which was a global recession that depressed demand for the products of Kerala's traditional industries. Nonetheless, when examined on an
industry-by-industry basis, labor militancy did adversely affect the rate
and quality of capital investment.

Because the unorganized sector is structurally diverse, capital's response
to labor militancy has varied across sectors. Three broad responses can be
identified: capital flight, capital reorganization, and capital boycott. The
first scenario is largely limited to some traditional manufacturing industries. As production is labor-intensive and physical investment low, capital
is footloose and has responded by shifting its operations to neighboring
states. The cashew industry, in which a predominantly female labor force
of some 110,00 workers roast and peel cashew nuts destined for export
markets, is a textbook example (M. Oommen 1979). Responding to labor
union pressure, the government first intervened in the industry in 1960 by
notifying a minimum wage. As wages rose, the "Cashew Kings," mostly
Quilon-based Christian entrepreneurs, responded by reorganizing production through cottage processing (*kudivarappu*) to circumvent the reach of
the unions and the law. When the state banned the practice in 1967, capital fled to Tamil Nadu where government officials openly boasted of lax
labor laws and where the supply of child labor was known to be abundant.[2] In a careful comparative study of factories in both states, M. A.
Oommen concludes that "it is the excessively high labour exploitation
that works to the advantage of the units located in Tamil Nadu"
(1979:83).[3]

---

[1] Calculated from GOK, *Statistics for Planning* 1988 and CMIE 1996.
[2] "Ministers . . . in several public announcements have made it clear that no efforts will be
made to implement minimum wage legislation in the cashew industry with a view to attracting this industry from Kerala" (M. Oommen 1979:82).
[3] By 1972, 107 of 390 factories were located in Tamil Nadu (GOK, State Planning Board
1984:295). The tide of capital flight has since been stemmed by state regulation of the movement of raw cashew nuts and direct takeover of thirty-four factories.

Where production is dependent on the supply of local primary resources, and is thus limited in its geographical mobility, capital's response to labor militancy has been to reorganize and, specifically, decentralize and "informalize" production. The coir industry is the classic case and is examined below in detail.

Finally, because the construction and service industries depend entirely on local demand, capital has no exit options. The effect of militancy here has been indirect. High wages in the construction and headload sectors have been passed on to consumers and to the manufacturing sector and a highly chaotic and disruptive form of union militancy has crippled markets and shut down construction projects. The overall effect has been to fetter accumulation by discouraging new investment.

The Coir Industry and the Reorganization of Capital

With an estimated 383,000 workers, concentrated mostly along the state's coastal belt, the coir industry is the largest source of employment in Kerala. Much like the cashew industry, it is a labor-intensive agro-processing industry that depends primarily on export markets. It is, however, more location-bound. Coconut husk, which provides the fiber from which coir yarn is spun, is produced locally. The industry's highest quality of yarn, spun from "white" fiber, is obtained through a process unique to Kerala. Coconut husks are treated ("retted") through immersion in the state's brackish backwaters, a bacteriological process that produces a particularly fine quality of fiber. Such locational factors have limited capital's ability to relocate production, although some shifting has taken place. Capital's response to labor militancy has instead taken the form of a reorganization of production, which has not only resulted in the de-development of the industry (it has quite literally regressed to a more rudimentary form of production) but has also jeopardized its ability to compete with new sources of coir production.[4]

No industry provides a better illustration of the argument that the borders between the formal and informal sectors are historically constituted through social struggles (Portes and Castells 1989). The coir industry spans both sectors and is made up of vertically integrated but organizationally distinct production activities, divided between processing and

[4] In the past fifteen years or so international competitors (primarily Sri Lanka) and neighboring states (Tamil Nadu and Karnataka) have challenged Kerala's dominant position in the supply of coir yarn, especially in the production of lower-quality brown fiber.

manufacturing. By one estimate, processing accounts for roughly 90 percent of workers.[5] The two basic processing activities are the removal of the fiber from the husk (defibering), which consists of both the retting and beating of the husk, and the spinning of coir yarn. The extraction of fiber is unskilled work in which only the most basic tools are used. It is generally performed by female labor within the household compound. Spinning, which alone accounts for 70 percent of workers in the industry, is done both by hand and on spinning wheels called ratts. Hand spinning is done by household producers, and ratt spinning, which requires the cooperation of four or five workers, is a cottage industry.[6] The processing sector is a highly fragmented and localized industry dominated by petty production consisting of both household units and various putting-out systems. This production system is integrated through dense networks of middlemen, including large suppliers of husks (mostly copra merchants), petty traders collecting and disposing of yarn, and wholesalers and commission agents providing the link with the larger manufacturers.

Most coconut-producing countries export only processed coir (yarn); the distinctiveness of Kerala's industry is to have developed a manufacturing sector in which yarn is woven into finished goods, primarily mats and carpets. Production is organized in both cottage units and registered factories. The wages and work conditions of workers in the registered sector have been subject to periodic agreements negotiated through an industrial relations committee (IRC). Wage revisions have been based on a formula first adopted in 1961.

In its industrial structure, the coir industry bears the imprint of its colonial origins. Though the processing base of the industry is wide and dispersed, it has historically been controlled by a small number of exporter-manufacturers, originally dominated by British capital. Located in the port town of Alleppey, the British trading houses, with their baling technologies, ties to European export markets, control of shipping lanes, and investment capital, had a commanding position in the industry, monopolizing the export of yarn and finished products. Until the 1960s the trading houses also operated large manufacturing units, employing over thirty thousand workers (Raveendran 1989:173). As we shall see, capital's capacity to extract surplus was more critically tied to its control over export

[5] All employment numbers are based on a 1988 survey (GOK, State Planning Board 1997a).
[6] A survey conducted by the Government of India Coir Board in 1960 found that 98 percent of hand spinners were household workers and 75 percent of wheel spinners were hired workers. Hand spinners constituted 60 percent of all spinners (GOI, Coir Board 1963).

markets and its links to precapitalist petty production units than to the actual organization of production.

Coir workers in Alleppey's factories were among the first workers in India to organize and were at the forefront of the CPI's political and organizational activities (see Chapter 2). In 1944 the Travancore Coir Factory Workers Union (TCFWU) had seventeen thousand members, roughly 90 percent of all coir factory workers in the Alleppey area (K. Nair 1973:96). The union was successful in securing annual bonus payments, cost-of-living increases ("dearness" allowances) and protection under the Factories Act. With the postwar period came increasing tension between capital and labor. Lower prices for coir products and increasing competition from Indian entrants put the factory sector of the coir industry at a comparative disadvantage to the small-scale rural units that paid lower wages and were not subject to factory legislation. The large manufacturer-exporter houses found it increasingly profitable to subcontract work to the rural sector.[7] Factory foremen were provided with severance packages and loans to start their own production units. Rural entrepreneurs, mostly of the local Ezhava landed gentry, relied on patronage ties to secure labor from small Ezhava tenants and agricultural laborers (Thomas Isaac 1982a). Capital could thus organize production outside the organizational reach of the unions. A memorandum submitted by coir factory unions in 1955 summarizes the strategic logic behind decentralization:

> They disorganize the well established industry and sabotage all agreements on labor relations. The workers employed by them are not organized and by the time they organize themselves the employer would have gone into liquidation or changed the place. The employees are recruited from the poor peasant class or from those who had been retrenched from well established factories. The owners . . . do not respect any of the provisions of the Factories Act, Maternity Benefit Act, and such other obligations, under the various labor legislation. They would refuse to pay the standardized wage rates that are laid down for the industry. They defy the decisions of the Coir Industrial Relations Council regulating industrial relations in the industry. (Government of Travancore-Cochin 1955:16–17)

---

[7] Though the large coir factories were only protoindustrial units that used little machinery, they were highly integrated and organized. In some factories, the entire coir production process from retting to matting was carried out (Raveendran 1989). Thus though the decentralization of the industry did not involve technological downsizing (the technology used in rural units was essentially the same as in the factories), it did involve the relocation and fragmentation of labor.

In a relatively short period of time the coir industry was reorganized from top to bottom. Factories were closed down and thousands of workers were retrenched. A fragmented labor movement found itself almost powerless to resist the defactorization of the industry. Until the banning of the CPI and its unions in 1946 (following the Punnapra-Vayalar uprising), coir workers had been a unified and militant force. But during the ban (1948–51) the Congress Party union successfully penetrated the coir industry, and throughout the 1950s interunion rivalry weakened the movement (Raveendran 1989). By 1965, large manufacturers had practically vanished from the coir industry (Thomas Isaac 1982b:23). Production units with fewer than twenty workers increased from 653 in 1955 to 3,425 in 1980 (1982b). The manufacturing sector began a steady decline as its share of total coir exports fell, while the share of yarn exports, destined for factories in Europe, increased (Das 1983:281).

Because large manufacturing-shipping houses controlled the coir market through their control of transportation and access to European markets,[8] they could extract surplus from coir producers without directly controlling production. Thus when labor militancy imposed social limits on the rate of surplus extraction in large-scale factories, industrial capital withdrew in favor of merchant capital, as the organization of production regressed from the stage of factory production to cottage-industry production. The existence of a precapitalist hinterland with large reserves of surplus labor had defeated the organized power of coir factory workers and set the stage for the de-development of the manufacturing sector of the coir industry.

Though capital was successful in displacing manufacturing from the organized to the unorganized sector, it could not ultimately prevent the reemergence of class struggle. By the late 1960s, having made organizational inroads into rural manufactories, the CITU organized a series of strikes, culminating in a general strike in 1971. The state intervened to impose cost-of-living adjustments and paid holidays in small-scale establishments and the Factory Act was amended to bring coir establishments employing more than two workers within its purview. Having reasserted their organizational power, the unions allied themselves with small manufacturers and successfully lobbied the central government to have the purchase price of coir increased, a move that was resisted by the export

---

[8] In 1940 the newly formed Travancore Coir Mats and Matting Manufacturers' Association had thirty-two members who together controlled more than 80 percent of the total marketing overseas (Das 1983:254).

houses.[9] The combined effect of these interventions was to increase the viability of small-scale units and curtail the market power of the exporters (Thomas Isaac 1982a). Thus a strategic alliance of workers and small producers had challenged the power of merchant shippers to extract profits through oligopolistic pricing (Sathyamurthy 1985:360). The strategy of decentralizing production had reached its political and social limits. Once again, large-scale capital sought to reorganize production, this time by mechanizing.

The cycle of militancy and capital reconfiguration was replicated in the processing sector. Until the 1950s, the retting, extraction, and spinning of coir had not evolved beyond what has been described as an "archaic" technological and social base (Thomas Isaac 1990). Production was dominated by traders, labor was supplied on a household or casual basis by an impoverished rural population, and technology consisted of little more than simple tools. In the mid-1950s, however, the recommendations of the Minimum Wages Committee triggered local organizing efforts, and within a decade unions were actively demanding enforcement of minimum-wage legislation for spinners. The movement received a further boost from the intervention of the CITU and the formation of the CPM-led 1967 government. Workers in the processing sector participated in the general strike of 1971 and successfully disrupted the movement of coir products to shippers. Wages rapidly increased, and by 1971 the Minimum Wages Committee concluded that prevailing wages were 100 to 125 percent above the notified minimum (Thomas Isaac, Van Stuijvenberg, and Nair 1992:39). As in the case of the manufacturing sector, capital's response was to decentralize production. Some of the larger husk-beating workyards run by copra merchants were closed, and the number of spinning establishments with more than twenty workers declined precipitously (40). But it was efforts in both the manufacturing and processing sectors to mechanize production that became the focal point of conflict.

The coir industry is a classic case of underdevelopment. Although it established itself at an early stage as Kerala's dominant industry, was well integrated into the world market by the turn of the century, and was built on a solid base of artisan labor (Kerala's principal comparative advantage to this day is the high quality of spinning), its technological base has stag-

---

[9] When exporters attempted to circumvent paying the higher floor prices set by the Coir Board, the unions led joint agitations by workers and small producers. This eventually resulted in the passage of the Kerala Coir Products Price Fixation Order under the Defense of India Rules of 1975 (Thomas Isaac 1982a).

nated. With the exception of a few power looms in the larger factories and baling machines used for packaging and export of yarn, the coir industry relies entirely on handicraft technology. As the industry's most astute scholar has surmised: "[E]ach unit of coir produced is soaked with simple human labor" (Thomas Isaac 1990:4–5). The low-level technological trap into which the industry has fallen is rooted in its precapitalist relations of production. Although machine technology for defibering and weaving was available in the 1930s, the availability of an abundant supply of cheap rural labor checked any impetus toward innovation. Failed efforts by European firms to introduce power looms in the 1930s have been tied directly to the low-cost advantages of cottage production. "Rural labor was so cheap that traditional technologies out-paced large-scale mechanized production systems" (Thomas Isaac, Van Stuijvenberg, and Nair 1992: 34). In 1961 the Coir Board offered licenses to the private sector for power looms, but by the end of the decade, only one shipping company had made use of a license (43).

The impetus for mechanization thus came only as a result of the class struggles that pushed up wages in both the processing and manufacturing sectors. By the late 1960s rural entrepreneurs were introducing defibering machines,[10] and by the mid-1970s shipping interests were pushing for the introduction of power looms in the weaving sector. Fearing labor displacement, the unions resisted.[11] Violent protests broke out, in which machinery was destroyed (42). And much as with the introduction of tractors in agriculture, the state, alarmed by the social costs inherent in the technological rationalization of a traditional labor-intensive industry, banned the use of husk-beating machines in all the principal coir-producing districts in 1973. When one of the leading coir houses in Kerala proposed to set up a power-loom factory in the state, it was refused a license.[12] Subsequently, the Kerala Coconut Husks and Fibre Order of 1975 prohibited the movement of husk for processing in defibering units established in Tamil Nadu.

In addition to these direct regulatory interventions, the state actively

[10] By one estimate the number of defibering machines reached four hundred in 1971 (Pylee 1976:6).
[11] A GOK State Planning Board study (1973) estimated that complete mechanization of husk beating would displace 81,562 of the 112,000 manual workers.
[12] The proposal to introduce power looms was opposed not only by labor but by small manufactures, which had a particularly strong voice on the Coir Board. Interview with K. Sugunendran, manager of Kerala Balers, May 15, 1992, Trivandrum. The factory was ultimately set up in Tamil Nadu. Although the production workers were recruited locally, the entire managerial and clerical staff were recruited from Kerala. Wages for production workers were much lower than those in Kerala (M. Oommen 1979:149).

promoted the development of a cooperative sector in the coir industry. Unions also pushed for cooperatives to bring production under worker control, eliminate middlemen, and arrest the process of fragmentation. Though the economic performance of the cooperatives has been poor, they have raised wage levels, increased the average size of spinning and defibering units by bringing workers together in workshops, and curtailed the power of traders to manipulate prices (Varkey 1981).

Changes in the coir industry in the post-Independence period have been driven by cycles of struggle and reconfiguration. In a first iteration, capital was able to meet the challenge of organized factory workers by exploiting the uneven development of the labor movement and devolving production to the sweatshops of the unorganized sector. In abandoning direct control of production while extracting surplus through its control of markets, capital reinforced the logic of underdevelopment. A second round of labor organizing and state intervention imposed new limits (market regulation and some social protection) on capital's ability to squeeze the traditional sector. This set the stage for modernizing the industry's productive base. But negotiating such a transition proved to be socially and politically difficult. Because the coir industry has functioned as a residual employment sector providing a supplementary source of income to underemployed rural households, the social costs of modernization remain high. Moreover, struggles in the coir sector have been particularly bitter, and organized labor remains wary of giving free rein to market forces. The result has been a standoff, a new contradiction in which labor's concerted opposition to mechanization has left capital idle. Brought to a technological standstill, the coir industry in Kerala in the 1980s was in a severe crisis. Its share of world exports dropped dramatically in the face of increasing competition from Tamil Nadu and Sri Lanka and product innovation in Europe and the United States.

Unbounded Militancy: Unionization in Casual Labor Markets

If labor militancy in the cashew sector led to capital flight, and in the coir sector to capital reorganization and then stagnation, in two other important sectors of the unorganized economy—construction and headload work—it has not created internal contradictions (since capital has limited exit options) but has become a significant barrier to new investments. Labor conflict in this sector has proven particularly difficult to manage. The semipermanent or casual nature of work has made labor particularly vulnerable to market fluctuations and the often despotic power of labor contractors. Because the sector has few formalized ties of employment, there are few institutional structures for mediating conflicts.

Headload workers, known elsewhere in India as "coolies," have historically been among the most degraded, socially and economically, of all occupational groups.[13] Although physically demanding, the work is unskilled and tied to the volume of commercial activity. These conditions favored the development of spot markets in labor, with no barriers to entry, although hiring often occurred along communal or caste lines. Headload workers first organized as part of the larger political developments that came with the 1957 Communist ministry. Through the 1960s local struggles succeeded in establishing unions as bargaining units, and in the subsequent decade local unions established a "complex system of work sharing, compartmentalization of the labor market, specification of tasks and elaborate wage schedules" (Vijayasankar 1986:23). What had been a labor market embedded in patron-client relations was replaced by a web of union jurisdictions. And what had been a form of undifferentiated labor power was now carefully divided into specific skills and functions.[14] As early as the mid-1970s, negotiated wage agreements had become the norm in many large markets. Nonetheless, the sector remained highly volatile. Agreements were based strictly on local-level bargaining power and did not benefit from any legislation or institutional support. The competition for worker support among rival unions made it difficult to develop and maintain workable agreements. To complicate matters, headload workers in Kerala have a long history of serving as the muscle men (*goondas*) that are a part of every political party in India. Interunion conflicts thus often draw in local political bosses, mixing political turf battles into an already potent concoction.

In contrast to headload workers, the impetus for unionization in the construction sector came from the labor federations rather than from local forces. Until the early 1980s, unionization was largely limited to skilled craft-workers (Harilal 1986). A migrant work force and the transitory nature of construction projects made it difficult to organize workers. But as the construction industry boomed in the 1970s, so did unionization. The CITU, having specifically targeted the unorganized sector at its Kanpur Conference in 1980, launched a highly effective organizing drive, which

---

[13] The use of the term "headload worker" (*chumattu thozhilali*) is an explicit rejection of the low social status associated with the term "coolie."

[14] In a major commercial market, Vijayasankar (1986) found that the wage schedule covered 350 separate items.

was immediately copied by rival federations.[15] This initiative, as in the case of headload workers, produced intense rivalries as unions vied for control of local labor markets. But because the labor federations are less indebted to local political bosses, and in general more disciplined, construction unions have been able to develop relatively effective and stable job-sharing arrangements.[16]

Union control over labor markets and the immobility of capital have provided labor with the leverage to secure dramatic wage increases. The real wages for headload workers have increased steadily since 1964 (Vijayasankar 1986). In the mid-1980s, skilled construction workers earned wages roughly equivalent to those of factory workers while urban headload workers commanded wages that were 75 percent higher than those of factory workers (Kannan 1992:17). Considering that most of these workers are semipermanent or casual, are traditionally from lower caste groups, and are not covered by labor legislation, their wage gains are all the more exceptional.

But wage inflation has taken a toll on the wider economy. High wages in this sector have been passed on to consumers as well as to the organized sector. Fixed capital expenditures are higher in Kerala for new projects because of the high cost of transport, unloading, and construction (Kannan 1992:33). Thus while wages in the organized sector are competitive, high wage levels in the construction and headload sectors have adversely affected Kerala's investment profile. The problem, moreover, extends to the question of labor control. Not only has labor militancy been on the increase (in contrast to the decline in the organized sector), but it is also highly disruptive in nature. Headload workers have in particular developed a reputation for extortionate practices and "irresponsible" demands.[17] They can and do paralyze large markets, disrupt the flow of

[15] In Trivandrum district alone, membership increased from one thousand workers in 1981 to 13,500 in 1992. Statewide membership for the CITU construction union was 65,000 in 1992 (CITU District Office, Trivandrum).

[16] Union officials from both the INTUC and the CITU insisted that worksite negotiations between unions are no longer a source of conflict. Work is allocated according to existing local membership levels. All unions keep lists of unemployed workers and distribute jobs on a priority basis.

[17] One newspaper columnist noted that "some sections of these headload workers were holding the business community to ransom by demanding unreasonable wages and not allowing anybody else to work in their areas of operation, especially in the export processing zones and in huge godowns [warehouses] where lightning strikes brought all work to a standstill for days. Export orders have been known to be canceled as a result of expired deadlines and the entire economy of the State was affected adversely by this section of workers." *Indian Express*, Cochin, June 23, 1993.

goods, and close down factories. Construction unions will occupy a site before construction begins and demand a hiring quota. An industrialist told me that "the red flags are planted even before the foundation stone is laid." Protracted negotiations with multiple unions can delay projects for months. Construction unions also often strike to invoke the "sons of the soil" right, demanding that employment in the unit under construction be reserved to members. Such "obstructionist" practices are often cited as the major deterrent faced by prospective investors (Sankaranarayanan and Bhai 1994:312). A government task force, summarizing the findings of a survey of industrialists, concluded: "Most of the respondents were of the opinion that labor problems outside the factory, especially at the construction stage and at the time of loading and unloading constitute a serious threat that gives the wrong message to prospective entrepreneurs, more particularly to those from outside the state who are not familiar with what is called '*Attimari*.' The government may immediately address this issue on a priority basis"[18] (GOK, State Planning Board 1991b:53).

Institutional Transformation and Class Compromise

Across Kerala's largest traditional industries and casual labor markets, the extension of social rights and the formalization of wage relations have produced a standoff: capital is now confronted with limits to its absolute power, but labor must still contend with capital's power to withdraw or remain idle. If the current balance of class forces rules out a return to past configurations, it also presents the possibility of reaching new combinations. Yet, while Kerala's economic woes, and in particular its high level of unemployment, have given pro-growth strategies a new urgency, short-term interests and ongoing conflicts make reaching the necessary accommodations difficult.

For one thing, a history of labor militancy and state interventions has made capital wary of making significant investments. For another, though labor leaders and the CPM have openly embraced the need to create a more attractive investment environment by reining in militancy and relaxing their opposition to the modernization of traditional industries, the stumbling block remains the social costs that such transformations will inevitably involve. Moreover, the dispersed and unregulated nature of the unorganized sector makes it particularly difficult to organize any kind of

[18] *Attimari* traditionally referred to the skilled arranging and stacking of sacks or cartons. The term is now widely used to describe any work carried out by headload workers.

accommodation. Class compromise can not be struck directly between labor and capital. On both sides of the equation there are collective action action problems. Capital is anything but unified, often divided between merchant and industrial interests. The uneven development of the trade union movement, fierce interunion rivalries, and the sheer insecurity of employment encourages opportunism rather than cooperation. The prospects for class compromise thus rest critically on the capacity of the state to create the political and institutional conditions under which posi-tive-sum trade-offs can be negotiated. Where capital is extremely mobile, as in the cashew industry, the state's maneuverability is severely con-strained. In other sectors where labor and capital are more interdepen-dent, there is room for accommodation.

Engineering a Social Pact in the Coir Industry

The current predicament of the coir industry reflects its tortuous history. Though labor failed to block the decentralization of the industry, it did subsequently reassert some control through the cooperative movement, and then successfully resisted mechanization. In strictly economic terms, this stalemate had the makings of a classic negative-sum game. But class interests are not given by economic circumstances alone. They are lived, experienced, and, under certain conditions, learned from. Though labor's defensive posture was at odds with the industry's long-term economic via-bility, it did make imminent social and political sense for unfettered mar-kets and mechanization promised large-scale labor displacement.[19] Past struggles, moreover, had bred distrust. The dismantling of the coir factory sector had exposed the vulnerability of labor, practically destroying what had been the cradle of Kerala's trade union movement.[20]

Yet by the late 1980s, as demand for coir products fell and the crisis of the industry deepened, unions had not only endorsed a program of phased mechanization but had also accepted the need to adopt market-conform-ing measures to revitalize the industry. The outline of this modernization program, formulated as part of Kerala's eighth five-year plan, is set out in the recommendations of the Task Force on Coir Industry, appointed by

---

[19] The unions' opposition to technological innovation was, it should be noted, practically identical to the position expressed by the central planning commission team that studied the coir industry in 1978 (cited in Thomas Isaac and Raghavan 1990:4).

[20] All four union secretaries I interviewed, two from the CITU, one from the AITUC, and one from the INTUC, specifically invoked the decentralization of manufacturing as a source of continuing bitterness and distrust.

the CPM government in 1990.[21] The task force recommendations cover a wide-range of issues, from reorganization of the cooperative sector and export promotion to technological choices and product development. The recommendations reflect the emergence of a class compromise in the form of an industrial policy that balances mechanization and market deregulation with worker-retraining programs and social control through the development of the cooperative sector.

Recognizing the need to improve the industry's competitiveness, the task force called for the subsidized mechanization of spinning, husk beating, and handlooms. The choice of recommended technologies itself reflects a compromise: arguing that the most advanced technologies would provide only marginal increases in productivity while displacing a far greater number of workers, the task force settled for intermediate technologies. In the spinning sector, half of the traditional ratts were to be replaced by treadle ratts, rather than with spinning machines with self-feeding mechanisms. In the manufacturing sector, power looms, which would require extraordinary investments, were rejected in favor of semiautomatic looms. Finally, in order to compete with Tamil Nadu's expanding share of the yarn market, one hundred combing machines for the production of brown fiber and one hundred defibering machines for retted husk were to be introduced.

If one considers that well into the 1980s yarn was produced with the use of a simple spinning wheel, that power looms and defibering machines were banned, and that notwithstanding minor innovations the coir industry had not progressed beyond archaic technologies, the task force's plans for modernization are indeed ambitious. How, then, was labor's acquiescence secured?

When I asked the secretary of the INTUC—which was in effect the "opposition union" in a CPM-appointed committee—why his union had accepted modernization, he replied, "The workers have never opposed modernization. They just insist that they have a right to a share of the extra profits that result from increased production. This is the only way that we can convince workers that they have a stake in increased productivity."[22]

The plan addresses these concerns by introducing the new technologies (with the help of subsidies) primarily through the cooperative sector. Though the 423 spinning, retting, and manufacturing cooperatives operating in 1990

---

[21] The task force consisted of sixteen members, including three union officials, two large manufacturers, a representative of export interests, three officials from the cooperative sector, and six officials representing various government agencies.
[22] Interview with P. X. Gregory, secretary of the Coir Labor Union (INTUC), May 15, 1992, Alleppey.

have not performed well economically, they have provided a job-sharing mechanism, consolidated various production processes, and raised wages above those in the private sector. Most crucially, the cooperative societies are run by elected officials, generally from the ranks of the union leadership. A majority of the societies, including the powerful apex cooperative, Coirfed, are controlled by the CPM. Thus in designating the cooperative sector as the principal point of entry for new technologies, the task force institutionalized labor's capacity to capture a share of future profits.[23]

The task force's second key recommendation is the lifting of the coconut levy and price-control system, which is a particularly dramatic departure from the policies of the past. In order to stem the outflow of husks to Tamil Nadu and provide cooperative societies with husks below market prices, various levy systems had been imposed. Though price regulation was somewhat successful in restricting the movement of husks as well as breaking the trading monopolies of some of the larger husk merchants, the task force recognized that it also created artificial scarcities, resulting in a shortfall of supply to cooperative societies. The unions responded by demanding monopoly procurement, which was rejected by both Congress-led and CPM-led governments. Instead, the committee chair noted, "We would prefer to make utmost use of the market channels to ensure the collection and distribution of husks" (GOK, State Planning Board 1990a:13). Conceding in effect the need to give capital greater flexibility in allocating resources, the task force thus parted with what had been a long-standing policy orthodoxy.[24]

It is of course too early to determine whether this "social consensus project," as one task force member called it, will actually succeed. The future of the coir industry depends in large part on factors beyond the control of any class compromise.[25] In the eighth five-year plan, 400 million ru-

---

[23] In a paper coauthored by the chair of the task force, this rationale was explicitly stated: "It is important therefore that the scheme of revitalization of the coir industry would minimize the displacement of labor and ensure [that] the maximum of the increased surplus accrue to the workforce. Cooperative industrial structure is the ideal one that would ensure that the sharing of the reduced work and the increased surplus to the maximum number of workers" (Thomas Isaac and Raghavan 1990:17).

[24] In southern Kerala, where most of the coir industry is concentrated, there is a shortage of husks. In northern Kerala, it is estimated that only 15–20 percent of husks are used for industrial purposes. By removing price and regulatory restrictions on the movement of husks, market signals should provide for a more adequate supply in the south (presently being partly fulfilled by imports of fiber from Tamil Nadu).

[25] Among these are future demand for traditional coir products, development and demand for new coir products (e.g., geo-fibers), and technical and financial assistance from the center (often a sticking point in the past).

pees were allocated to the coir sector, a threefold increase over the seventh five-year-plan expenditure. By 1996, monies had been disbursed to 124 spinning units and forty-six defibering mills in the cooperative sector (GOK, *Economic Review* 1996:96). A planning board study noted in 1997 a recent "mushrooming of retted husk defibering machines" in the private sector and predicted that this part of the industry (which involves the most arduous work and has experienced localized labor shortages) would soon be fully mechanized (GOK, State Planning Board 1997a:15).

The larger point here is that after five decades of particularly acrimonious conflict, organized labor and the various fractions of capital have brokered a negotiated solution. The genesis of this compromise is located in the convergence of historically specific structural, political, and institutional developments. The limits of labor's opposition to mechanization were exposed by market forces. The technological obsolescence of coir production had eroded Kerala's monopoly position in the industry as it lost ground to Tamil Nadu and other upstart producers. As production began to decline dramatically in the 1980s, wages and total employment declined.[26] Developing a strategic response, however, required political opportunities and realignments. The Communist party's conversion to the politics of class compromise and its return to power in 1987 created the opening that reformers seized on. When the first draft of the eighth five-year plan made only timid proposals for reform of the industry, the union-sponsored Coir Workers Centre commissioned a study from researchers at the Centre for Development Studies (CDS). The CPM government then appointed the task force, nominating T. M. Thomas Isaac, a widely respected expert on the coir industry and one of the party's more influential young reformers, as its chair.[27] Party leaders also played an instrumental role in convincing the unions of the need to mechanize production.[28]

But most critically, the unions were willing to make concessions because they were in a position to negotiate with capital. Their capacity to bargain, impose wage floors, and pressure the state to regulate markets had

[26] It is noteworthy that many of the task force's recommendations address not only current problems but anticipated ones. For instance, the introduction of combing machines for the production of brown fiber is an effort to develop a competitive position in a new product market. Similarly, the introduction of treadle ratts is in response to the assumption that spinning operations—long a Kerala monopoly—will soon be taken up in Tamil Nadu.

[27] The final report bears the strong imprint of a policy framework originally elaborated in an earlier paper by Thomas Isaac and coresearcher Pyaralal Raghavan (1990).

[28] One party leader took a group of CPM union officials to Pollachi in Tamil Nadu to tour the new defibering units that are exporting fiber to Kerala. The officials came away convinced that the coir industry had little choice but to follow suit.

reversed the informalization of the industry and institutionalized labor's voice, thus creating the necessary balance of forces that underlies any negotiated settlement. Moreover, the union leadership had provided a highly decentralized and fragmented work force with a more or less coherent voice, thus creating a social partner with whom the state could coordinate the terms of modernization. That unions are playing such a critical role in implementing the modernization package (through cooperative societies as well as training and educational programs) has made the transformation much more palatable to the rank and file.

Lastly, the material, institutional, and political terrain of compromise was provided by the state. The state had actively promoted the development of a cooperative sector as a means "to avoid middle men and ensure fair return to the workers." Though the cooperative societies did not perform to expectations, providing employment to only 20 percent of the work force, they nonetheless opened a gateway through which labor could exercise some control over an ambitious modernization project. And in providing financial support for mechanization of the cooperatives, the state is in effect subsidizing the social pact. Finally, by mediating institutionally and politically between labor and the different fractions of capital, the state has helped resolve the collective action problem that characterizes any industrial policy, especially one in which the number and spectrum of interests are so great. The plan adopted for the modernization of the industry is thus a carefully negotiated one which rests on the coordinating role of the state. The authors of the task force report note: "The consensus on these issues were [*sic*] reached on the understanding that all the recommendations would be carried out as a package. Any attempt at piecemeal implementation of the recommendations, out of financial or other considerations can result in serious unrest and jeopardize the whole scheme for revitalization" (GOK, State Planning Board 1990a:vi).

Formalizing the Informal: The Institutionalization of Headload Work

By the early 1980s the militancy of headload workers had emerged as Kerala's most serious labor problem. Unrestrained militancy has not only disrupted production and pushed up the costs of construction and transportation, it has also resurrected Kerala's reputation as a "problem state." The political and economic fallout of labor militancy in this sector is particularly difficult to contain. Because the costs of labor militancy can be passed on (either to consumers or producers), the return to militancy is exceptionally high. This problem was further exacerbated by the historical peculiarities of worker mobilization. Although the headload workers' movement piggybacked on larger working-class struggles, it was rooted in local unionism, and most struggles were carried out in the marketplace. With no political mediation at a higher level and worker gains resting solely on the strength of local bargaining power, there was little uniformity in agreements and no supra-local points of reference or legitimation. The intensity of local conflicts escalated when merchants, some of whom had ties to communal organizations (Vijayasankar 1986), began to organize and to resist union demands.[29] Vijayasankar notes that "the lack of governmental legislative regulation of employment conditions and wage levels was leading to a state of anarchy in the headload labor market all over the state" (1986:120).

Class struggle had invited state intervention. It also invited action by the CPM. The militancy of local unions threatened not only the control of the CITU (to which most headload workers' union's were loosely affiliated), but also the CPM's new project of accommodation. The party had come to power in 1980 promising to bring its unions into line, but violent clashes between headload party workers and activists of the Rashtriya Swayamsevak Sangh (RSS, the paramilitary organization of the BJP Hindu fundamentalist party) and a number of highly disruptive strikes demonstrated just how little control the party had over this element of the work force. The militancy of headload workers had become a serious political liability. John even argues that the contradiction between the party's accommodative line and headload-worker militancy was the ultimate cause of the government's downfall in 1982 (1991:212).

It is in this context that the Kerala Headload Workers Act (enacted in 1980) and its companion bill, the Kerala Headload Workers (Regulation of Employment and Welfare) Scheme of 1983, were introduced to provide an institutional structure for formalizing labor relations in headload work. The scheme represents by far the most ambitious effort in India to systematically formalize wage relations and conditions of employment in the unorganized sector.[30] It is in effect an effort to institutionalize, through state

[29] The situation reached a crisis point in 1981. A six-week strike in Trichur paralyzed the town's central market, involved outbreaks of violence, and required ministerial intervention (Kerala Institute of Labor and Employment 1982:5).

[30] Following a series of strikes in Bombay, headload workers (*hamalis*) were brought under a 1968 law designed to formalize work conditions. A "milestone in the jurisprudence on informal sector labor in west India. . . . In practice, the regulation of head loaders' labor was probably fated to be short, undoubtedly linked to the absence of a strong trade union movement" (Breman 1996:190). Breman specifically notes that union involvement in Kerala has made regulation of industry more effective.

intervention and a tripartite corporatist formula, contractual relations of employment.[31]

The Act and scheme have four basic components. The first regulates conditions of work, fixing the workday at eight hours, limiting work loads (not to exceed seventy-five kg), and setting mandatory retirement at age sixty. The second greatly strengthens the mediating role of the Labour Department by creating grievance and conciliation machinery. The most novel provision here is the granting of statutory powers and binding authority to conciliation officers in settling disputes, a notable departure from the nonbinding character of conciliation in Indian industrial-relations legislation. Third, the Act establishes a broad range of welfare measures including educational grants, accident insurance, house loans, and a pension plan. Finally, and most important, the Act creates local self-governing tripartite committees charged with registering, pooling, and compensating workers.

The committees are constituted in major markets and are composed of equal numbers of Labour Department officials, union representatives, and merchants. Workers and merchants must by law register with the committee. The committee then creates pools of workers assigned to a specific junction or market. Employers request workers from the committee and deposit a week's worth of wages in advance. Each pool elects a gang leader who is responsible for maintaining work cards, which are submitted to the committee for disbursement of salary.[32] Wage levels are negotiated bilaterally and fixed for two-year periods. Agreements on bonus payments, once a source of annual conflict (usually at the approach of the Onam festival season), are also set. Mandatory contributions to the welfare fund are collected from workers and employers and the various welfare programs are administered by the committee.

Though the general provisions of the Act (registration of workers, conciliation machinery) have been in effect since 1983, the committee scheme,

[31] The scheme directly addresses the principal demand of workers in the unorganized sector. In the words of one party official: "As rightly characterized by the headload workers movement a worker in the informal sector is a *'Nathan Illatha Thozhilali,'* i.e., a worker without a master or a citizen disowned by the society. This movement had declared its primary objective to be to discover or identify a master for the headload worker." Interview with K. Vijayachandran, July 6, 1992, Ernaukulam.

[32] Wages are paid twice a month and directly deposited into bank accounts. This strategy, according to the chief executive of the fund, is intended to promote savings and discourage drinking, a problem for which headload workers are notorious. (Monthly salary payments have been advocated by many women's groups as a means of curtailing liquor consumption, which some studies have identified as the largest consumption item of low-income households.)

which involves significant organizational start-up time, has been implemented incrementally.[33] By 1994, committees had been established in forty-five urban markets, covering 16,387 workers, and the fund amounted to 74 million rupees. An additional 112 market centers were slated for coverage, and the board was formulating a new scheme to cover mostly rural and unattached headload workers. Only administrative bottlenecks, specifically the recruitment and training of administrative staff, have kept coverage from increasing more rapidly (GOK, State Planning Board 1996a:27).

At first the implementation of the schemes elicited resistance from some unions. Though the pooling system has largely been patterned after the segmented labor markets carved out by the unions, there have been fears that this institutionalization will erode the unions' capacity to enforce entry barriers. Some local union bosses also opposed the formalization of transaction costs because it effectively eliminated their brokerage fees. As one Labour Department official put it, "With this regulatory system, there is less room for unscrupulous practices." But the committee system has been aggressively promoted by the labor federations, in particular the CITU. Welfare board officers readily credit the CITU with having successfully mobilized worker support for the scheme.

From all indications, merchants have also benefitted from the scheme. Though in some markets there are reports of evasion, usually in complicity with a renegade local labor leader, the dramatic decline in conflicts, the steady supply of labor, and the regularization of pay scales have greatly reduced the uncertainties associated with the previous system. The secretary of the Ernaukulam Chamber of Commerce noted that with fixed wages, there is less room for arbitrary exactions. "Even in cases where the costs to merchants are higher [because of the 25-percent administrative and welfare levy], they still prefer the new system because it operates more smoothly."[34]

In a relatively short period of time the headload sector has progressed from a classic case of an informal, unorganized spot market in labor, embedded in paternalistic, patron-client networks, to an open, competitive, but conflict-ridden and disorganized exchange among local power groups, and finally to a formalized and bureaucratized exchange relation governed by tripartite corporatist institutions. The rationalization of this sector

[33] This account is based on interviews with the finance officer and the chief executive of the Kerala Headload Workers Board, July 14 and November 18, 1992, Ernaukulam, and on records maintained by the board.

[34] Interview with P. P. Thomas, November 20, 1992, Ernaukulam.

began with the mobilization of labor. Unorganized workers with undifferentiated skills in a surplus-labor economy were at the mercy of traders. Insofar as unions gave workers a voice, carved out segmented markets, and elaborated job definitions, they created the basis for negotiated exchange. But because the impetus for unionization came from below, and evolved in a sector with few uniformities and no institutional or legal moorings, the movement developed unevenly. In an insecure environment, exercising direct control over conditions of work through labor agitation brought immediate returns to organized workers, but at a high price to economic and political stability. This situation ultimately necessitated the intervention of the state, which through legislative and administrative reforms secured an institutional basis for formal contractual relations.

Formalization and bureaucratization have allowed for the institutionalization of labor gains while reducing transaction costs. Payoffs to intermediaries, downtime resulting from disputes, and the costs of negotiation have been replaced by a relatively streamlined administrative system. Because the scheme is entirely self-financing (all administrative costs are covered by levies), the state exchequer is spared further strain.[35] And the forced savings and deferred wages of the welfare fund guarantee the type of long-term security generally reserved for the organized sector.

State intervention has thus helped secure collective goods that were beyond the logic of the previous system of labor relations. This extension of bureaucratic authority in the headload sector should not, however, be interpreted as some ineluctable process of rationalization. The state was drawn in through its ties to organized labor, and reforms were shaped by existing arrangements. The pooling system is thus little more than an administrative revamping of the market barriers the unions had already secured. Moreover, implementation of the scheme relies entirely on the organizational capacity of the unions. The chief executive of the welfare board was categorical on this point: "There is no possible way for the Labour Department to supervise the working of the scheme at the field level. We have neither the financial nor the administrative capacity. The scheme can only work if is actually implemented by the workers."[36]

---

[35] Not all workers see the new bureaucracy as an improvement. One commented that "the entire staff are maintained with the sweat and tears of the workers." It should be pointed out that the Rs. 2,500 monthly salary of headload workers in the busier markets is significantly higher than the pay for lower division clerks.

[36] As originally designed, the labor pools were to be directly administered by staff members. This system proved too expensive, and it lacked flexibility. Elected pool leaders, acting as intermediaries between the pools and the committees, have proven to be the linchpin of the pool system.

The Kerala Headload Workers Scheme has been so successful that a government committee recommended its extension to all casual labor markets (GOK, State Planning Board 1990b). Most casual labor markets in India remain well beyond the reach of the state, but in Kerala, a general consensus has now emerged that the state's economic woes can be addressed only by institutionalizing labor's bargaining capacity and formalizing labor relations in the unorganized sector. An editorial entitled "Tempting the Investor" noted that "the State's labor problem is confined to the unorganized sector (primarily headload workers) and cannot be solved unless their demands—security of tenure, wages, welfare schemes and so on—are met."[37]

Kerala's industrial base remains backward, dominated by agro-processing and labor-intensive industries. Production is organized, for the most part, in domestic units or small rural manufactories. Technological progress has been slow. Most workers in this sector remain by any comparative standards (excepting those of the rest of India) poor. Nonetheless, in the past four decades the politicization and empowerment of the working class have exposed the social limits of the existing economic order. The forms of domination and dependence that provided capital—whether merchant or industrial—with a cheap, captive, and inexhaustible supply of labor have been directly challenged. Unionization and state intervention have transformed the balance of class power and with it the social conditions of production. Wage floors, social rights, union control over labor markets, and direct administrative intervention in product markets have all combined to curtail the ability of capital to extract surplus by squeezing labor.

To fully appreciate the significance of these developments, one has but to consider the dead weight that the unorganized sector represents for India's developmental prospects. Four decades of planned development and massive public investments have created an impressive modern industrial sector. But the progress of this sector pales in comparison to the sheer size and inertia of the unorganized sector. Abysmally low wages and exploitative work conditions have taken a human toll that defies description. The economic consequences have also been severe. The failure to raise wages and increase aggregate demand for domestically produced consumer goods has dampened economic expansion. The persistence of a subsistence wage economy has also blunted any movement toward innovation and rationalization of production (Holmström 1993). As long as labor

[37] *Indian Express*, Cochin, September 22, 1992.

markets are embedded in social vulnerabilities, a cheap, fragmented, and plentiful supply of labor will continue to favor labor-sweating strategies of production. Under these circumstances, the unorganized sector will continue to swallow up the bulk of investable surplus, reproducing the logic of underdevelopment.

The demise of despotic capitalism in Kerala has not come without costs. The contradictions of labor militancy in Kerala have been particularly pronounced because uneven rates of mobilization within Kerala and uneven development in India have provided capital with a renewable lease on finding absolute forms of surplus extraction. Under these conditions, the problem of finding a material base for compromise is difficult. In the footloose cashew-processing industry, the high cost of Kerala labor will continue to result in capital flight as long as subsistence-level wages prevail in Tamil Nadu. The problem of capital flight in the coir industry is less acute given Kerala's locational advantages. But social limits to exploitation and increasingly competitive market conditions have triggered the inexorable decline of the traditional handicraft production system. Modernization has become socially and economically imperative.

If the material conditions of the unorganized sector provide only a very narrow margin for accommodating labor's demands while maintaining competitiveness, emerging institutional and political arrangements in Kerala have made it possible to work within that margin. At the all-India level, institutional conditions in the unorganized sector could not be less inviting of class compromise or a managed transition. Employment conditions are informal, semipermanent, and subject to severe market fluctuations. Both capital and labor are fragmented, with the later being completely disorganized. In Kerala, however, unions have provided labor a degree of unity and bargaining power, confronting capital with a collective agent. Political pressure from the labor movement has paved the way for state penetration, leading to the formalization, through bureaucratic and administrative intervention, of employment relations. The unorganized sector in Kerala is thus no longer constituted of fragmented workers tied to employment through patron-client relations or traditional forms of social domination, but of formal interest groups whose interactions are now in large part framed by the authority of a rational-legal state.

The unorganized sector has thus been formalized, not as a result of some immutable logic of capital or bureaucratic rationalization, but as a result of working-class struggles demanding the extension of democratic rights—of both citizen and worker—to all sections of society. In this respect, the case of Kerala confirms the claim of Portes and Castells that the boundaries of the informal are socially and historically constituted, evolving "along the borders of social struggles" (1989:27), and it provides an illustration of how democratic social pacts can effectively reverse the trend toward informalization that has been observed in Latin America and Africa (Portes and Schauffler, 1993; Meagher 1995).

7

Accumulationist Strategies: The Decline of Militancy in the Organized Factory Sector

At first glance, the organized factory sector offers the greatest opportunities for class compromise. In contrast to the unorganized sector, players on both sides are more likely to be capable of aggregating their interests. More permanent and formal conditions of employment increase the state's capacity for mediating conflicts. The higher proportion of capital (and technology) enlarges the material basis for class compromise. And because labor is especially dependent on continued investment, and capital in turn depends on skilled labor and shop-floor cooperation, the interdependency of class interests is pronounced and the returns to coordination are high.

But there are also significant obstacles to class compromise, particularly in an industrially underdeveloped economy. Because the industrial base is poorly developed and the local business class weak, industrial development in Kerala depends on attracting national and foreign investors. This need poses two collective action problems. It requires making concessions in the present to secure uncertain returns in the future, and it requires securing the cooperation of a segment of the labor force that is already relatively well off and well protected in order to extend the benefits of industrial growth to other segments of the work force. The task of attracting private capital to Kerala is especially daunting. The presence of a powerful Communist Party and labor's near-mythical reputation for militancy have kept investors at bay. "Labour recalcitrance," a typical editorial noted, "has come to be regarded as the biggest hurdle to industrialization in the State."[1] Indeed, why would capital invest in a state in which labor is so

---

[1] *Indian Express*, Cochin, September 10, 1992.

well organized and so politically influential, when other Indian states offer a far more docile labor force?

In this chapter I explore these questions by developing two general arguments. First, labor militancy in this sector, in contrast to the unorganized sector, has not been a direct cause of slow growth. Independently of class dynamics, a number of structural and historical factors have contributed to Kerala's sluggish industrialization. And though there is indeed a relationship between high levels of militancy and low levels of investment, the relationship is not a direct trade-off between wages and profits. Capital has stayed away because in India it remains fundamentally conservative, paternalistic, and risk-averse—disinclined to cope with organized workers even when profits can be made.

Second, despite the obstacles noted above, the past decade has witnessed the emergence of class compromise. As one State Planning Board document recently declared, "the era of militancy has come to an end." In its place has emerged an industrial-relations system that not only has demonstrated a capacity to effectively mediate industrial disputes, but also, by encouraging collective bargaining, has laid the institutional basis for forging class compromises. Concretely, these institutional developments have resulted in a dramatic decline in militancy and an increase in long-term wage agreements. A stable labor front based on the coordination of class interests, coupled with the most highly skilled work force in the subcontinent, has seen Kerala's investment profile improve significantly in the 1990s.

The Causes of Industrial Backwardness

By national standards, Kerala's industrial economy is underdeveloped. In 1994–95 Kerala contributed only 2.45 percent of national industrial production, well below its 3.4 percent share of population. Its per capita net value added in the manufacturing sector in 1992–93 was only 74 percent of the national average, though it did rank ahead of six of the fourteen major industrial states (CMIE 1996:tab. 15). Moreover, the state's industrial base is lopsided, with the bulk of industries located in low-value-added industries. Much of Kerala's industrial backwardness can be attributed to historical and structural factors.

Kerala has been described as a classic colonial enclave economy (M. Pillai and Shanta 1997:9). As late as 1959, industry was dominated by traditional industries, with the food-processing, beedi, cotton-weaving, coir, and ceramics industries accounting for 79 percent of the work force

(Thomas Isaac and Tharakan 1987:45). The dominance of merchant capital, a large supply of cheap labor, and the state's natural resource base of high-value agricultural commodities favored extractive over productive patterns of investment (Thomas Isaac and Tharakan 1987). During the nineteenth century, British capital transformed Kerala into a major supplier of primary materials by developing the plantation economy (tea, coffee, and rubber), and until the late 1940s manufacturing remained largely confined to export-oriented agro-processing industries dominated by European merchant capital. Though indigenous trading groups prospered with commercialization, the formation of a local bourgeoisie was stymied by the monopoly of European interests over export trade and by the socially fragmental character of Kerala's economic elite. The landed Hindu castes were parasitic rent-extractors, and the commercially oriented Syrian Christians concentrated their economic activities in the banking and plantation sectors. Thus, in contrast to the caste-based business groups that emerged throughout India in the nineteenth century, at the time of Independence no social group in Kerala was predisposed to take on the mantle of an industrializing bourgeoisie. Furthermore, Kerala has always been on the geographic and economic periphery of the national market. The spatial character of industrial development in India has been extremely skewed. Private industrial capital has been largely controlled by caste communities with close social and cultural ties to historic growth centers. Modern industrial production is highly concentrated in core metropolises. In 1992–93, the three states of Maharashtra, Gujarat, and Tamil Nadu alone accounted for over 43 percent of the India's total manufactured output. Kerala's skewed industrial profile (heavy on agro-processing, low on engineering industries) and its distance from national markets have been tied to adverse agglomeration and linkage effects (Subrahmanian and Pillai 1986).[2] The steady flow of Gulf remittances since the mid-1970s stimulated consumption for largely out-of-state goods and drew capital into speculative activities and quick-return investments in the service sector, including construction and a booming entertainment business (Kannan 1990a; P. Nair and Pillai 1994).[3]

[2] The example of rubber is telling. Despite producing 90 percent of the country's natural rubber, Kerala has captured only a negligible share of the industry's forward linkages. Although labor and capital productivity levels in rubber-based industries in Kerala are more than competitive, the bulk of value-added production is concentrated in Maharashtra, Tamil Nadu, and West Bengal (T. George and Joseph 1992).
[3] The adverse economic effects of the "post-office" economy appear in its inverse correlation with growth cycles. Remittances reached a peak between the late 1970s and mid-1980s—a period of stagnant growth—and their recent declines correspond to a period of fairly vigorous growth (for a summary of studies of remittances see Ramachandran 1996:219–20).

The pace of industrial growth in Kerala has been uneven, and has moved in cycles counter to the national pattern. Table 6 provides summary figures (in constant prices) for growth in the manufacturing (organized and unorganized) and registered factory sectors. The most striking pattern is the reversal of the 1965–75 trend, when Kerala outperformed India. The anemic 1.7 percent growth rate of the manufacturing sector during 1975–85 spawned a veritable boom in studies of Kerala's industrial "stagnation" and led many commentators to conclude that the contradictions of Kerala's redistributive path of development had come home to roost.[4] The problem certainly cannot be tied to the pattern of public expenditures. Public capital investments have been high. Kerala today has the largest number of public-sector units in the country. And Kerala's infrastructure—power supply, transportation, and communications—is among the best in India.[5] In dissecting the problem of industrial stagnation, analysts have focused on the labor question.

To what extent did labor militancy contribute to this period of industrial decline and more generally to Kerala's low level of industrial development? The most obvious link would of course be the cost of labor, but a number of studies have explicitly discredited the high-wage argument. Wages in Kerala's organized factory sector in 1986–87 were only 86 percent of the national figure.[6] Even taking into account the high proportion of low-wage processing industries (especially cashew), Subrahmanian (1990) found that factory wages in Kerala were on average marginally lower than for India and in contrast to agriculture were noticeably lower than in neighboring Tamil Nadu. Where the high-wage hypothesis does carry weight is in the unorganized sector. As we saw in Chapter 5, wages in this sector have indeed risen well above the national average, and it is interesting to note that when the 1975–85 statistics are disaggregated, the unorganized sector accounts for most of the slowdown. Thus, while the registered (factory) sector grew at a respectable 4.4 percent a year, the unregistered sector (which accounted for 55 percent of manufacturing output in 1975) limped along at .7 percent a year.[7]

Of course, the decision to invest is not a function of absolute wages but

[4] See in particular the special series entitled "Kerala Economy at the Crossroads?" (Kannan 1990a) that appeared in *Economic and Political Weekly*, September 1–8 and September 15, 1990. For studies that specifically draw a link between industrial decline and labor militancy see Raj 1991, Sankaranarayanan and Bhai 1994, and Prakash 1994.

[5] On the CMIE's infrastructure index (1991) Kerala ranks behind only Punjab and Haryana, and is comfortably ahead of major industrial states such as Gujarat and Maharashtra.

[6] GOI, *Annual Survey of Industries* 1986–87.

[7] Calculated from GOK, *Statistics for Planning* 1988:S2.

TABLE 6. Percentage growth in manufacturing and registered factory sectors, Kerala and India.

	Kerala		India	
	Registered	Manufacturing	Registered	Manufacturing
1965–75	4.7	6.8	3.4	3.6
1975–85	4.4	1.7	6.7	5.8
1985–93	5.8	5.9	5.6	5.5

Sources: For Kerala: various issues of *Economic Review* and *Statistics for Planning.* For India: CMIE, *India's Industrial Sector* 1996:table 5.
Note: All figures are annual compounded growth rates.

of the ratio of wages to productivity. Productivity is notoriously difficult to define and measure. In India there is only one reliable data source, the Annual Survey of Industries (ASI). Using this data, one can make a case that levels of productivity growth have been somewhat higher in Kerala. My purpose here, however, is simply to demonstrate that in terms of the wage-productivity ratio labor in Kerala does not offer capital comparatively unfavorable terms.

In separate studies based on ASI data, Khera (1991), Arun (1992), Subrahmanian and Pillai (1986), and Subrahamanian (1990) all found that productivity growth in Kerala has been higher than for India. Between 1976 and 1987, labor productivity growth in Kerala increased annually by 6.9 percent, compared to 3.9 percent for India, and easily surpassed the growth rates of all four south Indian states (Arun 1992). In a disaggregated study of industry groups, Subrahmanian found that in 1985–86, two-thirds of Kerala industries with higher than average wages also had higher productivity (and accounted for 58 percent of total value added) and out of ninety-five industries only seventeen (accounting for 9 percent of value added) had higher wages and lower productivity when compared with India. He also found that efficiency wages (defined as the ratio of money wage to productivity) improved absolutely and comparatively between 1970–71 and 1985–86, and he concluded that "Kerala has enhanced its competitive advantage for industrial location" (1990:2055). My own calculations also point to sustained productivity growth. Between 1970 and 1993, net value added per factory worker in Kerala climbed from 66.4 percent to 84 percent of the national average. The fact that it has fluctuated significantly (reaching as high as 94.5 percent in 1985) suggests that other factors, such as supply of inputs, power, and capital, have played a large role in determining productivity.

To be sure, net value added per worker in Kerala is below the national norm, a fact that has been cited to argue that Kerala's labor force remains, in comparative terms, unproductive (Albin 1990). But this argument fails to take into account the capital composition of industry. The disproportionate weight of traditional, labor-intensive industries in Kerala depresses the amount of value added per worker. If the contribution of the food-processing sector (in which cashew processing, the largest labor-intensive industry, is located) is excluded from national and state figures, value added per factory workers in Kerala jumps from 84 to 114 percent of the national figure for 1993.[8] If not for the predominance of traditional industries then, labor productivity in Kerala would be higher than the all-India level. This observation is supported (though not proven) by responses from a cross-section of industrialists in Kerala. Interviews yielded the consensus opinion that workers in Kerala are the most skilled and productive in the country.[9]

Labor militancy in Kerala has certainly been higher and work rules more rigid than in other states, but these have arguably been compensated for by higher, or at least faster-growing, levels of productivity.[10] The balance of the evidence, then, does not support the argument that labor militancy has been the major cause of Kerala's relatively slower pace of industrial development. The strongest evidence that labor and capital within the boundaries of Kerala have reached an accommodation and are capable of generating growth is in the proverbial pudding. Just as the "stagnation" thesis was gaining acceptance, the industrial sector took off. All of the studies of industrial decline draw conclusions based on an end year—1986–87—that proved to be a low point. Kerala's industry has since recorded its highest growth rate since Independence. Between 1986–1987 and 1993–1994, the factory sector grew at an annual average of 9.8 percent, well above the national average of 5.6 percent. Though inflated by an excessively low base year, this figure certainly points to a dramatic recovery. With an index of industrial production that reached 265.3 in 1993–94 from a base of 100 in 1980–81, Kerala, according to the State

[8] Calculated from tables 15, 16, and 52 in CMIE, *India's Industrial Sector* 1996. I found almost identical results using data from the *Annual Survey of Industries* for 1987–88.

[9] I conducted eleven in-depth interviews with the chief executives or general managers of factories with a minimum of two hundred workers. This nonrandom sample included units in the textile, chemical, electronics, tire, and metals industries. The sample included three public units. Six of the respondents had managed factories in other Indian states and made explicit comparisons.

[10] An industrialist with factories in three different states made this point explicitly when he explained to me that strikes in Kerala were not a major concern because once they were settled, the higher productivity of the Kerala unit could more than adequately make up for the shortfall.

Planning Board, has achieved "a strong foundation for the systematic growth of the industrial sector" (GOK, *Economic Review* 1995:76).

Coming back to the problem of Kerala's comparative industrial under-development, the case can now be made that capital, not labor, has been the problem. The dearth of invested capital in Kerala is acute. In 1987, fixed capital per worker amounted to 69.2 percent of the national aver-age, in contrast to value added per worker that was 91.4 percent of the national figure.[11] The problem has worsened since the 1970s and appears to be the most obvious cause of the "stagnation decade." Until recently, public capital has driven industrial growth in India, and Kerala's share of investments from the central sector have been in a free fall, dropping from 3.24 percent in 1975 to 1.29 percent in 1992 (GOK, *Economic Re-view* 1995). Private capital has amounted to little more than a trickle, contributing only 4 percent of the total investment in manufacturing in 1984 (CMIE, *Shape of Things to Come* 1984). In one factory manager's words, "Kerala has the most industrial worker, but the least industrial-ized state."

Thus we come back to the problem of labor militancy. Whatever its real effects on profitability, the *perceived* effects have been pronounced. Though militancy declined dramatically throughout the 1980s, Kerala continues to suffer an image problem. Until 1992, the Securities and Ex-change Board of India required that all companies based in Kerala identify labor as one of the "risk factors" in advertising new public issues. A gov-ernment task force in 1991 noted that "although the labour situation has dramatically improved, the state has to resort to a major publicity cam-paign to dispel the historically rooted apprehension about Kerala as a state prone to labour disputes" (GOK, State Planning Board 1991b:53). Based on a survey of industrialists from outside Kerala, Mani found that "the fear of the militant nature of trade unions" was the most important deterrent to investing in Kerala (1996:2324). In sum, Communist govern-ments and three decades of organized class struggle have created the com-mon perception, routinely aired in the media, that Kerala workers are the most militant, the most assertive, and the least pliable in India. "They know their rights, but not their duties" was the rather typical assessment of one textile chief executive. Given the paternalistic and highly traditional character of Indian management, and the wide availability throughout the country of less organized and less politicized workers, it follows that In-dian capital would shy away from Kerala. That the problem in this sense is more political than economic is certainly the consensus view in policy

[11] Calculated from the *Annual Survey of Industries*.

l circles in Kerala and has become the guiding assumption be-
to reform industrial relations.

Class Compromise and the Industrial-relations Regime

The organized factory sector in India has been described as an "island of privilege." India's post-Independence factory workers have generally enjoyed more legislated protection and political patronage than most industrial working classes at comparative stages of economic development. Because units in this sector fall under the control of either the state or monopoly capital, they have been sheltered from market competition. Jalan estimates that there are no less than one hundred regulations at the central and state levels that directly or indirectly regulate the employment and dismissal of workers (1991:85). Large-scale retrenchment is all but ruled out by a policy of rescuing "sick" units. In the absence of hard budget constraints, moreover, the logic of administrated wages that prevails in the civil service has been extended to public- and private-sector industries. Furthermore, unions in the organized sector have benefited from extensive political patronage. Every major political party sponsors its own union federation, and party leaders often build a political base through their trade union activities. Unions are also important contributors to party war chests and provide the foot soldiers for political protests and campaigns. For all their political clout however, workers in the organized sector have not built a strong labor movement. Though the trade union movement has demonstrated a capacity to engage in militant action and has translated its mobilizational power into support from political elites, the movement as a whole has failed to coalesce organizationally and politically. Organized labor has not significantly influenced development policy nor successfully expanded labor legislation or welfare measures to other sectors. In contrast to the success with which European labor movements sponsored labor parties, or the successes of the South African or Brazilian industrial unions in moving from trade unionism to the broader agenda of what Seidman (1994) calls "social movement unionism," the Indian trade union movement remains economistic in its outlook and fragmented in its structure.

At the heart of this problem are the insularity of the organized labor movement and the weak impulse of class politics. As we have seen, the organized sector remains small, accounting for only 9.3 percent of the total work force. Workers in registered factories account for only 2.9 percent of the total work force and only 29 percent of all manufacturing workers (see

table 5). Given this structural weakness and the threat posed by the existence of vast reserves of unskilled labor, "organized labor has elected to
follow the path of least resistance, to work with the conscious and acces-
sible rather than with vulnerable and dependent unskilled laborers in industry and agriculture" (Rudolph and Rudolph 1987:268). This timidity
is compounded by political factors. The most influential union federation
in India is the Congress Party–affiliated INTUC, a federation that has entrenched itself on the strength of state patronage rather than by organizing
the working class. Congress Party governments have consistently opposed
secret balloting and majority unionism out of fear that INTUC unions
would be displaced by the more activist left-wing unions (Chatterji
1980:10). In keeping with the Congress Party's accommodative politics,
the INTUC has downplayed class struggle and hard bargaining by supporting a strong role for the state and by consistently rejecting legislative
efforts to encourage bilateral collective bargaining (Bhowmik 1996).

The emergence of class politics has been further stifled by a state-dominated industrial-relations system that has fostered what Lloyd and Susan
Rudolph (1987) call "involuted pluralism." Industrial-relations legislation, fashioned by a state bent on securing rapid industrial development
and maintaining industrial peace, heavily favors "state controlled compulsory procedures rather than open-ended bargaining among interested parties" (1987:270). The result is that "state policy has created a legal and
procedural environment that encourages unions to depend for recognition
and benefits on government and management more than on their membership and the capacity to represent its interests" (273). This dependence on
the state, coupled with trade union laws that grant equal legal status to
any registered union (for which only ten members are required), has fueled
multiunionism (there were eleven national federations at last count) and
has given strategic power to union bosses acting more as brokers—strategically placed between their membership, management, and the state—
than as organizers. With no provisions for authorizing a majority bargaining agent, "employers usually have to deal with those who shout the
loudest" (Ramaswamy 1983:978).

The politics of fragmented incorporation and appeasement, which have
prevailed over the more classic industrial-relations model of mobilization
and regulated conflict, have created an unstable labor climate. The Emergency of 1975–77 was in large part a response to a sudden upsurge of organized labor militancy, and the volume of strikes and lockouts in the
1980s was much higher than in the 1970s. Both Ramaswamy (1983) and
the Rudolphs (1987) note that labor-management relations in general
have become increasingly chaotic. Pervasive state guidance and control,

the Rudolphs conclude, have "shortcircuited the development of responsible representation and bargaining by denying or obfuscating real conflicts of interest behind a facade of economic and administrative rationality. The failure of collective bargaining and regulated conflict to strengthen industrial democracy and the further narrowing of the right to strike will continue to drive conflicts of interests among employees, employers, and the state into the streets" (1987:271–72).

The organizational weakness of unions, argues Ramaswamy (1983), has only encouraged management to further rely on paternalistic relations or compliant in-house unions—often affiliated to the local ruling party— to maintain labor peace. This form of passive compromise has relied on co-optive short-term strategies and thus has failed to develop the institutional basis for concretely mediating interests. Compromises imposed from above have failed to secure worker loyalty, and in the hyperpluralistic environment of Indian industrial relations this failure has only exacerbated opportunistic union-switching. In this thinly institutionalized environment unions compete for membership loyalty by upping the ante and routinely violating negotiated agreements. To make matters worse, the problem of fragmentation (which the Rudolphs contrast to the "oligopolistic" forms of representation that characterize the stronger European labor movements) has of late been further aggravated by the rise of nativist and communal unions. The regional chauvinist Shiv Sena Party has muscled its way, with the help of organized crime, into the Bombay labor scene, once a Communist stronghold (Heuze 1990), and reports in the Indian press suggest that the fastest-growing labor federation in the country is the Hindu nationalist BJP-affiliated Bharatiya Mazdoor Sangh.

In contrast, the circumstances of the birth of Kerala's labor movement created, as we saw in Chapter 5, a highly politicized form of mobilization, squarely rooted in the politics of class struggle. Repeated cycles of militancy, fueled in particular by competition between the CPI and the CPM, consolidated the class character of the movement. Precisely because the terms of conflict were class-based, the labor movement in Kerala did not become dependent on the hyperpluralistic framework of Indian industrial relations. Conflicts between labor and management became the object of hard bargaining rather than backroom deal-making and patronage. At the same time, because the state found itself confronted with organized demands that could not be co-opted or channeled into the legalism of compulsory adjudication, intervention took the form of "facilitating joint consultation and joint regulation," the pillars of collective bargaining (K. Nair 1994). The effective representation of class interests and concerted state action institutionalized a framework that encouraged compromise over co-optation and provided a fulcrum for aggregation and regulated conflict rather than involution. Thus, as early as 1973, K. Ramachandran Nair, the most noted scholar of industrial relations in Kerala, wrote: "Organized trade union activity at the level of the undertaking seems to have been reduced considerably in recent years due to the emergence of industry-wide conciliation, joint consultations and negotiated settlements. For instance, major issues like standardization of wages, D. A., bonus, gratuity etc., are settled mostly through centralized negotiations" (1973:131).

Kerala has certainly not been spared the problems of multiunionism that flow from the "involuted pluralism" of national labor legislation, but a professionalized union leadership with strong ties to political parties has minimized the influence of self-styled "broker" unionism. In addition, despotic or paternalistic labor regimes have been vitiated by shop-floor militancy, a literate and highly politicized work force, and the subordination of communal and caste interests to class-based solidarity. This balance of forces has ruled out co-optive strategies in favor of a more adversarial climate in which conflict resolution has perforce become dependent on developing effective bargaining relations. The chief executive of a large manufacturing concern in Kerala, with ten years experience in Bombay, drew the comparison with the rest of India explicitly: "In the north, management is concerned with inventories and accounting. They don't understand industrial relations because they are used to getting their way with unions. When there is a problem with unions, they just fire or buy off the leader. Such practices are impossible in Kerala. In Kerala you have to adopt modern management techniques."[12]

Thus, in contrast to the forms of state corporatism that often characterize the relationship of the state to organized labor in developing countries, unions in Kerala, born of political mobilization, have maintained their organizational autonomy. While the Indian state has obfuscated class conflicts, the state in Kerala has condensed them. The role played by IRCs is a case in point. The committees, which cover nineteen industries in all, were instituted in explicit recognition of the futility of imposing agreements from above in a climate of highly antagonistic class relations. They now have a long track record of brokering agreements on wages, bonuses, working conditions, and welfare plans, and they have also played a critical role in preempting strikes (K. Nair 1973, 1994). The overall effect has been to emphasize voluntarily negotiated settlements over the compulsory adjudication of the Indian industrial-relations system. The Indian state took the initiative of controlling labor by encouraging pluralism. In Ker-

[12] Interview with P. V. S. Namboodiripad, Apollo Tyres, November 26, 1992.

ala, state intervention was a response to organized conflict, and the institutional forms that emerged were attuned to managing, rather than demobilizing, class interests. In his most recent evaluation of Kerala's industrial relations, Nair remarks that "the remarkable degree of trade union unity and the constructive role played by the state in giving autonomy to employers and trade unions to jointly determine the terms and conditions of employment are unique features of industrial relations in Kerala that have contributed positively to the growth of collective bargaining (1994:345).

The role of the Labour Department has also been critical. Trade unions in Kerala have come to rely heavily on the conciliation role of department officials. The majority of disputes brought to the department are raised by labor, and conciliation officers are generally praised by trade unionists and management alike for their impartiality. The effectiveness of the department in mediating conflicts is reflected in the extremely low incidence of cases referred to labor tribunals or the courts. During 1987–89, of a yearly average of 9,643 disputes recorded by the department only 4 percent were referred to adjudication (there were no cases of arbitration). Thus, in contrast to the national picture in which compulsory referrals have become a crutch and a source of stalemate, the norm in Kerala is direct or mediated bargaining. Since the 1960s, moreover, there has been a marked increase in direct labor-management negotiations. During 1987–89 the Labour Department was called upon to conciliate only 24 percent of all disputes, compared to 61 percent between 1965 and 1968, and the rest were settled by bilateral agreements.[13] The brokerage role of the state has so diminished that the Labor Department in 1997 suggested to the government that its conciliation functions be reduced in favor of increasing its welfare functions, including bringing new unorganized sectors under legislative protection.

Having discussed the form, we can now examine the actual content of class compromise in the organized factory sector. Given the conventional comparative and historical points of reference for discussing class compromise, however, doing so is somewhat tricky. In the classic case of European social democracies, compromise has taken the shape of peak-level accords in which, typically, labor parties and their highly centralized labor federations negotiate income transfers and a full employment policy in exchange for wage restraint and labor discipline. In Kerala, the mechanisms for eliciting and organizing class cooperation at this level are limited. For one thing, Kerala lacks the macroeconomic policy tools and fiscal leverage

[13] GOK, *Labour Statistics at a Glance* 1991; Labour Department, Administration Report.

of a nation-state and has virtually no control over the mobility of capital. For another, the liberal-constitutional structures of the Indian legal and political system inherited from the British rule out the forms of state-sanctioned monopolistic or oligopolistic representation associated with continental European corporatism.

These obstacles notwithstanding, changes in government policy and in the strategic orientation of unions, particularly those affiliated with the CPM, do clearly point to the emergence of negotiated class compromises in Kerala's factory sector. The two most notable developments conform closely to what has generally been identified as the defining characteristics of working-class compromise, namely labor's strategic "quiescence"—to use Cameron's term (1984)—and the self-conscious embrace of increased productivity as the positive-sum basis for coordinating profits and wages. The term "negotiated compromise" is particularly appropriate since, in contrast to Latin American cases in which "corporatist patterns of interest representation . . . are frequently the consequence of political structures consciously imposed by political elites on civil society" (Stepan 1978:47), the process here begins with the mobilization of workers and finds expression through, and not outside of, democratic institutions. The state's role in mediating conflicts between capital and labor was not initiated from above, but rather emerged in response to the political imperatives of managing class struggles in a parliamentary setting. This "democratic" variant of corporatism, in which the relationship of wages to profits is subject to organized mediation among state, labor, and capital, bears another important similarity to European social democracy. The growth strategy undergirding class compromise specifically seeks to build on the comparative advantages in labor productivity and social organization that reside in the democratic welfare state: advanced human-capital resources and a highly developed institutional capacity for fostering cooperative labor-management relations.

The quiescence of labor—or more correctly its strategic withholding of militancy—is reflected directly in the decline of strike activity as well as in the increase in negotiated long-term agreements. As table 7 shows, on all the key measures of militancy—numbers of strikes, workers involved, and man-days (the government term) lost—there has been a notable decline since the 1970s. Moreover, if one excludes the years of the Emergency (1975–76), during which industrial actions were severely restricted, the yearly average of man-days lost in the 1970s was actually much higher at 1.7 million, making the figure of the 1990s (.9 million) all the more significant. This decline, it should be emphasized, has occurred against the

TABLE 7. Labor militancy in Kerala, annual averages.

	Strikes	Workers Involved	Man-days Lost
1971–80	309	136,386	1,332,562
1980–90	133	78,845	1,180,325
1990–96	44	56,738	908,231

Source: GOK, Labour Department, Administration Report (annual).

backdrop of ever higher levels of unionization.[14] The comparative picture is also telling. Throughout the 1970s Kerala had the distinction of ranking only behind West Bengal in total number of man-days lost (M. Kumar 1989); the three-year average of 1990–92 places it ninth out of fourteen major states.[15]

To these quantitative measures of declining militancy—which should be treated with caution because some smaller strikes go unreported and other forms of industrial action are unaccounted for—can be added the observations of labor officials, union leaders, industrialists, and students of labor relations. In a survey of businessmen and representatives of industry associations conducted by the State Planning Board, the vast majority agreed that the industrial climate in Kerala has improved (1991b:51). Of the eleven chief executives I interviewed, ten categorically asserted that labor militancy in the 1980s and early 1990s had noticeably declined. Although interunion conflicts were cited as an ongoing problem, the modal opinion was that unions had become more predictable and reliable. None of the respondents reported a problem with spontaneous job actions. Every strike reported over the previous five-year period (1987–92) was duly notified and carried out in conjunction with the renegotiation of long-term contracts.

Trade union leaders are no less categorical. S. C. S. Menon, the most prominent independent trade union leader in Kerala and a forty-two year veteran of the movement, notes that ever since the 1981–82 Left Democratic Frout government "tamed the unions," the Cochin-Ernaukulam industrial belt (where the majority of Kerala's large manufacturing units are located) has been a model of industrial peace. The president of over nine large factory unions in the area, Menon added that industrial relations have become so routinized that unions now rarely call on the Labour Department for conciliation.[16] Clearly, because labor has politically and insti-

[14] Between 1975–76 and 1991, the number of registered unions increased from 4,491 to 7,998 (GOK, Labour Department, Administration Report).
[15] Calculated from CMIE, *Basic Statistics*, vol. 2, 1993:tab. 8.10.
[16] Interview, November 12, 1992, Ernaukulam.

tutionally secured the right and the power to bargain with capital, militancy has lost much of its strategic saliency. The president of the CITU, T. N. Ravindranath, who publicly took issue with the CPM ministry's capital-friendly industrial policy in 1988, asserted that the "principle that wages and bonuses have to be negotiated is widely accepted. The phase of militancy is over."[17] Equally telling has been the determination of the political establishment to publicize the decline in militancy. The last two governments have gone to great pains to advertise Kerala's "peaceful" labor front.[18]

The decline in militancy is closely tied to the increasingly common practice of negotiating long-term labor-management agreements, which now routinely include bonus schemes linked to productivity. The question of bonuses has been the most explosive source of industrial conflict in Kerala. Legislation passed in 1946 guaranteed a minimum bonus of 4 percent of yearly wages, but set no ceiling. In the climate of intense distrust that prevailed between labor and management, bonus demands became the focal point of conflict, a critical test of forces fueled by the one-upmanship of interunion rivalry. The bonus question was also ideologically loaded. In the dominant Marxist discourse of the trade unions, profits were equated with exploitation, and bonuses became the means through which workers could secure their "rightful" share of surplus. In 1962–63, 121 of 141 work stoppages were precipitated by the bonus issue (K. Nair 1973:85). The labor process itself was also a contested issue. Unions demanded and for the most part secured work rules and opposed efforts to increase productivity. The idea of tying wages to performance was specifically rejected because, as one prominent union leader remarked, it "would result in the workers working themselves out on the jobs" (S. Menon ca. 1979).

A political climate of class struggle did not rule out factory-level compromises, however. As early as 1957, following a protracted strike, unions and management at the Indian Aluminum Company agreed to the first long-term agreement in the state that included a productivity-linked monthly bonus scheme. Similar agreements were soon adopted in other factories, and by the mid-1970s most large factories in the Cochin-Ernaukulam industrial belt had long-term agreements with either monthly

[17] Interview, November 22, 1992, Ernaukulam.
[18] CPM's chief minister, E. K. Nayanar, having noted the recent period of labor peace, said to a conference of industrialists in Bombay, "[L]et us work together on the principles of fair wages and fair profits," and he reassured prospective investors that "our Labour Department would act swiftly in case of any dispute" (cited in Herring 1991a:723).

or yearly productivity-linked bonus schemes.[19] Reviewing the state of industrial relations in Kerala at the time, Nair concluded that "in no other state in India are there so many long-term collective bargaining agreements operating so successfully as in Kerala" (1973:391). By the 1990s, Labour Department policy was to encourage the signing of five-year agreements and to refuse to conciliate agreements that did not have productivity clauses.

The degree to which these institutions have helped underscore the basis for formal coordination of interests is reflected in the sheer detail, complexity, and comprehensiveness of long-term agreements.[20] The standard agreement covers not only basic pay scales and bonuses, but also work rules, grievance procedures, and a wide array of benefits. The actual document, which is drawn up with the assistance of a Labour Department officer, often represents the culmination of months of careful negotiation. As both sides are determined to avoid the referral of disputes to arbitration, agreements are carefully worded to facilitate voluntary conciliation. Labour Department officials I interviewed noted that the success of these agreements was in large part facilitated by the bargaining skills of professionalized union leaders who are armed with intimate knowledge of the businesses' financial workings that is routinely provided by unionized company accountants.

The significance of these agreements is twofold. First, they have dramatically reduced the uncertainty and distrust that have been the root cause of the more spontaneous forms of labor agitation. With bonus incentive schemes fixed for a three- to five-year period and work rules carefully defined, there is less room for friction between management and labor. There is also less room for interunion rivalry. Labour Department officials report a significant drop in go-slow tactics, wildcat strikes, and other forms of shop-floor conflict. They also note that whereas national legislation still has no provisions for compulsory recognition of majority unions as bargaining agents, multiunionism in Kerala has been curbed by a widespread

[19] At the national level, the Bonus Act (1965), while including provisions for productivity linking, ties bonuses to profits. A series of case studies and commentaries by industrialists and trade unionists collected in Suri 1981 indicates that only a small percentage of factories in India have adopted effective wage-productivity schemes. The existing practice of negotiating bonus payments on a yearly basis is generally viewed as the most common cause of industrial conflict.
[20] A scholar of industrial relations in the United States and former labor-relations manager in a Kerala textile unit described such long-term agreements as far more carefully worded than in the United States and far more comprehensive than similar agreements in other Indian states. Sarosh Kuruvilla, Cornell University, personal communication, April 1994.

informal practice of negotiating only with unions that represent more than 20 percent of workers in a given factory. Second, in tying bonuses to productivity, what was once an object of explosive class conflict has been parlayed into the basis of a cooperative class compromise.[21] S. C. S. Menon summed up the change succinctly: "The CPM had always advocated resisting capitalists. Workers were urged to not cooperate with management. Productivity increases were seen as inherently exploitative. But that philosophy has changed. Now the CPM is even educating workers about productivity."[22]

Learning Class Compromise

The decline of militancy and the widespread adoption of productivity agreements signal an important new phase in labor-capital relations in Kerala. The politics of class struggle are a thing of the past. The organized labor movement still possesses an extraordinary capacity for mobilization, and by all accounts, levels of unionization are on the rise and the degree of politicization remains high, as witnessed by the numerous one-day general strikes that have been organized to protest the center's liberalization policies. Yet by and large, workers are less inclined to strike and more inclined to cooperate with capital than in the past. How can one explain this strategic retreat from militancy?

In part, the consolidation of collective bargaining machinery has limited the arbitrary power of management and provided workers with institutional channels for redressing their grievances. The increasingly rule-bound character of labor-management relations, secured as we have seen in comprehensive long-term productivity agreements, has circumscribed the terrain of shop-floor struggles. Today, every sizable factory in Kerala has a labor relations officer, and wildcat actions are on the decline. The dynamics of factory-level compromises, however, derive for the most part from developments that have taken place in the political arena. Much as in the case of the European social democracies, compromise has been both learned and enforced through the strategic capacity and organizational re-

---

[21] The material basis for these compromises is, in comparative terms, quite large. Bonuses in Kerala represent 10.64 percent of the total wage bill, the highest percentage in all major states and significantly higher than the national average of 4.43 percent (GOI, *Indian Labour Yearbook* 1990:34). A high share of overall surplus is thus subject to direct negotiation and tied to performance.

[22] Interview, November 12, 1992, Ernaukulam.

sources of a disciplined, quasi-Leninist political party and its trade union wing.[23]

India's fragmented and paternalistic industrial-relations system has fostered economistic and unstable unions. The emphasis on compulsory adjudication (over bilateral bargaining) and the reliance on state patronage have decoupled negotiating leverage from mobilizational capacity. Rather than build strong organizations with loyal and committed followings, most trade union leaders have competed for members by inflating demands and breaking agreements. Only politically committed and ideologically cohesive unions have nurtured a more loyal and stable following, securing concessions on the strength of negotiated agreements (Ramaswamy 1983:978). Lloyd and Susan Rudolph conclude that efforts by the state to impose social order from above through a model of pluralistic representation have been a failure. Instead, they argue, India would be better served by an industrial-relations system of "regulated conflict" with a more European-like "oligopolistic pattern of interest aggregation" in which more politically oriented unions take up the interests of the working class (1987:289). One such union, they note, is the CITU, which, along with its CPI counterpart, the AITUC, is the only federation in India to have consistently opposed state corporatism in favor of bilateral collective bargaining (288).

The CITU has a substantial presence only in West Bengal, Kerala, and Tamil Nadu.[24] Judging by the percentage of factory workers who are members, it is strongest in Kerala. Its organizational strength and class-based character is best gauged by the simple fact that, having exhausted the potential for unionization in the factory sector, the CITU successfully turned to the unorganized sector. With its cohesive ideological positions, its programmatic orientation, and its close ties to the CPM, the CITU has resisted incorporation from above, thus retaining its associational autonomy and strategic capacity.

The CITU's recent conversion to the politics of class compromise is clearly tied to the lessons learned from the Communist Party's experiences

---

[23] Among the characteristics that differentiate the Swedish labor movement from its British counterpart, Pontusson emphasizes its "strategic capacity" to formulate and systematically pursue long-term policies. This capacity, he argues, is "embedded in the organizational structures of the labor movement," which include its more political, "class-oriented" unionism, the absence of factionalism within the Swedish Social Democratic Party, and the close integration of party and union (1990:58).

[24] In 1986, CITU membership was 709,708 in West Bengal, 381,522 in Kerala, and 120,042 in Tamil Nadu (CPM, *Political Organizational Report* 1989). Membership in Kerala had risen to 415,000 by 1990. *India Today*, March 15, 1990.

in the agricultural sector. In a series of commentaries in 1992 that appeared in the CPM daily, *Desabhimani*, E. M. S. Namboodiripad, while carefully applauding the wage gains made by workers, acknowledged Kerala's industrial woes and went on to endorse the practice of tying wages to productivity. Interestingly, he framed his discussion primarily around agriculture, pointing to the cooperative venture of the "labour-farmer" (*thozhilali-karshaka*) class. In 1972, the CITU explicitly rejected the idea of tying wages to productivity at its state conference. Seven years later, the federation's president, K. N. Ravindranath, elaborated the rationale for class compromise by pointing to the agrarian situation and noting that the interests of agricultural laborers and farmers could be productively reconciled (Conference of Indian Trade Unions 1979:4).

As is largely true of its agrarian counterpart, the KSKTU, the CITU has learned from the hard lessons of capital's boycott that there are structural limits to militancy. Instances of capital flight from Kerala's organized factory sector have actually been rare. The dramatic deindustrialization of West Bengal, which has long experienced the highest rate of strike activity in India, has not gone unnoticed, however.[25] Stagnant employment growth and the inadequacy of public-sector investment has led the CITU to accept the need for private investments. Though privatization is still officially opposed (a position shared by all the union federations), since 1982 the CITU has embarked on a program of commissioning studies of chronically unprofitable public-sector units and proposing specific revitalization measures. A CITU leader, R. Raghavan Pillai, succinctly identified the dilemma underlying the union's willingness to compromise with capital: "Without increasing investment and production there can be no prosperity. We don't want the redistribution of poverty."[26]

Beyond the conversion to left corporatism, the capacity of the CPM, and with it the CITU, to underwrite class compromise also resides in its ability to actually affect the behavior of the rank and file. Given the strength of shop-floor unionism and a history of often bitter struggles, labor quiescence has not been easy to come by. The rank and file, for whom militancy has secured significant economic and political dividends, have scuttled more than one agreement. Workers on the shop floor have also jealously guarded hard-won work rules, resisting efforts by management to modernize or streamline production. CITU leaders talk about the need "to educate workers about productivity" and complain about the

---

[25] From 1970–71 to 1988–89, West Bengal's share of the national output of manufacturing fell from 13.5 to 6.7 percent (CMIE, *Basic Statistics* 1993:tab. 8.6–1).
[26] Interview, April 3, 1992, Trivandrum.

difficulty of making "fair" wage demands when other unions continue to press for unrealistic gains. At its 1990 state council meeting, the CITU deplored the number of unions that violate the terms of negotiated agreements. Overall, though, the dramatic decline in militancy in recent years suggests that the federation has been successful in eliciting compliance with its new strategic line. Officials in the Labour Department were unanimous is singling out the CITU as the most disciplined of the labor federations, and its member unions as those least likely to engage in unauthorized job actions.

Class-based unionism alone does not suffice to explain why workers have forgone militancy and accepted compromise. Organized class struggle produced immediate gains, but the outcome of organized class compromise is less certain. As Przeworski writes, "There is nothing structural about the capitalist system of production that would guarantee that future interests of any particular group be satisfied. *Appropriation of profit by capitalists is a necessary but not a sufficient condition for the future realization of interests of any group.*" (1985:139–40). Under the conditions of a private-property economy, there can be no certainty that wage and other concessions made to capital will actually translate into higher future levels of investment and growth. Within the absolute boundaries set by the imperative of accumulation, it is possible, however, to reduce the degree of "uncertainty" involved in the trade-off between wages and profits. The politically hegemonic position of labor does provide some guarantees. The sheer power of the unions and the extent of protective legislation have secured a high degree of social and political control over the distribution of surplus, thus minimizing the risks involved in making concessions to capital. A leveled playing field reduces the chances of unilateral and opportunistic behavior and increases the chances of cooperation. Thus working-class organization and the collective representation of its interests have been a critical ingredient of European-style neocorporatist arrangements. As Schmitter notes, "the relevant interlocutors must be in a situation of mutual deterrence, each sufficiently capable of organized collective action to prevent the other from realizing its interests directly through social control and/or economic exploitation" (1985:35). This balance of power, however, does not establish the rules of the game.

The organized character of labor in Kerala has certainly created a situation of mutual deterrence, but it has also shaped the evolution of an industrial-relations system that has facilitated the kind of hard bargaining and the coordination of interests that reduces the uncertainty and hazards of interclass transactions. Such coordination is not given by some larger economic necessity, however. It must be concretely shaped and managed.

It must be institutionally and politically embedded. And the historical process through which this embedding took place was marked by two key patterns. First, because neither repression nor co-optation was ever a politically viable option, the state had little choice but to give institutional expression to the class power of labor, that is, create a playing field on which the threat of militancy, rather than actual militancy, would define labor's bargaining position. Second, responding to the programmatic character of the labor movement, state actions tended to facilitate what Cohen and Rogers call an "artful democratic politics of secondary associations" in which "public powers are used to encourage less factionalizing forms of secondary associations" (1992:395). The more encompassing forms of interest representation that emerged in Kerala are reflected in the extent to which the industrial-relations system favors collective bargaining between organized interest groups and tripartite mediations over the "involuted pluralism" and compulsory adjudication of the national labor scene. And as the respective positions of labor and capital have become increasingly institutionalized, formal bargaining practices have evolved and become more acceptable to both parties through iteration and the demonstration effect of success. The legitimation of industrial relations in Kerala, and more broadly of democracy, has reduced the degree of uncertainty. "In the past," remarked the manager of OEN Industries, Kerala's most successful electronics manufacturer, "labor would demand impossible bonuses. Management would offer nothing. A strike or lockout would follow. Now negotiations are over a 1- or 2-percent increase. The total bonus package is well defined and always in the 15–16-percent range. All these norms have removed items of conflict."[27]

Toward an Accumulationist Strategy of Development

In agriculture as well as industry, the CPM's stated position is that redistributive gains can no longer be sustained without increases in output. Moreover, party leaders have explicitly identified productivity as the material basis for building corporatist class alliances. The party's most prominent new theorist, T. M. Thomas Isaac, summed up the new tactical position: "The significance of the LDF [CPM-led Left Democratic Front] (1987) platform lies in the attempt to reorient the mass movements to consciously participate in a strategy for expanding the production base itself. The politics of such a reorientation lies in the realization that it is neces-

[27] Interview, November 19, 1992, Ernaukulam.

228 The Labor of Development

sary not only to defend the redistributive gains of the past but also for the continued advance of the radical forces themselves" (Thomas Isaac and Kumar 1991: 2703).

The determination of the party and its unions to secure "growth in the commodity producing sectors" through class compromise came into sharp focus during the tenure of the Left Democratic Front government (1987–91). K. R. Gouri, arguably the party's most popular leader and the architect of the aborted 1957 land reforms, was made minister of industry and charged with the task of breathing new life into Kerala's industrial development. She actively courted private capital and used her political clout to restrain the unions. Summarizing her pitch to the trade unions, Gouri said, "We [the party] explained to workers that unless they increased productivity, their industries couldn't survive. They were told they have a stake in the industry, and that more cooperation was necessary."[28] The CPM secretariat specifically called upon the working class to develop a new "work culture"[29]—the party's euphemism for labor discipline—and the government declared that "according to the new labour policy, the workers should attach as much importance to their duties and responsibilities as to their claims and demands. They alone can foster a better labour-management relations" (GOK, Public Relations Department 1987:23). The CITU echoed the ministry's policy by emphasizing the importance of worker discipline and denouncing the practice of protecting workers who violate rules as threatening "not only productivity, but the industry itself."[30] Gouri's "no-nonsense" approach was warmly welcomed by industrialists.[31]

The state's new commitment to growth-led strategies of development is reflected in a wide range of policy initiatives. The eighth five-year plan (1992–97), for example, explicitly argued that Kerala, with its high levels of social development in contrast to the rest of the country, could afford

[28] Interview, November 27, 1992, Alleppey.

[29] *Indian Express*, Ernaukulam, March 19, 1990.

[30] The new strategic line, as it has evolved, clearly originates more from the party than from the CITU. Gouri's pivotal role has a clear lineage. Her deceased husband, T. V. Thomas, was the CPI minister of industry in the 1967 United Democratic Front (UDF) government, and had earned the wrath of the CITU by advocating labor disciple and calling for more private investment. Gouri's relationship to the unions was also not without tension. The CITU in particular was opposed to her efforts to privatize a loss-making state government unit. In the end however, the minister clearly prevailed, signing important investment agreements with, among others, the Tatas and Birlas.

[31] See *India Today*, September 30, 1990. The 1987 ministry also opened a stock exchange in Cochin (currently the fastest-growing exchange in India) and established Kerala's first export-processing zone.

the luxury of no longer committing the bulk of its resources to social welfare measures. The plan also recognized the limits of state-led accumulation in a dependent subnational economy, and emphasized instead the need to attract private capital. In a break with the fixed sectoral allocations of past plans, the share of total outlay for the social services sector was reduced from 23.7 percent in the seventh five-year plan to 19.73 percent, while the allocation to industry was increased from 11.8 percent to 14.83 percent (GOK, State Planning Board 1991c: 10).

The Kerala government's *Statement of Industrial Policy* of 1991 also marked a turning point. Departing from its dirigiste days of directly sponsoring productive activities, the state committed itself to a market-nurturing strategy of industrial promotion. Noting that "our strategy for industrial development, quite simply, is to use our own limited budgetary allocation to attract as much investible resources as possible from within the State as well as outside" (GOK, Statement of Industrial Policy 1991: 4), the government introduced a package of financial incentives for new investors that included tax holidays and power subsidies. According to one study, Kerala's incentive package is currently the most competitive in south India (Mani 1996). The Kerala State Industrial Development Corporation (KSIDC) has also been given a more prominent role as the "nodal agency" for promoting medium and large industries. A byzantine maze of clearance procedures for investors has been streamlined into a "Green Channel Scheme" under the single authority of the KSIDC. In collaboration with the private-sector Tata Consultancy Services, the corporation has identified six strategic areas in which to promote investment: food processing, biotechnology, textiles, electronics hardware and software, tourism, and mineral development. Between 1990–91 and 1995–96, total financial assistance in the form of loans and share capital disbursed by the corporation increased 270 percent (GOK, KSIDC 1996).

Next to labor militancy, the most often-cited disincentive to investing in Kerala is the problem of land acquisition, followed by the problem of securing a stable power supply.[32] High population density as well as a vociferous environmental movement have made it particularly difficult to acquire large tracts of land. The state has accordingly emphasized the development of integrated industrial parks with dedicated services, including power supply. Targeted at industries with potential linkage effects, the most high-profile of these parks has been the 180-acre Technopark in

---

[32] Power supply continues to be the Achilles' heel of Indian industrialization, and Kerala is no exception. Although its power tariffs are amongst the lowest in the country, current supply meets only 81 percent of demand (GOK, *Economic Review* 1995:70).

Trivandrum, India's only fully integrated hardware and software production and research facility, and the first with a general-use earth satellite sta-
tion.[33] The success of Technopark has spawned other initiatives including
a "walk-in-and-manufacture" industrial park in Cochin, a rubber park in
Ernaukulam, a techno-industrial park for agro-processing in Malappuram, and a four-hundred-acre "textile city" in Palghat that is absorbing
outgrowth from Tamil Nadu's hosiery industry in Coimbatore. In the
hope of capitalizing on Kerala's biodiversity and its stock of scientific personnel, the state is also promoting biotechnology. In a clear break with the
past, a government task force recently rejected the idea of setting up a
state-sector unit in favor of promoting basic R and D and establishing a
biotech park with ties to university research institutes (GOK, State Planning Board 1997b). The current CPM ministry has also agressively taken
on the power supply problem by restructuring the notoriously corrupt
State Electricity Board (against the initial opposition of the CITU) and for
the first time signing agreements with the private sector to expand installed capacity.

Though it is still too early to assess the actual effects of these initiatives,
they clearly mark a watershed in the transformative role of the state. The
model of the state as demiurge, that is, surrogate capitalist directly involved in productive activities, has been quietly and unceremoniously re-
tired in favor of a model of state intervention more akin to the midwifery
functions of the East Asian developmental state (Evans 1995). From regulation and substitution of capital, the state has moved decisively in the direction of nurturing private capital by providing selective incentives and
reducing entry costs. There have been a number of determined efforts to
develop close partnerships with the private sector and adopt more competitive managerial practices. Nowhere are these trends better illustrated
than in the case of Technopark. In contrast to the political patronage and
bureaucratic micromanagement that have historically plagued state projects in Kerala, Technopark was built on time and within budget. The project's CEO was recruited from the private sector and was given carte
blanche to hire his own staff, contract for administrative services from the
private sector, solicit construction bids, and negotiate directly with construction and headload unions. Though the project has now spanned three

[33] High cost of living and infrastructure problems have reduced the attractiveness of Bangalore and Bombay, India's principal software centers. Salaries for engineering graduates in
Trivandrum are 40 percent lower than in Bangalore, and power tariffs and rents are 50–60
percent lower (Mani 1996:2327).

different governments, it has been largely free of political meddling, and key ministers, including Susheela Gopalan, a CITU leader known for her militant pro-labor positions, have played an active role in pressuring the center to relax restrictions on foreign investments.[34]

Of course Kerala is not alone in undertaking these efforts. The acceleration of liberalization in 1991 has seen all of India's states develop more capital-friendly policies in the race to attract both national and foreign capital. There are two critical differences, however. Throughout most of the country, states have only a fragmented and narrowly based labor movement to contend with and have accordingly pursued the "low-road" strategy of competitiveness by deregulating labor markets, weakening protective legislation and in general promoting the informalization of labor (Candland 1995). Because of its ties to labor, the state in Kerala is constrained to take the "high road." Most Indian states, moreover, have well-established ties to select elements of private capital. But with a history of mutual suspicion and hostility, and given the very weakness of the local bourgeoisie, the state in Kerala must develop these linkages from scratch. Thus although the shift to an accumulationist strategy has been necessitated by the constraints as well as opportunities of the logic of private investment in an increasingly open economy, the modalities of the shift have been fashioned by very different political and institutional equations and with a very different set of anticipated trade-offs.

Developing the institutional linkages and carefully calibrated forms of intervention that are the hallmark of the developmental state is not simply a matter of following a blueprint. Because the state in Kerala is accountable to a broader range of social partners than is true of most developmental states, nurturing state-capital partnerships will require painstaking negotiation and confidence-building. And as we have seen, in a market economy there are no absolute guarantees, even under the most favorable of institutional circumstances, that class compromise will result in long-term growth. Yet the political commitment by the state and the organized Left to promoting more stable labor relations, as well as the initiatives in the direction of midwifery described above, represent a significant departure from a past in which the role of the state was almost exclusively dictated by the political imperatives of social reform and accumulation strategies were entirely subordinated to redistributive demands.

[34] Interview, with G. V. Raghavan, CEO, Technopark, December 5, 1992 and August 7, 1997, Trivandrum.

Will Capital Come?

Though it is clear that *within* Kerala labor and capital have come to terms, it remains unclear whether labor's strategic concessions, the state's market-augmenting initiatives, and local human capital resources will suffice to overcome capital's historic aversion to Kerala. With a weak industrial base, Kerala's economy does not enjoy the agglomeration effects of more developed regions of the country, a problem compounded by its geographical isolation from national markets. Of even greater significance, however, are the bounded rationality and relative immobility of capital itself. Investment decisions in India are constrained by information barriers, and the lack of uniformity and transparency in the regulatory environment puts a premium on developing close ties to state officials and political brokers. Indian capital in this sense is very parochial, embedded in dense networks that are both cultural and political. Though Indian businesses have certainly become more adventurous since liberalization, the lack of ties to Kerala's political establishment and the mythical proportions that labor's militancy has assumed in the business press continue to be significant deterrents.

Since liberalization in 1991, Kerala's performance in securing investment from the private sector has been mixed. Data from the Secretariat of Industrial Assistance (May 1998) show that between August 1991 and April 1998 Kerala attracted only 1.2 percent of total private proposed investment, well below its share of population (3.4 percent). Still, this is a significant improvement over the 1980s, when Kerala consistently ranked last among all states and barely registered on the investment map. In 1984, for example, only two private projects were established, attracting a miserable Rs. 8.5 per capita compared to Rs. 214 per capita in India (CMIE, *Shape of Things to Come* 1984). Total private investment in 1984 and 1986 (no data is available for 1985) came to Rs. 1.23 billion. By contrast, in 1993 and 1994, the two most recent years for which disaggregated data are available, total private investment came to Rs. 30.6 billion.[35] In a study using KSIDC data, Mani concludes that there has "been a tremendous increase in industrial investment in the state since 1991–92" (1996:2326).

CMIE investment figures, which can be broken down by year and which include projects under implementation as well as proposed projects, provide the most disaggregated picture and reveal a sharply upward trend. In

---

[35] All figures are from CMIE, *Shape of Things to Come* (various years), and include investments proposed, announced, and under implementation.

TABLE 8. Per capita investments on hand in manufacturing sector and total economy, in current rupees.

	1990	1991	1993	1994	1995	1996	1997
India							
Manuf.	2,002	2,478	3,012	3,277	4,410	5,350	5,324
Total	3,497	4,234	6,759	8,460	10,181	12,773	13,268
Kerala							
Manuf.	931	1,552	1,278	1,586	1,931	4,172	4,379
% of India	(46)	(63)	(42)	(48)	(44)	(78)	(82)
Total	1,413	2,069	2,069	5,172	7,000	13,551	13,655
% of India	(40)	(49)	(31)	(61)	(69)	(106)	(103)

Source: CMIE, *Profile of States* 1997.
Notes: India = fourteen major industrial states. "Investments on hand" includes proposed, announced, and under implementation. Data for 1992 not available.

the first half of the decade, Kerala continued to lag behind the national average (see table 8). Since 1994, however, there has been a marked acceleration, in both absolute and relative terms, and for both total investment and manufacturing investment. In fact, in 1996 and 1997, investment levels in Kerala were slightly higher than the national average. The picture with respect to other states is also instructive. Taking a three-year average (1995–97), per capita investment on hand in Kerala was Rs. 11,402, putting it well behind the leaders, Gujarat, Karnataka, and Orissa (25,000 to 31,000), but placing it squarely in the middle of fourteen other states, alongside Andhra Pradesh (11,850) and Madhya Pradesh (11,470), and surprisingly close to Maharashtra (13,806). Kerala is of course starting from a low base point, so one must be cautious about drawing conclusions. But clearly there has been some movement, and what was a trickle in 1980s has become a stream, if not a river, in the 1990s.

The pattern of investment suggests that Kerala may have broken the deadlock in two critical respects. First, sectors in which Kerala is most likely to capitalize on its human-capital endowments appear to be doing well. The electronics sector has attracted some new investments, and is beginning to play a more dominant role in the state's economy. A survey by the State Electronics Development Commission found that in 1992–93 electronics production in the state grew by 47 percent.[36] The industry

[36] From a national market share of 2.9 percent in 1990–91, Kerala jumped to 4.3 percent in 1992–93, increasing its share of national exports from .5 to 3 percent. The production per employee in Kerala was 65 percent higher than the national average. *Hindu International Edition*, July 10, 1993.

group BPL, a leading electronics manufacturer in India, has committed to an investment package of Rs. 4.5 billion (fiberoptic terminal equipment, pagers, and so forth) for various electronics production units. In 1997, BPL's electronic equipment plant in Palghat ranked first among private companies in total sales (estimated at Rs. 8.6 billion). AMP, a Fortune 500 company, has built a totally export-oriented electronic unit in Cochin's export processing zone (EPZ). Electronics is now the largest sector in the EPZ, and exports increased by 72 percent in 1997. Software is also emerging as a growth sector. The U.S.-based Information Management Resources (IMR), a key player in India's software exports, is setting up a 300-million-rupee development and training facility. Technopark has to date attracted twenty-eight different companies including a 500-million-rupee semi-conductor plant, and a 550-million-rupee joint venture with two U.S. firms for export-oriented production of PCB copper foil and software development projects with Swedish, Swiss, and Japanese partners. Most telling, however, has been the decision by Tata Consultancy Services, which accounts for more than 50 percent of software exports in India, to set up its main software training facility, which will be the largest corporate training facility in Asia, in Trivandrum. Turnover at Technopark alone was expected to reach Rs. 1 billion in 1998.[37] Because of increased demand, three more software technology parks are now planned for Cochin, Calicut, and Cannanore.

Second, the state's efforts to attract capital in thrust sectors appears to be paying off. In addition to the success of Technopark, the state also recently signed an agreement with Tata-Lever Ltd. to build a 6.3-billion-rupee international biotechnology park designed to attract investments in the high-tech processing of marine and agricultural exports. Most critically, the state's decision to court private power providers has seen total investment in that sector jump from Rs. 8 billion in 1993 to Rs. 182 billion in 1996 (CMIE, *Profile of States* 1997).

Though Kerala continues to lag behind major industrial states, and traditional growth centers continue to attract the lion's share of capital, Kerala's investment profile has certainly improved markedly over the years. When the Indian biweekly *Business Today* conducted a survey of states in 1997, it ranked Kerala fourth (out of twenty-seven states and territories) in twenty-eight objective measures of physical and social infrastructure, labor, government, and fiscal incentives.[38] Revealingly, Kerala's ranking on the "perception" index, based on CEO interviews and using nineteen indi-

---

[37] *Frontline*, November 6, 1998.
[38] *Business Today*, December 22, 1997.

cators, was much lower at eighteen, resulting in the largest discrepancy by far between "objective" and "perception" ranks of any state. The ranking was, however, an improvement over the 1995 rank of twenty-third. Moreover, though the survey report summarized Kerala's investment profile by noting, predictably, that labor relations and minimum wages were the major "investment weaknesses," the political situation was deemed to be "remarkably stable" and the state was considered the least corrupt in the country.

The economic and institutional circumstances of the organized sector in India have proven to be quite favorable to class accommodations. As is the case in Latin America (Deyo 1987:198), workers in India's modern industrial sector, are politically privileged, economically included, and well organized. The protected markets and regulated competition of India's autarkic industrialization strategy have offered a generous material base for a high-wage, high-profit class compromise. That compromise is, however, a passive one, engineered on the strength of state patronage and protected labor markets. Class contradictions have been obfuscated and their reconciliation deferred, not negotiated. Traditional managerial practices have been left intact and productivity performance has been lackluster. Moreover, quasicorporatist structures of labor incorporation erected against a background of political pluralism have weakened the institutional hold of labor unions, resulting in increasing organizational disarray and rank-and-file restlessness. As India embarks on the uncertain path of liberalization, the industrial-relations system seems less capable than ever of coping with class conflict. The danger, as O'Donnell has argued in relation to Latin America, is that a weak state combined with economic uncertainty favors "disaggregated" strategies and "pragmatic non-solidaristic" behavior (1993). Pervasive fragmentation, the incapacity to expand beyond the organized sector, and the increasing influence of communal organizations suggests that such disaggregation is precisely what is happening to the labor movement in India.

Somewhat ironically, as a direct consequence of a long history of labor mobilization, Kerala's labor-capital relations have become institutionally embedded. The institutionalization of a formal bargaining culture, in which the rights and interests of labor and capital have been specifically recognized, has promoted class coordination. The compromises that have been struck in Kerala's factory sector are proactive, carefully negotiated around concrete class interests that have centered on the issue of productivity. In addition, working-class redistributive gains have served to stabilize and broaden the material base for class compromise.

As India continues to confront the social and economic dilemmas of capitalist development in a democratic society, social-protection legislation, the role of unions, and the size of the welfare state will inevitably become objects of contestation. If the experiences of Latin America, Africa, and Sri Lanka are any indication, liberalization will only aggravate these conflicts (Walton and Seddon 1994). In India the political entrepreneurialism born of fifty years of democratic politics has provided mechanisms for brokering intra-elite conflicts (Jenkins 1995). But in the absence of cohesive lower-class organizations, "mass politics" continues to be dominated by communalism and parochial solidarities. Varshney argues that in the national election of 1996 economic reform was a nonissue. Mass political discourse was instead dominated by "expressions of India's identity politics [which] have led to mass mobilization, insurgencies, riots, assassinations, desecrations and destructions of holy places. In popular perceptions, the significance of identities has been far greater than the implications of economic reforms" (1996:3). In this climate of political fragmentation the capacity of democratic institutions to effectively address the pressing distributional dilemmas that India faces will be severely tested. If nothing else, the institutionalization of class compromise in both the organized and unorganized sectors suggests that this is a test Kerala has already passed.

Conclusion:
The Democratic Development State

Kerala's trajectory of development has been marked by social investment and redistributive reform. As a model of what Dreze and Sen (1989) have called "support-led security," it is by no means a unique case. Sri Lanka, Costa Rica, and China are among the better-known countries in which remarkable levels of social development have been achieved largely on the strength of public intervention. For countries starting at low levels of income, the comparative evidence suggests that effective and broad-based public intervention provides a more certain and more rapid road to increasing basic human capabilities than growth-led strategies.[1] Despite these and other findings, including an increasingly large body of literature that points to the growth-enhancing effects of social investment, the paradigmatic dominance of neoliberalism and the perceived crisis of the welfare state continue to inform the view that redistribution and growth are locked in a zero-sum game. The stagnation of Kerala's economy in the 1970s and 1980s was interpreted in precisely these terms, and raised serious questions about the viability and sustainability of its developmental trajectory.

The post–World War II "golden age" of Fordism, in which increasing levels of social consumption were structurally tied to productivity-led growth, suggests that capitalism need not be a zero-sum game. If there is a lesson to be drawn from the ascendant period of European social democ-

[1] In their comparative study of the relationship between growth and social development, Dreze and Sen conclude that "given the very large 'growth equivalent' of public support, only the existence of some remarkably powerful (and negative) trade-off between public support and economic growth would seriously undermine the case for extensive involvement in public support at an early stage of development" (1989:202).

237

racy (which, whatever its much-debated current state, did underwrite sustained economic expansion for at least three generations), it is that a politically empowered working class and an interventionist state can reconcile growth with redistribution. Of course, to draw a parallel between Kerala and the European welfare states raises obvious problems of units of analysis, levels of development, and sequencing. Kerala enjoys few of the macroeconomic instruments of the nation-state. India itself remains dependent on a capitalist world economy in which it may not be condemned to peripheral status (the jury on liberalization is still out) but where the pathways out of the periphery, even in a best case scenario, remain cluttered. Moreover, in India the classic capitalist developmental sequence has been turned upside down. Democracy and the demand for distributive justice have predated industrialization and accumulation on an expanded scale. If in Europe the rise of organized labor movements raised the problem of how to make capitalism more democratic and more equitable, in Kerala the question has become how to make a redistributive democracy more conducive to accumulation.

In exploring this question, we must begin with a brief review of how redistribution has actually affected growth in Kerala. In the broadest terms, class mobilization has transformed the relations of production, uprooting precapitalist institutions, most notably landlordism and the traditional caste-based labor regime. Class mobilization has also accelerated the consolidation of institutions and governance structures that the literature of comparative political economy has long argued are necessary for modern capitalism. Such consolidation includes not only the development of a modern bureaucratic state capable of providing a generalized and predictable environment of legality and order, but also countervailing institutions that limit the self-destructive forces of the market. If the long-term effects of these structural and institutional developments are conducive to the emergence of dynamic capitalism, the immediate effects, especially as measured in growth rates, have been mixed. As much as class mobilization triggered transformations (eroding the social bases of first the precapitalist, and then the despotic labor regimes), militancy and state intervention did undoubtedly discourage investment. Much has been made of the stagnation of the economy between 1975 and 1990. Production levels have since rebounded, suggesting that the crisis had more to do with the birth pangs of a new economic order than with an intractable class stalemate. In agriculture, the cycle of crisis and recovery was clearly tied to a massive shift of land from food crops to commercial nonfood crops. Labor's bargaining capacity and social-protection schemes helped manage the costs (declining employment) of making that transition. Contrary to Moore's dictum (see p. 51), the peasantry in Kerala has not been made to pay the price of modernity. In industry, the outcome remains uncertain. But insofar as the politics of wage militancy and the dirigiste state have given way to organized class compromise and to state strategies of nurturing the market, Kerala's industrial prospects have certainly improved.

Returning to the question of the effects of redistribution, a prima facie case can be made that redistributive reforms and public expenditures represent significant investments in future growth. Building a welfare state has of course required substantial public outlays which have diverted resources from the commodity-producing sectors. But in a surplus-labor economy, where the price ratio of wages to capital is low, labor-intensive social development expenditures have a significant comparative cost advantage. Doctors and teachers come cheap in the developing world and, assuming they are used efficiently, have high marginal returns. Moreover, creating universal entitlements to health and education reduces the unit cost of providing these services and hence reduces the cost of reproducing labor power.[2] Endogenous-growth theories have highlighted the importance of basic education, and it is now widely recognized that the high growth rates of the East Asian NICs can in large measure be attributed to high levels of human capital formation, both in primary education and health (Bajpai and Sachs 1996). The consensus on India (Lewis 1995) is that its growth performance has been significantly dampened by its dismal primary education record (in 1995, 291 million adults were illiterate and forty-five million children were not receiving primary schooling). In contrast, broad-based and relatively cost-effective investments in social overheads have created Kerala's most important economic asset: a skilled, educated, and highly mobile labor force, including a large supply of postgraduate professionals. These investments have already generated significant rewards. Remittances from Malayalee workers abroad and in other Indian states are often treated as exogenous to Kerala's economy, yet they represent nothing less than a return on Kerala's most significant investment and profitable export, skilled labor.

The impact of Kerala's welfare state on social development has been sustained more by the state's efficiency than by its size. In both health and education, Kerala has consistently outspent all other Indian states, but the difference in expenditures can explain only a portion of the dramatic difference in output. Clearly, the state's delivery systems have been excep-

---

[2] Education expenditures in Kerala have fallen from a high of 37 percent of total expenditures in 1959–60 to 26.9 percent in 1992–93 (Ramachandran 1996:322). The literacy rate over this period increased from 56.8 percent (1961) to 89.8 percent (1991).

tionally proficient by the standards of the subcontinent (Dreze and Gazdar 1996; Ramachandran 1996; Kannan 1990b). With respect to every significant measure of social provisioning, Kerala has outperformed all other Indian states.[3] Because it was born of sustained political mobilization from below, public intervention has been marked by the synergy of state capacity and social capital (Evans 1996; Heller 1996). The high levels of accountability that have resulted from competitive and organized participation have minimized the leakage and maximized the spread of public expenditures.[4] The point here is that much of Kerala's developmental success can be explained by good governance and high levels of social capital, resources that, far from infringing on economic efficiency, are now generally seen as essential to sustaining economic activity.[5] Kerala's current challenge of harnessing these resources to a project of accumulation pales in comparison to the challenge of redressing the abysmally low rates of social development that continue to plague the Indian subcontinent.

Having made a case for both the immediate and potential positive economic spillover of redistribution, I now return to formulating a more general critique of economistic and zero-sum formulations of the growth-versus-equity debate. There have been two fundamental critiques of the market as a self-regulating system of exchange. Economic sociologists and economic historians have argued that in order for markets to work at all they must be embedded in social structures and enabling institutions. Marxists have argued that markets are structured by the power relations among classes, and that even where the labor form is fully commodified, labor's share of the social surplus is fixed by the rate of what Marx called

[3] Three telling Kerala indicators compared to South India (which has outperformed north India): percentage of rural female children aged 12–14 who have been enrolled in school—98.2 vs. 72; per capita supply of food grains provided through the public distribution system—60 kg per year vs. 28; percentage of recent births in medical institutions—92 vs. 50 (Dreze and Gazdar 1996:tab. 6).

[4] In their study of Uttar Pradesh, where literacy rates are 25 percent for women and 49 percent for men, Dreze and Gazdar found that primary education suffers from endemic teacher and student absenteeism, interference by local landed elites, dilapidated physical structures, caste discrimination in the classroom, and hiring patterns characterized by patronage and social privilege. In Kerala, on the other hand, they found that "most primary schools there closely monitored school attendance, and contacted parents in the event where a child fails to turn up at school for a number of days. Similarly, most schools provided midday-meals, had an active parent-teacher association, and were supported by creche facilities for pre-school children" (1996:87).

[5] In contrast to Putnam's influential thesis on northern Italy (1993), where he argues that the origin of social capital lies in a distant past and has a fundamentally cultural, almost essentialist quality, social capital in Kerala has specifically political origins and indeed was born of sustained conflict.

"socially necessary labor," which is as much a function of the history of social struggles as of the forces of supply and demand. The differences in these two approaches notwithstanding, the basic point remains that even if there is a calculable "optimal trade-off" (a doubtful claim in and of itself, given the intractable problem of valuating and measuring social costs), the process of actually balancing accumulation against consumption is an inherently political one. Every trade-off between taxes and investment, wages and profits, and efficiency and justice is a socially and institutionally mediated exchange, shaped by established rules of the games, existing relationships and forces, and bounded rationality.

So in addressing the question of redistribution and growth we must begin by exploring underlying political and social configurations. Variations in either will define the realm of possible trade-offs. What distinguishes capitalism from all previous economic systems is precisely that the relationship between those who appropriate and those who produce surplus can be, within limits, positively coordinated. In precapitalist economies and in the early stages of capitalism, absolute surplus is produced through undynamic, labor-squeezing forms of extraction. The production of relative surplus value, however, is by definition based on a social organization of production that increases productivity and expands the pie. The problem, of course, is that the slicing of the pie is, a priori, a function of private property, which precludes socially organized distribution. The terms and modalities under which distribution and accumulation can be positively coordinated thus depend on the role of extramarket mechanisms.

In a democratic capitalist system, the modalities and substance of such negotiated allocations are shaped, to varying degrees, by three factors. The first concerns procedural forms of democratic representation (including the actual degree and scope of citizenship rights) through which propertyless groups are provided a say over how surplus is distributed. The second is the degree of the state's autonomy in formulating public interests and insulating itself from particularistic forms of political influence (rent-seeking), as well as its authoritative and organizational capacities to intervene effectively. The third is the organizational/political character of labor itself, especially the degree of solidarity and capacity for collective action in securing concessions either directly from capital or through the state. One can debate relative weights, but all three factors clearly play a role in determining the extent to which the trade-offs of a capitalist economic system are effectively mediated. My claim with respect to Kerala is that its institutional and power configurations—the embedded character of the state, the degree of democratization, and the hegemonic position of the working class—have all contributed to creating what is, in comparative terms, a particularly effective model for organizing class compromise.

Thus, even if one must remain cautious about economic prospects, the Kerala "model" is viable precisely because it is more capable of addressing the contradictions of development in a capitalist democracy than most developing states. First, significant redistributive gains have removed the most debilitating and potentially explosive sources of social conflict. While the oft-asserted relationship between economic insecurity and heightened ethnic or religious conflict should hardly be treated as axiomatic, the virtual absence of civic strife in Kerala is certainly tied to the encompassing nature of a welfare state that has weakened the link between economic insecurity and social position. Second, because political institutions in Kerala developed in response to a series of social movements that culminated with the articulation of class interest, ongoing distributional conflicts can be directly addressed and effectively mediated. This institutional capacity fulfills a critical requirement of negotiating the double transition. As Przeworski notes, "if reforms are to proceed under democratic conditions, distributional conflicts must be institutionalized: all groups must channel their demands through the democratic institutions and abjure other tactics" (1995:70).

The national picture provides an instructive comparison. The "centrism" of Indian politics has often been identified as the pillar of stability and order in the world's largest and most challenging democracy (Rudolph and Rudolph 1987). Yet it is precisely the weak articulation of organized class interests that not only explains India's dismal record on the social and redistributive fronts but also threatens to unravel the Indian polity (Kohli 1990:396). As formal democracy has slowly but surely eroded traditional forms of social and political authority, new social groups have been mobilized. In the absence of genuine and effective lower-class organizations, the centrifugal forces of fragmented and parochial interests have prevailed, leading to what O'Donnell (1993), in the Latin American context, has called the "disaggregation" of civil society. The "competitive demagogy" (Brass 1994:24) that characterizes mass mobilizations, the privatization of violence, the personalization of politics, the resurgence of regionalisms, and the predominance of "status injury" political claims have all been interpreted as the signs of a disintegrating polity. Because democratic institutions in India are deeply entrenched, and because democratic forms of contestation have provided elites mechanisms for settling their own differences and subordinate groups with constrained but legitimate channels for expressing their grievances, alarmist claims that democratic governance itself is at risk are clearly unwarranted. It is appropriate, however, to point to what might be called the disembodied character of the political system, one in which political processes fail to give expression to fundamental interests and the state's developmental efficacy is severely compromised. What sets Kerala apart from other Indian states and, indeed, from most developing societies is its history of organized class politics. The developmental character of the state, the success of social and redistributive reforms, and the ability of institutions and politics to manage distributional claims can all be tied to the mobilization of workers and peasants.

There is an important parallel here with European history. Luebbert concludes his comparative survey of the social origins of liberalism, fascism, and democracy in Europe by writing that:

> One of the correlates, indeed a central premise, of much development theory is that fragile societies need time to build political institutions—the institutions of the state, the economy, and parties—before mass participation can be effectively managed. The European experience suggests that this vision is flawed. It suggests, in the first place, that the institutions that are built on conditions of restricted participation will be swept away or otherwise fundamentally undermined by the participatory breakthrough. It suggests, further and even more emphatically, that stabilizing democratic institutions are only built *through* mass participation (1991:314).

If, as E. P. Thompson has so famously put it, the English working class "did not rise like the sun at an appointed time" (1963:9), but made itself, much the same can be said of the conditions under which tenants, field laborers, and factory workers formed a cohesive political force in Kerala. Class formation was the product of the timely convergence of agrarian discontent, anti-imperialism, and social reform movements. And it was given shape by the strategic interventions of a Communist Party that was a uniquely indigenous amalgamation of democratic Leninism, agrarian populism, and Indian nationalism. Broader forces also played a determinate role. Had Kerala not been a subregion of a larger national entity with parliamentary institutions that bounded political action, it is conceivable that reactionary forces would have gained the upper hand and taken Kerala the way of the reactionary dictatorships examined by Moore (1966).

If the circumstances and dynamics of mobilization are best left to historical analysis, the case of Kerala does suggest some interesting lessons about the relationship between development and lower-class mobilization. Much of the recent literature on development more or less implicitly assumes that the presence of an organized and politically empowered wage-

244 The Labor of Development

earning class is antithetical to capitalism. Neoliberal policy advocates, as well as some comparative political economists, explicitly argue that successful market reforms require strong and determined states that enjoy a high degree of insulation from popular demands. At the heart of such an equation is a strong, autonomous state that enjoys a high degree of rationality and capacity. But such states are hard to come by. As I argued in Chapter 1, the process of state formation is a long and contested one, and powerful transformative states can hardly be conjured up by the institution-building blueprints of the international development community. The developmental credentials of the East Asian states underscores the problem. Not only were they born of exceptional geopolitical circumstances and a unique historical lineage, but their transformative powers were largely a function of their authoritarian character. The so-called third wave of democratization has all but ruled out the authoritarian trajectory of rapid development.

But if democracy is now broadly seen to be a necessary part of development—a view bolstered by the increasingly influential claim that good governance is good for the economy—there is little consensus on what form democracy should take. In the neoliberal view too much democracy unleashes distributional demands and thus threatens the process of shifting allocative powers from the state to market forces. Accordingly, a case is made for pushing through reforms in a hurry or at least before the next elections (that is, before populists can mobilize support) or, alternatively, giving greater institutional autonomy to critical decision-making technocracies (strong executives, powerful central banks) or simply removing vital macroeconomic powers from sovereign control (for example IMF conditionalities). The problem here, as Przeworski and O'Donnell have so convincingly argued, is that under such autocratic policy regimes where governance is reduced to rule by decree, "society is taught that it can vote but not choose" (Przeworski 1992:56). The discrediting of popular representation, coupled with the imposition of austerity measures—both of which take place against a backdrop of pronounced socioeconomic inequalities—severely threatens the process of democratic consolidation. In sum, the delayed substantive incorporation of popular classes inevitably discredits the reform project and eventually weakens the authoritative legitimacy of the state's transformative mandate.

On what grounds, then, can one make a case for an alternative scenario, in which lower-class interests are democratically coordinated with a market-conforming project of economic transformation? The point of departure is to reiterate the central analytical focus of political economy: the role of the modern bureaucratic state and democratic institutions in mediating the social and economic crises that dynamic capitalism generates. When left unchecked, the crisis tendencies of capitalism threaten not only social stability, but also accumulation. A working equilibrium between the logic of private appropriation and the logic of social consumption is not a structural given: it is the result of historically specific struggles that congeal into various institutional configurations. There are accordingly a wide range of empirical arrangements under which hegemonic capitalism can be reproduced. But the basic model of capitalist society, in which the state and the economy are institutionally separated but functionally integrated through political processes, remains the same. In one form or another, be it through Gramsci's hegemonic state which organizes this "equilibria of forces," Przeworski's class compromises, or Offe's functionally integrated subsystems, the contradictions of capitalism are politically managed. And for all the variation in analytical emphasis, what draws these arguments together are two basic presuppositions: that the precondition for integration is a balance of class forces, that can only result from the organization of the working class, and that democracy is the actual process through which "an uncertain but limited redistribution of resources" is negotiated (Burawoy 1989:71).

Why have these perspectives on political economy not been extended to the developing world where the challenge of reconciling private property with citizenship rights looms larger than ever? Primarily, I believe, because the politics of the developing world are never treated as an autonomous variable. On the one hand, there are those theories of development that practically discount the significance of politics and the nation-state, arguing that both are subordinated to the logic of capital or the world economy. On the other hand, the theories of development that do take politics seriously tend to operate with explicit or implicit Huntingtonian assumptions: the social and economic contradictions of developing societies are so acute that political processes and institutions stand little chance of actually being effective. Whether deployed to explain what Migdal calls the weak state, the fragility of Latin American democracies, or the predatory behavior of African states, the assumption is that political disorder (the failure to aggregate) reflects the resiliency of traditional identities, dependencies, and social groupings in developing societies. The only states that are defined as "developmental" are, accordingly, authoritarian regimes that have effectively silenced this cacophony of threatened interests and new demands.

Where these views fail is in their inability to articulate a theory of social change in the developing world, and specifically to acknowledge the independent effects of patterns of social mobilization. Between the strong-state authoritarianism of the NICs and the weak-state overload of India, there are the politics of society—of social movements as well as classes-in-formation—which not only shape associational life and transform civil society, but when successfully scaled up can also restructure the relationship between state and society.

In the case of Kerala, the formative stages of democratization and mass politics coincided with class formation. The sharply delineated discourses and issues of class-based interests displaced the clientalistic logic of the class-accommodation politics of the Congress Party which in turn produced a synergistic pattern of state-society engagements. Class conflict has an affinity with the procedural logic of democracy. As Offe notes, "the conduct of class conflict teaches people (i.e., *workers vs. employers, manufacturers vs. consumers*, etc.) that they depend upon those on the other side of the interest divide with whom they are, at the same time, in conflict" (1997:6). Also class-based movements make encompassing demands, usually framed by calls for social leveling and protection from the injustices of purely market-based resource distributions (Cohen and Rogers 1992). In a poor and deeply hierarchical society, such demands are in effect public goods which not only lend themselves to the instrumentalities and the universalism of the modern bureaucratic state, but also invite the expansion of democratic legality. The cumulative effect of iterated cycles of state interventions (which produced visible and concrete results) was to legitimate the effectiveness of democratic institutions and political solutions. With the proviso that the historical protagonist was the working class rather than the bourgeoisie, this mutually reinforcing interplay of state and society recapitulates the dynamic of developmental transformation that Evans describes in his theory of the autonomous but embedded state:

> The presence of organized social groups with something to gain from transformation enhances the prospect of sustaining a transformative bureaucratic state; effective bureaucracies enhance the prospects that would-be industrialists or "incipient gentry" will become organized social groups. Conversely, a society dominated by loose-knit webs of local power holders with a vested interest in the status quo will make it harder for coherent, cohesive state apparatus to survive, but the absence of a coherent state apparatuses makes it less likely that civil society will organize itself beyond a loose web of local loyalties. (1995:41)

If the East Asian NICs represent the symbiosis of coherent capitalist class interests and the developmental state, then Kerala represents the symbiosis of coherent *lower*-class interests and a *democratic* developmental state.

For all these reasons it is necessary to go beyond the conventional typologizing of Kerala as a model of "social development" and make a stronger claim: in its degree of social and political organization, Kerala is more developed than any other Indian state, displaying, in fact, many of the institutionally formalized linkages between state and society (including a high degree of both infrastructural and authoritative state capacity) characteristic of advanced democratic-capitalist states. State and society in Kerala are now functionally articulated, compared to the disarticulation of the rest of India, where politics have become disembodied from pressing questions of social and economic reform.

The relationship between lower-class mobilization and the development of institutions and political alignments capable of "managing" the tensions of the "double transition" is illustrated by other cases of late development. In the Spanish case, Maravall (1993) has argued that the Spanish Socialist Workers Party was able to successfully push through often painful market reforms by reducing social costs through the rapid development of a welfare state that effectively institutionalized social citizenship rights. Similarly, in post-Pinochet Chile, a left-center government has secured electoral support for ongoing market reforms by redressing some of the more severe distributive inequities that resulted from Pinochet's rule and by facilitating limited but important forms of social concertation (Roberts 1997). Though analyses of the actual degree of working-class integration differ (see Hershberg 1997), the state's capacity to negotiate and manage the terms of transition have visibly increased. In both cases, the authoritative capacity of the state, including its credibility in making strategic concessions, has depended in large part on its links to working-class movements.

Important parallels can also be drawn with South Africa and, to a lesser extent, Brazil. In the 1980s, both of these highly industrialized but unevenly developed countries reached developmental impasses. State-led industrialization under bureaucratic-authoritarian regimes created organizationally powerful and socially radicalized labor movements, which challenged the exclusionary character of peripheral capitalism. The resulting crises in turn paved the way for democratization (Seidman 1994). In Brazil, democratization has provided new opportunities for demanding equity-enhancing reforms. For the most part these reforms have been frustrated by the absence of broad-based support and by the resiliency of the clientalistic and segmented politics of the past (Weyland 1996). Nonetheless, in selective pockets of high working-class organization, unions have successfully developed new and flexible forms of negotiating compromises (Martin 1997). In South Africa, a far more powerful and cohesive working-class movement has empowered the state with more comprehensive powers for pursuing distributive reforms. Whether the political capacity for building class compromise in South Africa can survive structural pressures for a more neoliberal strategy of economic development is still an open question, but it is already clear that working-class mobilization has directly contributed to the consolidation of democracy (Adler and Webster 1995).

The circumstances under which each of these states must manage workable "equilibria of forces" vary significantly. Nascent democratic institutions coexisting with redoubts of authoritarianism make for narrow margins of maneuverability and heighten the potential cost of militancy. At the same time, new political opportunities for subordinate groups and more vibrant civil societies have given expression to pent-up demands, increasing the urgency of distributive reforms. Because each of these reforming states is, to some extent, embedded in labor, they enjoy significant strategic leverage in organizing social concertation and democratically managing the costs of transition. Whether South Africa, Brazil, and Chile will be able to satisfy distributive demands while pursuing market reforms remains as uncertain as Kerala's prospects of successfully embarking on the path to accumulation. What is certain in Kerala's case, however, is that democratic consolidation is a fait accompli, and that many of the demands for redistribution and social reform that are sure to shape the politics of development in India for much of the foreseeable future have already been successfully addressed. And just as important, the institutional and political processes that underwrote the politics of redistributive development have also set the stage for a strategy of economic development based on class compromise.

Works Cited

Primary Sources

Government of India (GOI)

Analysis of Work Force in India. 1988. Office of the Registrar General and Census Commission (Occasional paper no. 8 of 1988).
Annual Survey of Industries. 1986–87.
Census of India. 1991. *Kerala: Workers and Their Distribution.*
Coir Board. 1963. *Report on the Economic and Statistical Survey of Coir Industry.*
Labour Bureau. 1984. *Report on the Working of the Minimum Wages Act, 1948, for the Year 1984.*
——. *Indian Labour Yearbook* (annual).
Ministry of Labour. 1991. *Report of the National Commission on Rural Labour.* Vols. 1 and 2. New Delhi.
Planning Commission. 1952. *First Five Year Plan.* New Delhi.
——. 1993. Expert Group on Estimation of Proportion and Number of the Poor.
Reserve Bank of India. 1989. Agricultural Credit Review Committee. *A Review of the Agricultural Credit System in India.* Bombay: Reserve Bank of India.
Secratariat of Industrial Assistance. 1998. SIA Statistics. *Industrial Investment Proposals* (monthly).

Government of Kerala (GOK)

Agricultural Development Policy. 1992.
Department of Agriculture. 1996. *Agenda Notes: National Conference on Agriculture for Kharif Campaign.*
Department of Economics and Statistics. Various years. *Report on the Cost of Cultivation of Important Crops in Kerala.*

———. 1977, 1980, 1988, 1993. *Statistics for Planning.*

———. 1981. *Report on the Survey of Coir Workers.*

———. 1985. *Report of the Survey on Socio-Economic Conditions of Agricultural and Other Rural Labourers in Kerala (SSEC)—1983–84.*

———. 1987. *Growth of Factory Employment in Kerala.*

———. 1989. *Agricultural Census 1985–86.*

———. 1991. *Annual Survey of Industries, 1985–86.*

Kerala Agricultural Workers Act (KAWA). 1976.

Kerala Budget in Brief (annual).

Kerala State Industrial Development Corporation (KSIDC) (annual reports).

Labour Department. 1990. *Enforcement of Minimum Wages Act 1948 in Kerala.*

———. 1991a. Minimum Wages Committee.

———. 1991b. *Labour Statistics at a Glance.*

———. Administration Report (annual).

Nair, Janardhanan M. 1981. *Report of the One Man Commission on the Problems of Paddy Cultivators in Kerala.*

Public Relations Department. 1987. *The First 100 Days.*

Ramankutty, K. 1982. *One Man Commission Report on Land-Labour Ratio in Respect to Paddy Cultivation in Palghat District.* Palghat: Department of Labour.

Registrar of Co-operative Societies. *Handbook on Co-operative Movement in Kerala* (annual).

Report of the Kuttanad Inquiry Commission. 1971.

State Planning Board. *Economic Review* (annual).

———. 1969. *A Study of Tractor Use and Its Impact on the Farm Economy of Kerala.*

———. 1973. *Report of the Study Group on Mechanization in Coir Industry in Kerala.*

———. 1984. *Report of the High Level Committee on Industry Trade and Power.* Vol. 2.

———. 1986. *A Report on the Role of Small Scale Industries in the Seventh Five Year Plan.*

———. 1989a. *Eighth Five Year Plan—Report of the Task Force on Agricultural Employment.*

———. 1989b. *Report of the Steering Committee on Agriculture and Allied Sectors.*

———. 1990a. *Task Force on Coir Industry.*

———. 1990b. *Eighth Five Year Plan 1990–95—Report of the Steering Committee on Industry and Mining.* June.

———. 1991a. *Draft Eighth Five Year Plan.*

———. 1991b. *Report of the Task Force for Review of Implementation of Plan Schemes under the Industries Sector.*

———. 1991c. *Draft Eighth Five Year Plan 1992–1997 and Annual Plan 1992–93.* Vol. 1. November.

———. 1992. *Plan Outlays and Expenditure.*

———. 1996a. *Ninth Five Year Plan (1997–2002).* Task Force on Modern Small Scale Industries.

———. 1996b. *Social Security Initiatives in Kerala. Report of the Expert Committee.*

——. 1997a. *Ninth Five Year Plan* (1997–2002). *Report of the Task Force on Traditional Industries.*

——. 1997b. *Ninth Five Year Plan* (1997–2002). *Report of the Task Force on Biotechnology and Agro-based Industries.*

Statement of Industrial Policy. 1991.

Government of Travancore-Cochin

Report of the Committee on Coir Mats and Matting Manufacturing Industry. 1955.

Secondary Sources

Adler, Glenn, and Eddie Webster. 1995. "Challenging Transition Theory: The Labor Movement, Radical Reform, and Transition to Democracy in South Africa." *Politics and Society* 23(1): 75–106.

Ahluwalia, M. S. 1978. "Rural Poverty and Agricultural Performance in India." *Journal of Development Studies* (April): 298–323.

Alavi, Hamza. 1982. "The State and Class under Peripheral Capitalism." In *Sociology of "Developing Societies,"* edited by H. Alavi and T. Shanin, 289–307. New York: Monthly Review Press.

Albin, Alice. 1990. "Manufacturing Sector in Kerala: Study of Its Growth and Structure." *Economic and Political Weekly* 25 (37): 2059–70.

——. 1992. "Kerala Economy at Crossroads." *Economic and Political Weekly* 27 (12):606–8.

Alexander, Joseph K. 1972. "Kerala Labour Attitude: A Hindrance to Economic Development." In *Development of Kerala*, edited by P. K. B. Nayar. Trivandrum: University of Kerala.

Alexander, K. C. 1989. "Caste Mobilization and Class Consciousness: The Emergence of Agrarian Movements in Kerala and Tamil Nadu." In *Dominance and State Power in Modern India: Decline of a Social Order*, edited by F. Frankel and M. S. A. Rao, vol. 1, 362–414. Delhi: Oxford University Press.

Amsden, Alice. 1985. "The State and Taiwan's Economic Development." In *Bringing the State Back In*, edited by Peter Evans et al., 78–106. New York: Cambridge University Press.

——. 1989. *Asia's Next Giant: South Korea and Late Industrialization.* New York: Oxford University Press.

Anderson, Perry. 1974. *Lineages of the Absolutist State.* London: Verso.

Arun, T. G. 1992. "Growth and Structural Changes in the Manufacturing Industries of Kerala, 1976–87." M. Phil., diss. Centre for Development Studies, Trivandrum.

Attwood, D. W., and B. S. Baviskar. 1993. *Who Shares?* New York: Oxford University Press.

Baby, A. A. 1996. "Trends in Agricultural Wages in Kerala: 1960–1990." Occasional paper series, Centre for Development Studies, Trivandrum.

Bajpai, Nirupam, and Jeffrey Sachs. 1996. "India's Economic Reforms: Some Lessons from East Asia." Development discussion paper no. 532a, Harvard Institute for International Development, Cambridge, Mass.

Bandyopdhyay, Suraj, and Donald Von Eschen. 1993. "Villager Failure to Co-operate: Some Evidence from West Bengal, India." In *Who Shares?*, edited by D. W. Attwood and B. S. Baviskar, 112–45. New York: Oxford University Press.

Banerjee, Nirmala. 1988. "The Unorganized Sector and the Planner." In *Economy, Society and Polity*, edited by A. K. Bagchi. New Delhi: Oxford University Press.

Bardhan, Pranab. 1970. "Green Revolution and Agricultural Labourers in India." *Economic and Political Weekly* 5 (29–31): 1239–46.

———. 1984a. *The Political Economy of Development in India*. New York: Basil Blackwell.

———. 1984b. *Land, Labor, and Rural Poverty: Essays in Development Economics*. New York: Columbia University Press.

———. 1988. "Dominant Proprietary Classes and India's Democracy." In *India's Democracy*, edited by A. Kohli, 214–24. Princeton, N.J.: Princeton University Press.

———. 1997. "Sharing the Spoils: Group Equity, Development, and Democracy." Unpublished paper, University of California, Berkeley.

Bates, Robert. 1981. *Markets and States in Tropical Africa*. Berkeley: University of California Press.

Bhaduri, A. 1983. *The Economic Structure of Backward Agriculture*. London: Academic Press.

Bharadwaj, Krishna. 1985. "A View on Commercialization in Indian Agriculture and the Development of Capitalism." *Journal of Peasant Studies* 12 (4): 8–25.

Bhat, Mari P. N., and S. Irudaya Rajan. 1990. "Demographic Transition in Kerala Revisited." *Economic and Political Weekly* 25 (35, 36):1957–80.

Bhowmik, Sharit Kumar. 1996. "State Intervention and the Working Class Movement." *Economic and Political Weekly* 31(52): L39–L43.

Boone, Catherine. 1994. "States and Ruling Classes in Post-colonial Africa." In *State Power and Social Forces: Domination and Transformation in the Third World*, edited by J. Migdal, A. Kohli, and V. Shue, 108–42. Cambridge: Cambridge University Press.

Brass, Paul R. 1994. *The Politics of India since Independence*. Cambridge: Cambridge University Press.

Bratton, Michael. 1994. "Peasant-State Relations in Postcolonial Africa." In *State Power and Social Forces: Domination and Transformation in the Third World*, edited by J. Migdal, A. Kohli, and V. Shue, 231–54. Cambridge: Cambridge University Press.

Breman, Jan. 1985. *Of Peasants, Migrants and Paupers: Rural Labour Circulation and Capitalist Production in West India*. New Delhi: Oxford University Press.

———. 1996. *Footloose Labour*. Cambridge: Cambridge University Press.

Brenner, Robert. 1977. "The Origins of Capitalist Development: A Critique of Neo-Smithian Marxism." *New Left Review* 104: 25–92.

——. 1985. "Agrarian Class Structure and Economic Development in Pre-industrial Europe." In *The Brenner Debate*, edited by T. H. Aston and C. H. E. Philipin, 10–63. Cambridge: Cambridge University Press.

——. 1986. "The Social Basis of Economic Development." In *Analytical Marxism*, edited by J. Roemer, 25–53. Cambridge: Cambridge University Press.

Burawoy, Michael. 1985. *The Politics of Production*. London: Verso.

——. 1989. "Marxism with Micro-foundations." *Socialist Review* 19 (2): 53–86.

Burmeister, Larry. 1990. "State, Industrialization and Agricultural Policy in Korea." *Development and Change* 21 (2): 197–223.

Callaghy, Thomas. 1988. "The State and the Development of Capitalism in Africa: Theoretical, Historical, and Comparative Reflections." In *The Precarious Balance*, edited by Donald Rothschild, 67–99. Boulder, Colo.: Westview.

Cameron, David. 1984. "Social Democracy, Corporatism, Labor Quiescence, and the Representation of Economic Interests in Advanced Capitalist Democracies." In *Order and Conflict in Contemporary Capitalism*, edited by J. Goldthorpe, 143–78. Oxford: Oxford University Press.

Candland, Christopher. 1995. "Trade Unionism and Industrial Restructuring in India and Pakistan." *Bulletin of Concerned Asian Scholars*: 27 (4): 63–78.

Castells, Manuel. 1992. "Four Asian Tigers with a Dragon Head: A Comparative Analysis of the State, Economy, and Society in the Asian Pacific Rim." In *States and Development in the Asian Pacific Rim*, edited by R. Appelbaum and J. Henderson, 33–69. London: Sage.

Cawthorne, P. M. 1995. "Of Networks and Markets—The Rise of a South Indian Town: The Example of Tiruppurs Cotton Knitwear Industry." *World Development* 23 (1): 43–56.

Centeno, Miguel A. 1994. *Democracy within Reason: Technocratic Revolution in Mexico*. University Park: Pennsylvania State University Press.

Centre for Monitoring Indian Economy (CMIE). Various years. *Shape of Things to Come*. Bombay.

——. 1991. *Basic Statistics Relating to States of India*. Bombay.

——. 1993. *Basic Statistics Relating to the Indian Economy*. Bombay.

——. 1994a. *Basic Statistics Relating to States of India*. Bombay.

——. 1994b. *Basic Statistics Relating to the Indian Economy*. Bombay.

——. 1996. *India's Industrial Sector*. Bombay.

——. 1997. *Profile of States*. Bombay.

Chatterji, Rakhahari. 1980. *Unions, Politics and the State: A Study of Indian Labour Politics*. New Delhi: South Asian Publishers Pvt.

Chaudhry, Kiren A. 1993. "The Myths of the Market and the Common History of Late Developers." *Politics and Society* 21 (3): 245–74.

Cohen, Jean. 1982. *Class and Civil Society*. Amherst: University of Massachusetts Press.

Cohen, Joshua, and Joel Rogers, 1992. "Secondary Associations and Democratic Governance." *Politics and Society*, 20 (4): 393–472.

Collier, Ruth B., and David Collier. 1991. *Shaping the Political Arena*. Princeton N.J.: Princeton University Press.

Communist Party of India, Marxist (CPM). 1989. *Political Organisational Report of the Thirteenth Congress*. Trivandrum.

Conference of Indian Trade Unions. 1979. Kerala State Conference.

Cumings, Bruce. 1987. "The Origins and Development of the Northeast Asian Political Economy: Industrial Sectors, Product Cycles, and Political Consequences." In *The Political Economy of the New Asian Industrialism*, edited by F. C. Deyo, 44–83. Ithaca: Cornell University Press.

Das, Jayadeva D. 1983. *Working Class Politics in Kerala: A Study of Coir Workers*. Kariavattom: T. C. Lilly Grace.

Datt, Guarav, and Martin Ravallion. 1996. "Why Have Some Indian States Done Better Than Others at Reducing Poverty?" Policy research working paper no. 1594, World Bank, Washington, D.C.

de Janvry, Alain. 1981. *The Agrarian Question and Reformism in Latin America*. Baltimore: John Hopkins University Press.

Desai, D. K. 1988. "Institutional Credit Requirement for Agricultural Purchase—2000 A.D." *Indian Journal of Agricultural Economics* 43: 3.

Deshpande, L. K. 1983. *Segmentation of Labour Market: A Case Study of Bombay*. Bombay: Orient Longman.

De Soto, Hernando. 1989. *The Other Path*. New York: Harper and Row.

Deyo, Frederic C. 1987. "State and Labor: Modes of Political Exclusion in East Asian Development." In *The Political Economy of the New Asian Industrialism*, edited by F. C. Deyo, 182–203. Ithaca: Cornell University Press.

———. 1990. "Economic Policy and the Popular Sector." In *Manufacturing Miracles*, edited by Gary Gereffi and Donald Wyman, 179–204. Princeton, N.J.: Princeton University Press.

Dreze, Jean, and Haris Gazdar. 1996. "Uttar Pradesh: The Burden of Inertia." In *Indian Development*, edited by J. Dreze and A. Sen, 33–128. Delhi: Oxford University Press.

Dreze, Jean, and Amartya Sen. 1989. *Hunger and Public Action*. Oxford: Clarendon.

———. 1995. *India: Economic Development and Social Opportunity*. Delhi: Oxford University Press.

Duvvury, Nata. 1994. "Social Security in the Unorganised Sector." Centre for Development Studies, Trivandrum.

Economic and Political Weekly Research Foundation (EPW Foundation). 1993. "Poverty Levels in India: Norms, Estimates and Trends." *Economic and Political Weekly* (August 21): 1748–68.

Esping-Andersen, Gøsta. 1990. "Single-party Dominance in Sweden: The Saga of Social Democracy." In *Uncommon Democracies: The One-party Dominant Regimes*, edited by T. J. Pempel, 33–57. Ithaca: Cornell University Press.

———. 1991. *The Three Worlds of Welfare Capitalism*. Princeton, N.J.: Princeton University Press.

Evans, Peter. 1979. *Dependent Development*. Princeton N.J.: Princeton University Press.

——. 1987. "Class, State, and Dependence in East Asia: Lessons for Latin Americanists." In *The Political Economy of New Asian Industrialism*, edited by F. C. Deyo, 203–26. Ithaca: Cornell University Press.

——. 1992. "The State as Problem and Solution: Predation, Embedded Autonomy, and Structural Change." In *The Politics of Economic Adjustment: International Constraints, Distributive Conflicts, and the State*, edited by S. Haggard and R. Kaufman, 139–80. Princeton, N.J.:Princeton University Press.

——. 1995. *Embedded Autonomy: States and Industrial Transformation*. Princeton, N.J.: Princeton University Press.

——. 1996. "Government Action, Social Capital and Development: Reviewing the Evidence on Synergy." *World Development* 24 (6): 1119–32.

Evans, Peter, and Dietrich Rueschemeyer. 1985. "The State and Economic Transformation. Toward an Analysis of the Conditions Underlying Effective Intervention." In *Bringing the State Back In*, edited by Peter Evans et al., 44–78. New York: Cambridge University Press.

Evans, Peter, and John D. Stephens. 1988. "Development and the World Economy." In *Handbook of Sociology*, edited by N. Smelser, 739–73. London: Sage.

Ferguson, James. 1994. *The Anti-politics Machine: "Development," Depoliticization and Bureaucratic Power in Lesotho*. New York: Cambridge University Press.

Fic, V. M. 1970. *Kerala, Yenan of India: Rise of Communist Power, 1937–1969*. Bombay: Nachiketa Publications.

Francis, Shaji K. 1990. "Dynamics of Rural Labour Markets: An Analysis of Emerging Agricultural Labour Shortage in a Kerala Region." M. Phil. diss., Centre for Development Studies, Trivandrum.

Franke, Richard W. 1993. *Life Is a Little Better: Redistribution as a Development Strategy in Nadur Village, Kerala*. Boulder, Colo.: Westview.

Franke, Richard W., and Barbara Chasin. 1989. "Kerala: Radical Reform as Development in an Indian State." Food First Development Report No. 6, San Francisco.

Frankel, Francine. 1978. *India's Political Economy: 1947–1977*. Princeton, N.J.: Princeton University Press.

George, Alex. 1987. "Social and Economic Aspects of Attached Labourers in Kuttanad Agriculture." *Economic and Political Weekly* (December 26): A141–A150.

George, Jose. 1984. *Politicisation of Agricultural Workers in Kerala: A Study of Kuttanad*. New Delhi: K. P. Bagchi.

George, K. K. 1993. "Limits to Kerala Model of Development." Monograph series, Centre for Development Studies, Trivandrum.

George, P. S., and Chandan Mukherjee. 1986. "Rice Economy of Kerala: A Disaggregated Analysis of Performance." Working paper no. 213, Trivandrum.

George, Tharian K., and Joseph Toms. 1992. "Rubber-based Industrialisation in Kerala: An Assessment of Missed Linkages." *Economic and Political Weekly* 27 (1–2): 47–66.

Gereffi, G., and D. Wyman. 1989. "Determinants of Development Strategies in Latin America and East Asia." In *Pacific Dynamics: The International Politics of Industrial Change*, edited by S. Haggard and C. Moon, 23–52. Inha and Boulder, Color.: CIS and Westview.

Gold, Thomas. 1986. *Society and State in the Taiwan Miracle*. Armonk, N.Y. M. E. Sharpe.

Gopal Iyer, K., and R. Vidyasagar. 1986. "Agrarian Struggles in Tamilnadu." In *Agrarian Struggles in India after Independence*, edited by A. R. Desai. Delhi: Oxford University Press.

Gopalan, A. K. 1973. *In the Cause of the People*. Bombay: Orient Longman.

Gough, Kathleen. 1968–69. "Peasant Resistance and Revolt in South India." *Pacific Affairs* 41: 4.

———. 1981. *Rural Society in South East India*. Cambridge: Cambridge University Press.

Govindan, K. C. 1986. *Memoirs of an Early Trade Unionist*. Centre for Development Studies, Trivandrum.

Gramsci, Antonio. 1971. *Prison Notebooks*. New York: International Publishers.

Grindle, Merilee. 1986. *State and Countryside: Development Policy and Agrarian Politics in Latin America*. Baltimore: Johns Hopkins University Press.

Gulati, Leela. 1990. "Agricultural Workers' Pension in Kerala: An Experiment in Social Assistance." *Economic and Political Weekly* 25 (6): 339–43.

Gupta, Akhil. 1998. *Postcolonial Developments: Agriculture in the Making of Modern India*. Durham: Duke University Press.

Haggard, Stephan. 1990. *Pathways from the Periphery: The Politics of Growth in Newly Industrializing Countries*. Ithaca: Cornell University Press.

Haggard, Stephan, and Robert R. Kaufman. 1995. *The Political Economy of Democratic Transitions*. Princeton N.J.: Princeton University Press.

Hagopian, Frances. 1994. "Traditional Politics against State Transformation in Brazil." In *State Power and Social Forces: Domination and Transformation in the Third World*, edited by J. Migdal, A. Kohli and V. Shue, 37–63. Cambridge: Cambridge University Press.

Harilal, K. N. 1986. "Kerala's Building Industry in Transition: A Study of the Organisation of Production and Labour Process." M. Phil. diss., Centre for Development Studies, Trivandrum.

Harriss, John. 1982. *Capitalism and Peasant Farming: Agrarian Structure and Ideology in Northern Tamil Nadu*. Bombay: Oxford University Press.

———. 1991. "The Green Revolution in North Arcot: Economic Trends, Household Mobility, and the Politics of an 'Awkward Class'." In *The Green Revolution Reconsidered: The Impact of High-yielding Rice Varieties in South India*, edited by P. B. R. Hazell and C. Ramasamy, 57–84. Baltimore: Johns Hopkins University Press.

———. 1992. "Does the "Depressor" Still Work? Agrarian Structure and Development in India: A Review of Evidence and Argument." *Journal of Peasant Studies* 19 (2): 189–227.

Harriss, John, K. P. Kannan, and Gerry Rodgers. 1990. "Urban Labour Market Structure and Job Access in India: A Study of Coimbatore." Geneva: International Labour Organization.

Hart, Gillian. 1989. "Agrarian Change in the Context of State Patronage." In *Agrarian Transformations: Local Processes and the State in Southeast Asia*, edited by G. Hart, A. Turton, and B. White, 31–52. Berkeley: University of California Press.

Heller, Patrick. 1996. "Social Capital as Product of Class Mobilization and State Intervention: Industrial Workers in Kerala, India." *World Development* 24 (6): 1055–71.

Herring, Ronald. 1980. "Abolition of Landlordism in Kerala: A Redistribution of Privilege." *Economic and Political Weekly* 15 (26): A59–A69.

——. 1983. *Land to the Tiller: The Political Economy of Agrarian Reform in South Asia.* New Haven: Yale University Press.

——. 1989. "Dilemmas of Agrarian Communism: Peasant Differentiation, Sectoral and Village Politics." *Third World Quarterly* 11 (1): 89–115.

——. 1991a. "Contesting the 'Great Transformation': Land and Labor in South India." Manuscript. Cornell University.

——. 1991b. "From Structural Conflict to Agrarian Stalemate: Agrarian Reforms in South India." *Journal of Asian and African Studies* 26 (3–4): 169–88.

——. 1996. "From Fanaticism to Power: Ratchet Politics and Peasant Mobilization in South India, 1836–1956." Paper presented at the Association of Asian Studies annual meeting, Honolulu, April 14–16.

——. 1999. "Embedded Particularism: India's Failed Developmental State." In *The Developmental State*, edited by Meredith Woo-Cumings. Ithaca: Cornell University Press.

Hershberg, Eric. 1997. "Liberal Democracy, Market-Oriented Development, and the Future of Popular Sector Representation: Lessons from Contemporary Chile and Spain." In *The New Politics of Inequality in Latin America*, edited by D. Chalmers et al., 337–59. New York: Oxford University Press.

Heuze, Gerard. 1990. "Workers' Struggles and Indigenous Fordism in India." In *Work for Wages in South Asia*, edited by M. Holmstrom. New Delhi: Manohar.

Hirschman, Albert. 1984. *Getting Ahead Collectively: Grassroots Experiences in Latin America.* New York: Pergamon.

Holmström, Mark. 1993. "Flexible Specialisation in India." *Economic and Political Weekly* 28 (35): M82–M86.

Huntington, Samuel. 1968. *Political Order in Changing Societies.* New Haven: Yale University Press.

Jalan, Bimal. 1991. *India's Economic Crisis: The Way Ahead.* Delhi: Oxford University Press.

Jannuzi, F. Thomasson. 1994. *India's Persistent Dilemma: The Political Economy of Agrarian Reform.* Hyderabad: Orient Longman.

Jeffrey, Robin. 1976. *The Decline of Nayar Dominance: Society and Politics in Travancore, 1947–1908.* Dehli: Vikas.

——. 1992. *Politics, Women and Well-Being: How Kerala Became 'a Model'.* Houndmills, Basingstoke, Hampshire: Macmillan.

Jenkins, Robert S. 1995. "Sustaining Economic Reform under Liberal Democracy." *IDS Bulletin* 26 (2): 37–48.

John, K. C. 1991. *Kerala: The Melting Pot.* New Delhi: Nunes.

Johnson, Chalmers. 1982. *MITI and the Japanese Miracle.* Stanford, Calif.: Stanford University Press.

Jose, A. V. 1973. "Wages of Agricultural Labourers in Kerala." *Economic and Political Weekly* (Annual Number, February): 281–288.

———. 1977. "The Origin of Trade Unionism among the Agricultural Labourers of Kerala." *Social Scientist* 5 (12): 25–43.

———. 1988. "Agricultural Wages in India." *Economic and Political Weekly* (Review of Agriculture June 25): A46-A58.

Joseph, P. T. 1985. "Agricultural Labour in Kerala: A Case Study of Palghat Region." Kerala Institute of Labour and Employment, Trivandrum.

Ka, Chih-Ming, and Mark Selden. 1986. "Original Accumulation, Equity, and Late Industrialization: The Cases of Socialist China and Capitalist Taiwan." *World Development* 14 (11): 1293–1310.

Kahler, Miles. 1990. "Orthodoxy and its Alternatives: Explaining Approaches to Stabilization and Adjustment." In *Economic Crisis and Policy Choice: The Politics of Adjustment in the Third World,* edited by J. Nelson. Princeton N. J.: Princeton University Press.

Kannan, K. P. 1988. *Of Rural Proletarian Struggles: Mobilization and Organization of Rural Workers in South-West India.* Delhi: Oxford University Press.

———. 1990a. "Kerala Economy at the Crossroads?" *Economic and Political Weekly* 25 (N35-3):1951-56.

———. 1990b. "State and Union Intervention in Rural Labour: A Study of Kerala, India." Asian Regional Team for Employment Promotion (ARTEP). International Labour Organization, New Delhi.

———. 1990c. "Towards Understanding the Dynamics of Rural Labour Markets: An Approach Based on Indian Evidence." *Indian Journal of Labour Economics* 33 (3): 200–16.

———. 1992. "Labour Institutions and the Development Process in Kerala, India." Manuscript. Centre for Development Studies, Trivandrum.

———. 1994. "Levelling Up or Levelling Down? Labour Institutions and Economic Development in India." *Economic and Political Weekly* 29 (30): 1938–45.

———. 1995. "Declining Incidence of Rural Poverty in Kerala." *Economic and Political Weekly* (October 14–21):2651–62.

Kannan, K. P., and K. Pushpangadan. 1988. "Agricultural Stagnation in Kerala: An Explanatory Analysis." *Economic and Political Weekly* (September 24): A120–A128.

———. 1990. "Dissecting Agricultural Stagnation in Kerala: An Analysis across Crops, Seasons and Regions." *Economic and Political Weekly* 25 (N35-3): 1991–2001.

Kapadia, Karin. 1995. "The Profitability of Bonded Labour: The Gem-cutting Industry in Rural South India." *Journal of Peasant Studies* 22 (3): 446–483.

Katznelson, Ira, and R. Zolberg, eds. 1986. *Working-class Formation.* Princeton N. J.: Princeton University Press.

Kerala Institute of Labour and Employment. 1982. "Headload Workers' Strike at Trichur." Trivandrum.

Kerala State Karshaka Thozhilali Union (KSKTU). 1991. *Agricultural Workers Movement in Kerala. 50th Year Anniversary Souvenir.* (Malayalam) Alleppey.

———. 1988. *Report of the 11th State Conference.*

———. 1991. *Report of the 12th State Conference.*

Khera, R. N. 1991. "Growth of the Registered Manufacturing Sector at the State Level." *Journal of Income and Wealth* 13 (1): 114–22.

Knorringa, Peter. 1996. "Operationalisation of Flexible Specialisation: Agra's Footwear Industry." *Economic and Political Weekly* 31 (52): L50–L56.

Kohli, Atul. 1987. *The State and Poverty in India.* Cambridge: Cambridge University Press.

———. 1990. *Democracy and Discontent: India's Growing Crisis of Governability.* Cambridge: Cambridge University Press.

———. 1994. "Where Do High Growth Political Economies Come From? The Japanese Lineage of Korea's 'Developmental State.' " *World Development* 22 (9): 1269–93.

Koo, Hagen. 1987. "The Interplay of State, Social Class, and World System in East Asian Development." In *The Political Economy of New Asian Industrialism*, edited by F. C. Deyo, 165–81. Ithaca: Cornell University Press.

Kothari, Rajni. 1991. "State and Statelessness in Our Time." *Economic and Political Weekly* Annual Number.

Krishnaji, N. 1986. "Agrarian Relations and the Left Movement in Kerala: A Note on Recent Trends." In *Agrarian Struggles in India after Independence*, edited by A. R. Desai. Delhi: Oxford University Press.

Krishnan, T. N. 1991. "Wages, Employment and Output in Interrelated Labour Markets in an Agrarian Economy: A Study of Kerala." *Economic and Political Weekly* (June 29): A82-A96.

Krishnan, T. N., and M. Kabir. 1992. "Social Intermediation and Health Transition: Lessons from Kerala." Working paper no. 251, Centre for Development Studies, Trivandrum.

Kumar, Gopa G. 1986. *Regional Political Parties and State Politics.* New Delhi: Deep and Deep.

Kumar, Mohana S. 1989. "Industrial Disputes in India: 1951–1985." M. Phil. diss., Centre for Development Studies, Trivandrum.

Kurien, C. T. 1992. *The Economy: An Interpretive Introduction.* New Delhi: Sage.

———. 1994. "Kerala's Development Experience: Random Comments about the Past and Some Considerations for the Future." In *International Congress on Kerala Studies*, vol. 2, 21–34. Thiruvananthapuram: A. K. G. Centre for Research Studies.

Lewis, John. 1995. *Indian's Political Economy: Governance and Reform.* Delhi: Oxford University Press.

Lieten, G. K. 1982. *The First Communist Ministry in Kerala: 1957–59.* Calcutta: K. P. Bagchi.

Lubeck, Paul. 1992. "Malaysian Industrialization, Ethnic Divisions, and the NIC Model." In *States and Development in the Asian Pacific Rim*, edited by R. Appelbaum and J. Henderson, 176–98. London: Sage.

Luebbert, Gregory. 1991. *Liberalism, Fascism, or Social Democracy: Social Classes and the Political Origins of Regimes in Interwar Europe.* New York: Oxford University Press.

Lukose, Ani. 1991. *Labour Movements and Agrarian Relations*. Jaipur: Rawat.

Mahendra, Dev, S., M. H. Suryanarayana, and K. S. Parikh. 1991. "Rural Poverty in India: Incidence, Issues and Policies." Indira Gandhi Institute of Development Research, Bombay.

Mallick, Ross. 1992. "Agrarian Reforms in West Bengal: The End of an Illusion." *World Development* 20 (5): 735–50.

Mamdani, Mahood. 1996. *Citizen and Subject: Contemporary Africa and the Legacy of Late Colonialism*. Princeton N.J.: Princeton University Press.

Mani, Sunil. 1996. Economic Liberalisation and Kerala's Industrial Sector: An Assessment of Investment Opportunities." *Economic and Political Weekly* (August 24–31): 2323–30.

Mann, Michael. 1984. "The Autonomous Power of the State: Its Origins, Mechanisms and Results." *Archives Europeens de Sociologie* 25: 185–213.

Maravall, Jose L. 1993. "Politics and Policy: Economic Reforms in Southern Europe." In *Economic Reforms in New Democracies*, edited by L. C. B. Pereira, J. M. Maravall, and A. Przeworski, 77–131. Cambridge: Cambridge University Press.

Marshall, T. H., 1992. *Citizenship and Social Class*. London: Pluto.

Martin, Scott. 1997. "Beyond Corporatism: New Patterns of Representation in the Brazilian Auto Industry." In *The New Politics of Inequality in Latin America*, edited by D. Chalmers et al., 45–71. New York: Oxford University Press.

Marx, Karl. 1977. *Capital*. Vol. 1. New York: Vintage Books.

Meagher, Kate. 1995. "Crisis, Informalization and the Urban Informal Sector in Sub-Saharan Africa." *Development and Change* 26 (2): 259–84.

Mencher, Joan. 1978. "Agrarian Relations in Two Rice Regions of Kerala." *Economic and Political Weekly* (Annual Number, February): 349–66.

———. 1980. "The Lessons and Non-lessons of Kerala: Agricultural Labourers and Poverty." *Economic and Political Weekly* (Special Number, October): 1781–1802.

Menon, Dilip. 1994. *Caste, Nationalism and Communism in South India: Malabar 1900–1948*. New Delhi: Cambridge University Press.

Menon, S. C. S. ca. 1979. "Linking Annual Bonus to Production/Productivity: Employees' View Point." Cochin.

Mies, Maria. 1982. *The Lace Makers of Narsapur: Indian Housewives Produce for the World Market*. London: Zed.

Migdal, Joel S. 1988. *Strong Societies and Weak States: State-Society Relations and State Capabilities in the Third World*. Princeton, N.J.: Princeton University Press.

———. 1994. "The State in Society: An Approach to Struggles for Domination." In *State Power and Social Forces: Domination and Transformation in the Third World*, edited by Joel Migdal, Atul Kohli, and Vivienne Shue, 7–37. Cambridge: Cambridge University Press.

Migdal, Joel, Atul Kohli, and Vivienne Shue, eds. 1994. *State Power and Social Forces: Domination and Transformation in the Third World*. Cambridge: Cambridge University Press.

Miles, Robert. 1987. *Capitalism and Unfree Labour: Anomaly or Necessity?* London: Tavistock.

Minhas, B. S., et al. 1991. "Declining Poverty in the 1980s: Evidence Versus Facts." *Economic and Political Weekly* (July 6–13).

Mohan, Nanda V. 1994. "Recent Trends in the Industrial Growth of Kerala." In *Kerala's Economy*, edited by B. A. Prakash, 217–36. New Delhi: Sage.

Moore, Barrington. 1966. *Social Origins of Dictatorship and Democracy: Lord and Peasant in the Making of the Modern World.* Boston: Beacon.

Mouzelis, Nicos. 1988. "Sociology of Development: Reflections on the Present Crisis." *Sociology* 22: 1.

Mukherjee, Chandan, and T. M. Thomas Isaac. 1994. "Nine Observations on Educated Unemployment in Kerala." In *International Congress on Kerala Studies*, vol. 2, 66–68. Thiruvananthapuram: A. K. G. Centre for Research Studies.

Mukherjee, Vanita Nayak. 1989. "Socio-economic Conditions in Kuttanad: A Survey." Manuscript written for the Kuttanad Water-balance Study Project, Indo-Dutch Project, Trivandrum.

Muraleedharan, S. 1994. "Industrial Backwardness in Kerala—A Survey of Alternative Hypotheses." In *International Congress on Kerala Studies*, vol. 2, 28–29. Thiruvananthapuram: A. K. G. Centre for Research Studies.

Murray, Martin. 1994. *The Revolution Deferred: The Painful Birth of Post-apartheid South Africa.* London: Verso.

Murthy, Narayana J. L. 1988. "Institutional Finances." In *Multilevel Planning in India*, edited by V. Reddy. Hyderabad: Booklinks.

Nagesh, H. V. 1981. "Forms of Un-free Labour in Indian Agriculture." *Economic and Political Weekly* 16 (30): A109–A115.

Naidu, K. M. 1993. "Unemployment and Employment in India: An Overview." *Indian Journal of Labour Economics* 36: 8–29.

Nair, K. Ramachandran. 1973. *Industrial Relations in Kerala.* New Delhi: Sterling.

———. 1976. *Rural Politics and Government in Kerala.* Trivandrum: Kerala Academy of Political Science.

———. 1994. "Trade Unionism in Kerala." In *Kerala's Economy*, edited by B. A. Prakash, 331–48. New Delhi: Sage.

Nair, P. R. Gopinathan, and P. Mohanan Pillai. 1994. "Impact of External Transfers on the Regional Economy of Kerala." Centre for Development Studies, Trivandrum.

Namboodiripad, E. M. S. 1957. *Kerala: Problems and Possibilities.* New Delhi: Communist Party Publications.

———. 1959. *Twenty-eight Months in Kerala: A Retrospect.* New Delhi: People's Publishing House.

———. 1967. *Kerala Yesterday, Today and Tomorrow.* Calcutta: National Book Agency Private.

———. 1984. *Kerala Society and Politics: An Historical Survey.* New Delhi: National Book Agency.

———. 1985. *Selected Writings*, vol. 2. Calcutta: National Book Agency.

———. 1994. *The Communist Party in Kerala: Six Decades of Struggle and Advance*. New Delhi: National Book Centre.

Narayana, D. 1990. "Agricultural Economy of Kerala in the Post-seventies: Stagnation or Cycles?" Working paper no. 235, Centre for Development Studies, Trivandrum.

Natarajan, S. 1982. "Labour Input in Rice Farming In Kerala—An Inter-regional, Inter-temporal Analysis." In *Agricultural Development in Kerala*, edited by P. P. Pillai. New Delhi: Agricole.

Nayanar, E. K. 1982. *My Struggles: An Autobiography*. New Delhi: Vikas.

Nossiter, T. J. 1982. *Communism in Kerala: A Study in Political Adaptation*. Berkeley: University of California Press.

———. 1988. *Marxist State Governments in India*. London: Pinter.

O'Connor, James. 1973. *The Fiscal Crisis of the State*. New York: St. Martin's.

O'Donnell, Guillermo. 1988. "Challenges to Democratization in Brazil." *World Policy Journal* 5 (2): 281–300.

———. 1993. "On the State, Democratization, and Some Conceptual Problems: A Latin American View with Glances at Some Postcommunist Countries." *World Development* 21 (8): 1355–69.

Offe, Claus. 1984. *Contradictions of the Welfare State*. Cambridge: MIT Press.

———. 1997. "Homogeneity and Constitutional Democracy: Political Group Rights as an Answer to Identity Conflicts?" Paper presented at the Conference for the Study of Political Thought, April 4–6, Columbia University.

Offe, Claus, and Helmuth Wiesenthal. 1985. "Two Logics of Collective Action: Theoretical Notes on Social Class and Organizational Forms." In *Political Power and Social Theory*, edited by M. Zeitlin, 170–220. Greenwich, Conn.: JAI.

Onis, Ziya. 1991. "The Logic of the Developmental State." *Comparative Politics* 24 (1): 109–26.

Oommen, M. A. 1979. "Inter State Shifting of Industries: A Case Study of South India." Manuscript, University of Calicut, Trichur.

———. 1990. "Land Reforms and Economic Change: Experience and Lessons from Kerala." *Science and People* (March): 28–38.

———. 1991. "Development Experience, Development Priorities and Fiscal Resources of Kerala." *People and Development*, Centre of Science and Technology for Rural Development (Supplemental Issue, April–May): 1–30.

———. 1992. "The Acute Unemployment Problem of Kerala: Some Explanatory Hypotheses." *IASSI Quarterly* 10 (3): 231–55.

Oommen, T. K. 1985. *From Mobilization to Institutionalization: The Dynamics of the Agrarian Movement in Twentieth Century Kerala*. New Delhi: Sangam Books.

Paige, Jeffrey. 1975. *Agrarian Revolution*. London: Free Press.

Panikkar, K. N. 1989. *Against Lord and State: Religious and Peasant Uprisings in Malabar 1836–1921*. Delhi: Oxford University Press.

Papola, T. S. 1992. "Labour Institutions and Economic Development: The Case of Indian Industrialization." In *Labour Institutions and Economic Development in India*, edited by T. S. Papola and G. Rodgers. Geneva: International Institute of Labour Studies. Research series, no. 97.

Paranjothi, T., and K. N. Ushadevi. 1989. "Some Aspects of Loaning—A Study with Reference to Irinjalakuda Primary Co-operative Agricultural Development Bank Limited in Kerala." College of Co-operation and Banking, Kerala Agricultural University, Trichurm.

Patnaik, Utsa. 1986. "The Agrarian Question and Development of Capitalism in India." *Economic and Political Weekly* 21 (18):781–93.

Paul, Samuel. 1990. "Lessons from Kerala: How to Do Less with More?" *Economic and Political Weekly* 25 (51): 2907–2808.

Paulini, Thomas. 1979. *Agrarian Movements and Reforms in India: The Case of Kerala.* Ph.D. diss. Saarbruden: Verlag Breitenbach.

Pereira, Anthony. 1997. *The End of the Peasantry: The Rural Labor Movement in Northeast Brazil, 1961–1988.* Pittsburgh: University of Pittsburgh Press.

Peter, P. C. 1957. *Some Industrial Problems: With Special Reference to Travancore-Cochin.* Bombay: Popular Book Depot.

Pillai, Mohanan P., and N. Shanta. 1997. "Industrialization in Kerala." Kerala Studies series. Centre for Development Studies, Trivandrum.

Pillai, P. N. Krishna. 1972. "Industrial Relations in Kerala." In *Development of Kerala,* edited by P. K. B. Nayar. Trivandrum: University of Kerala.

Pillai, V. R., and P. G. K. Panikar. 1965. *Land Reclamation in Kerala.* New York: Asian Publishing House.

Polanyi, Karl. 1944. *The Great Transformation.* Boston: Beacon.

Pontusson, Jonas. 1990. "Conditions of Labor-party Dominance: Sweden and Britain Compared." In *Uncommon Democracies: The One-Party Dominant Regimes,* edited by T. J. Pempel, 58–82. Ithaca: Cornell University Press.

Portes, Alejandro. 1994. "The Informal Economy and Its Paradoxes." In *Handbook of Economic Sociology,* edited by N. Smelser and R. Swedberg, 426–49. Princeton N.J.: Princeton University Press.

Portes, Alejandro, and Manuel Castells. 1989. "World Underneath: The Origins, Dynamics, and Effects of the Informal Economy." In *The Informal Economy: Studies in Advanced and Less Developed Countries,* edited by A. Portes, M. Castells, and L. A. Benton, 11–40. Baltimore: John Hopkins University Press.

Portes, A., and R. Schauffler. 1993. "Competing Perspectives on the Latin American Informal Sector." *Population and Development Review* 19: 33–60.

Prakash, B. A. 1994. "Kerala's Economy: An Overview." In *Kerala's Economy,* edited by B. A. Prakash, 15–42. New Delhi: Sage.

Prasad, K. V. Eswara, and Anuradha Prasad. 1990. "State Legislations and Employment Relations in the Bidi Industry in India." In *Labour Landscape: A Study of Industrial and Agrarian Relations in India,* edited by V. Chandra Mowli. New Delhi: Sterling.

Przeworski, Adam. 1985. *Capitalism and Social Democracy.* Cambridge: Cambridge University Press.

———. 1989. "Class, Production, and Politics: A Reply to Burawoy." *Socialist Review* 19(2): 87–111.

———. 1992. "The Neoliberal Fallacy." *Journal of Democracy* 3 (3): 45–59.

———. 1995. *Sustainable Democracy.* Cambridge: Cambridge University Press.

Pushpangadan, K. 1992. "Wage Determination in a Casual Labour Market: The Case of Paddy Field Labour in Kerala." Working paper no. 224, Centre for Development Studies, Trivandrum.

Putnam, Robert. 1993. *Making Democracy Work: Civic Traditions in Modern Italy.* Princeton, N.J.: Princeton University Press.

Pylee, M. V. 1976. *A Study of the Coir Industry in India—Problems and Prospects.* Cochin: Coir Board.

Radhakrishnan, V., and K. Mukundan. 1987. "Supply and Utilization of Short-term Co-operative Agricultural Credit in Palghat District." Manuscript, Kerala Agricultural University, Vellanikkara.

Radhakrishnan, V., E. K. Thomas, and K. Jessy Thomas. 1994. "Performance of Rice Crop in Kerala." In *Kerala's Economy,* edited by B. A. Prakash, 160–78. New Delhi: Sage.

Raj, K. N. 1991. "Kerala's Pattern of Development." *People and Development* (January-February): 38–43.

Raj, K. N., and Michael Tharakan. 1983. "Agrarian Reform in Kerala and Its Impact on the Rural Economy—A Preliminary Assessment." In *Agrarian Reform in Contemporary Developing Countries,* edited by A. K. Ghose. New York: St. Martin's.

Ramachandran, V. K. 1990. *Wage Labour and Unfreedom in Agriculture: An Indian Case Study.* Oxford: Clarendon.

——. 1996. "On Kerala's Development Achievements." In *Indian Development,* edited by Jean Dreze and Amartya Sen, 205–356. Delhi: Oxford University Press.

Raman, Ravi K. 1986. "Plantation Labour in Kerala: Composition, Wage Trends and Wage-Productivity Relationship." *Indian Journal of Labour Economics* 28: 288–306.

Ramaswamy, E. A. 1983. "The Indian Management Dilemma: Economic vs. Political Unions." *Asian Survey* 23 (8): 976–90.

——. 1984. *Power and Justice: The State in Industrial Relations.* Delhi: Oxford University Press.

Ratcliffe, John. 1978. "Social Justice and Demographic Transition: Lesson from India's Kerala State." *International Journal of Health Services* 8:1.

Raveendran, N. 1989. "Social Background of the Trade Union Movement: A Study of the Trade Union Movement in Kerala with Special Reference to the Coir Industry." Ph.D. diss., University of Kerala, Trivandrum.

Roberts, Kenneth. 1997. "Rethinking Economic Alternatives: Left Parties and the Articulation of Popular Demands in Chile and Peru." In *The New Politics of Inequality in Latin America,* edited by D. Chalmers et al., 313–36. New York: Oxford University Press.

Rudra, Ashok. 1985. "Local Power and Farm-level Decision-making." In *Agrarian Power and Agricultural Productivity in South Asia,* edited by S. Rudolph, 251–80. Berkeley: University of California Press.

Rudolph, Lloyd I., and Susan H. Rudolph. 1987. *In Pursuit of Lakshmi: The Political Economy of the Indian State.* Chicago: University of Chicago Press.

Rueschemeyer, Dietrich, Evelyne H. Stephens, and John D. Stephens. 1992. *Capitalist Development and Democracy.* Chicago: University of Chicago Press.

Sankar, P. N. 1985. "Work, Wages and Well-being of Agricultural Labourers in Palghat District." M. Phil. diss., Kerala Agricultural University, Trichur.

Sankaranarayanan, K. C., and V. Karunakaran. 1985. *Kerala Economy*. New Delhi: Oxford and IBH Publishing Co.

Sankaranarayanan, K. C., and M. Meera Bhai. 1994. "Industrial Development of Kerala—Problems and Prospects." In *Kerala's Economy*, edited by B.A. Prakash, 298–315. New Delhi: Sage.

Sathyamurthy, T. V. 1985. *Centre-State Relations: The Case of Kerala*. New Delhi: Ajanta.

Scheper-Hughes, Nancy. 1992. *Death without Weeping: The Violence of Everyday Life in Brazil*. Berkeley: University of California Press.

Schmitter, Philippe C. 1985. "Neo-corporatism and the State." In *The Political Economy of Corporatism*, edited by Wyn Grant, 32–62. New York: St. Martin's.

Scott, James C. 1985. *Weapons of the Weak: Of the Everyday Forms of Peasant Resistance*. New Haven: Yale University Press.

———. 1998. *Seeing Like a State: How Certain Schemes to Improve the Human Condition Have Failed*. New Haven: Yale University Press.

Seidman, Gay W. 1994. *Manufacturing Militance: Workers' Movements in Brazil and South Africa: 1970–1985*. Berkeley: University of California Press.

Sen, Abhijit. 1991. "Shocks and Instabilities in an Agriculture-constrained Economy: India." In *Rural Transformation in India*, edited by J. Breman and S. Mundle, 490–522. Delhi: Oxford University Press.

Sen, Amartya. 1973. "Poverty, Inequality and Unemployment: Some Conceptual Issues in Measurement." *Economic and Political Weekly* (Special number, August).

Sen, Gita. 1992. "Social Needs and Public Accountability." In *Development Policy and Public Action*, edited by Marc Wuyts, Maureen Mackintosh, and Tom Hewitt, 253–78. Oxford: Oxford University Press in association with the Open University.

Sen, Sukomal. 1990. "For a Correct Class-composition of the Party." *The Marxist: Theoretical Quarterly of the CPI(M)* 8: 20–35.

Singh, Manjit. 1991. *Labour Process in the Unorganised Industry: A Case Study of the Garment Industry*. New Delhi: Manohar.

———. 1997. "Bonded Migrant Labour in Punjab Agriculture." *Economic and Political Weekly* 32 (11): 518–19.

Skocpol, Theda. 1985. "Bringing the State Back In: Current Research." In *Bringing the State Back In*, edited by Peter Evans, et al., 3–43. New York: Cambridge University Press.

Srinivas, M. N. 1967. *Social Change in Modern India*. Berkeley: University of California Press.

Srinivasan, T. N. 1985. "Neoclassical Political Economy, the State, and Economic Development." *Asian Development Review* 3: 38–58.

Stark, David, and Lásló Bruszt. 1998. *Postsocialist Pathways: Transforming Politics and Property in East Central Europe*. Cambridge: Cambridge University Press.

Stepan, Alfred. 1978. *The State and Society: Peru in Comparative Perspective.* Princeton, N.J.: Princeton University Press.

———. 1985. "State Power and the Strength of Civil Society in the Southern Cone of Latin America." In *Bringing the State Back In*, edited by P. Evans et al., 317–46. New York: Cambridge University Press.

Stephens, John D. 1979. *The Transition from Capitalism to Socialism.* London: Macmillan.

Subrahmanian, K. K. 1990. "Development Paradox in Kerala: Analysis of Industrial Stagnation." *Economic and Political Weekly* 25 (37): 2053–58.

Subrahmanian, K. K., and P. Mohanan Pillai. 1986. "Kerala's Industrial Backwardness: Exploration of Alternative Hypothesis." *Economic and Political Weekly* 21 (14): 577–92.

Sunanda, S. 1991. "Institutional Credit for Agriculture in Kerala: A Disaggregated Analysis." M. Phil. diss., Centre for Development Studies, Trivandrum.

Suri, G. K., ed. 1981. "Linking Bonus with Productivity." *Papers and Proceedings of a National Tripartite Seminar.* Sri Ram Centre for Industrial Relations and Human Resources, New Delhi.

Tarrow, Sidney. 1994. *Power in Movement: Social Movements, Collective Action and Politics.* Cambridge: Cambridge University Press.

Thampy, M. M. 1990. "Wage-cost and Kerala's Industrial Stagnation: Study of Organised Small Scale Sector." *Economic and Political Weekly* 25 (37): 2077–82.

Tharakan, Michael. 1998. "Socio-religious Reform Movements, Process of Democratization, and Human Development." In *Democratization in the Third World: Concrete Cases in Comparative and Theoretical Perspective*, edited by Olle Tornquist, 122–45. Houndmill, Basingstoke, Hampshire: Macmillan.

Tharamangalam, Joseph. 1981. *Agrarian Class Conflict: The Political Mobilization of Agricultural Labourers in Kuttanad, South India.* Vancouver: University of British Columbia Press.

———. 1998. "The Perils of Development without Economic Growth: The Development Debacle of Kerala, India." *Bulletin of Concerned Asian Scholars* 30 (1): 23–34.

Thomas Isaac, T. M. 1982a. "Class Struggle and Structural Changes in the Coir Mat and Matting Industry in Kerala." *Economic and Political Weekly* 17 (31): PE13–PE29.

———. 1982b. "Class Struggle and Structural Changes in the Coir Mat and Matting Industry 1950–1980." Working paper no. 142, Centre for Development Studies, Trivandrum.

———. 1985. "From Caste Consciousness to Class Consciousness: Alleppey Coir Workers during Inter-war Period." *Economic and Political Weekly* 20 (4): 5–17.

———. 1990. "Evolution of Organization of Production in Coir and Yarn Spinning Industry." Working paper no. 236, Centre for Development Studies, Trivandrum.

———. 1998. "Decentralisation, Democracy and Development: A Case Study of the People's Campaign for Decentralized Planning in Kerala." Unpublished paper. Kerala State Planning Board.

Thomas Isaac, T. M., Richard Franke, and Pyaralal Raghavan. 1998. *Democracy at Work In An Indian Industrial Cooperative.* Ithaca: Cornell University Press.

Thomas Isaac, T. M., and Mohana S. Kumar. 1991. "Kerala Elections, 1991: Lessons and Non-Lessons." *Economic and Political Weekly* 26 (47): 2691–2703.

Thomas Isaac, T. M., and Pyaralal Raghavan. 1990. "A Policy Framework for Revitalisation of Coir Industry in Kerala." Working paper no. 240, Centre for Development Studies, Trivandrum, India.

Thomas Isaac, T. M., and E. M. Shridharan. 1992. "Kerala's Development and its Politics." *Marxist Samvadan* 1:1.

Thomas Isaac, T. M., P. A. Van Stuijvenberg, and K. N. Nair. 1992. *Modernisation and Employment: The Coir Industry in Kerala. Indo-Dutch Studies on Development Alternatives—10.* New Delhi: Sage.

Thomas Isaac, T. M., and P. K. Michael Tharakan. 1987. "An Enquiry into the Historical Roots of Industrial Backwardness of Kerala—A Study of theTranvancore Region." Manuscript, Centre for Development Studies, Trivandrum, India.

Thompson, E. P. 1963. *The Making of the English Working Class.* New York: Vintage.

Thorner, Daniel. 1976. *The Agrarian Prospect in India.* Bombay: Allied Publishers.

Tilly, Charles. 1978. *From Mobilization to Revolution.* Reading, Mass.: Addison-Wesley.

——. 1984. *Big Structures, Large Processes, and Huge Comparisons.* New York: Russell Sage Foundation.

——. 1992. *Coercion, Capital, and European States, AD 990–1992.* Cambridge, Mass.: Blackwell.

Törnquist, Olle. 1991. "Communists and Democracy: Two Indian Cases and One Debate." *Bulletin of Concerned Asian Scholars* 23 (2): 63–76.

United Nations. 1975. *Poverty, Unemployment, and Development Policy: A Case Study of Selected Issues with Reference to Kerala.* New York: Department of Economic and Social Affairs.

——. 1978. *Population Growth and Agricultural Development: A Case Study of Kerala.* Rome: Food and Agriculture Organization.

United Nations Development Programme. 1994. *Human Development Report.* New York: Oxford University Press.

Varghese, T. C. 1970. *Agrarian Change and Economic Consequences: Land Tenures in Kerala 1850–1960.* Bombay: Allied Publishers.

Varkey, V. O. 1981. "Development and Working of Coir Cooperatives in Kerala." Ph.D. diss., University of Poona.

Varshney, Ashutosh. 1995. *Democracy, Development and the Countryside: Urban-Rural Struggles in India.* Cambridge: Cambridge University Press.

——. 1996. "Mass Politics or Elite Politics? India's Economic Reforms in Comparative Perspective." Paper presented at the Conference on India's Economic Reforms, December 13–14, Center for International Affairs and Harvard Institute of International Development, Harvard University, Cambridge, Mass.

——. Forthcoming. *Ethnic Conflict and Civic Life: Hindus and Muslims in India.* New Haven: Yale University Press.

Varughese, K. V. 1978. *United Front Government in Kerala: 1967–1969.* Madras: Christian Literature Society.

Vijayasankar, P. S. 1986. "The Urban Casual Labour Market in Kerala: A Study of Headload Workers in Trichur." M. Phil. diss., Centre for Development Studies, Trivandrum.

Wade, Robert. 1990. *Governing the Market: Economic Theory and the Role of Government in East Asian Industrialization.* Princeton, N.J.: Princeton University Press.

Walton, John, and David Seddon, eds., 1994. *Free Markets and Food Riots: The Politics of Global Adjustment.* Cambridge, Mass.: Blackwell.

Warren, Bill. 1980. *Imperialism: Pioneer of Capitalism.* London: New Left Books.

Weber, Max. [ca. 1927] 1981. *General Economic History.* New Brunswick, N.J.: Transaction.

———. 1946. *From Max Weber: Essays in Sociology,* edited by H. H. Gerth and C. Wright Mills. New York: Oxford University Press.

Weiner, Myron. 1991. *The Child and the State in India.* Princeton N.J.: Princeton University Press.

Weyland, Kurt. 1996. *Democracy without Equity: Failures of Reform in Brazil.* Pittsburgh: University of Pittsburgh Press.

White, Gordon. 1995. "Towards a Democratic Developmental State." *IDS Bulletin* 26 (2): 27–36.

Williamson, John. 1993. "Democracy and the 'Washington Consensus.' " *World Development* 21 (8): 1329–36.

Wolf, Eric. 1969. *Peasant Wars of the Twentieth Century.* New York: Harper and Row.

———. 1982. *Europe and a People without History.* Berkeley: University of California Press.

World Bank. 1997. *World Bank Development Report: The State in a Changing World.* New York: Oxford University Press.

Zachariah, K. C. 1984. "The Anomaly of the Fertility Decline in India's Kerala State: A Field Investigation." World Bank Working Paper 5700, Washington, D.C.

Index

Paddy cultivation. *See* Rice
Palghat, 90, 90n.1, 94, 96, 97, 98–103, 137; and agrarian movement history, 66–74, 80–82; and KAWA, 138–146, 147; and Minimum Wage Crisis, 108–109, 114. *See also* Malabar
Parayars, 59, 64. *See also* Caste
Patronage, 5, 29–30, 47, 187
Patron-client norms, 95n.6
Patron-client relationships, 11, 19, 25; in India, 54–56, 116; in Palghat, 143
Pattom Declaration of 1865, 63
PDS (Public Distribution System), 134
Peasants, 1–2, 5, 52; in East Asia, 32. *See also* Agrarian movements; Agrarian social structure; Agrarian transformation; Embourgeoisement of peasantry
Pereira, Anthony, 88
Permanency (Palghat), 143–145. *See also* Proletarianization
Pillai, P. N. Krishna, 173
Pillai, Raghavan R., 225
Pluralist theory, 47
Polanyi, Karl, 11, 93, 137n.29
Political mobilization, 48
Populist mobilization (India), 5, 54, 116. *See also* Mobilization: of traditional networks
Portes, Alexandro, 163n.4, 164, 169; and Manuel Castells, 169, 185, 206
Poverty: and comparison between Kerala and India, 35; in India, 56
Precapitalist classes, 24
Precapitalist institutions, 10–12, 36, 97–98; casualization (Travancore), 71; and class mobilization, 49; and coir industry, 190; demise of, 40; embeddedness of land and labor in, 37–40; reproduction of, 37–38; resilience of, 38. *See also* Agrarian social structures
Pre-capitalist societies, 29–30
Primary Development Banks, 126–128. *See also* Credit
Primitive accumulation, 38–39. *See also* Great Transformation
Proletarianization, 36–39, 152–154. *See also* Agrarian transformation; Casualization; Permanency
Przeworski, Adam, 43–45, 44n.10, 153–154, 226, 242, 244
Public legality, 11, 18–19, 114–116, 154;

in India, 90; in Palghat, 102. *See also* Citizenship; Democracy; Incorporation; Public legality; State
Pudunagaram, 100–102, 106, 142
Pulayas, 59, 64. *See also* Caste
Punnapra-Vayalar Revolt, 65–66, 173
Purdah, 167
Putnam, Robert, 20, 240n.5

Raj, K. N., 120
Ramachandran, V. K., 97
Ramankutty, K., 141
Ramankutty report (Palghat), 141–142
Ramaswamy, E. A., 215–216
Ravindranath, K. N., 104, 225
Ravindranath, T. N., 104, 221
Redistribution, 7, 17–18, 154, 227; and growth, 237–245. *See also* Capitalism; Class compromise; Democracy: and redistribution
Relative surplus value, 40–41, 241
Rhagavan, V. V., 151
Rice cultivation, 64, 90,121–125, 131, 145–146. *See also* Crop conversion
Rubber trees, 128–129. *See also* Crop conversion; Tree crops
Rudolph, Lloyd I., and Susan H. Rudolph, 47, 55n.3, 161, 215–216, 224

Satyagrahas, 149
Scheper-Hughes, Nancy, 76n.19
Schmitter, Philippe C., 226
Scott, James, 6, 137–138
Seidman, Gay W., 15, 214
Sen, Abhijit, 170n.14
Sen, Amartya, 135
Shiv Sena Party, 216
SNDP (Sree Narayana Dharma Paripalana), 62, 172. *See also* Caste; Ezhavas
Social capital, 127–128
Social citizenship. *See* Citizenship
Social development: difference between India and Kerala, 239–240
Social welfare (Kerala), 6–10
Socioeconomic indicators, 7–8, 135
Socioreligious reform movements (Travancore), 60. *See also* Caste: reform movements
South Africa, 5, 35, 247–248
South Korea, 31–35, 35n.8. *See also* East Asian NICs